FILM BUDGETING

Or, How Much Will It Cost To Shoot Your Movie?

FILM BUDGETING

Or, How Much Will It Cost To Shoot Your Movie?

Ralph S. Singleton
Edited by Alain Silver and Robert Koster

FILM BUDGETING
Or, How Much Will It Cost to Shoot Your Movie?

LONE EAGLE PUBLISHING CO.
1024 N. Orange Drive
Hollywood, CA 90038
Phone 323.308.3400 or 800.FILMBKS
Fax 310.471.4969
ifilm.com

Printed in the United States of America

Printing by McNaughton & Gunn
Cover design by Heidi Frieder

Library of Congress Cataloging-in-Publication Data

Singleton, Ralph S. (Ralph Stuart),
Film Budgeting, or, How much will it cost to shoot your movie?/ Ralph S. Singleton.
p. cm.
Includes index
ISBN 0-943728-65-7
1. Motion picture industry—United States—Finance. I. Title
PN1993.5.U6S52 1996
384'.83'0973 – dc20 96-25822
CIP

Materials from "The Conversation" reproduced with permission from Francis Ford Coppola.

For

Joan, Katherine and Elizabeth

NOTE: Words in **BOLD FACE SMALL CAPS** are defined in the glossary. Many terms which are not defined here are defined in the companion book *Film Scheduling* (Lone Eagle Publishing) as well as in the *Filmmaker's Dictionary* (Lone Eagle Publishing).

CONTENTS

ABOVE-THE-LINE

BELOW-THE-LINE

POST PRODUCTION

CONTRACTUAL COSTS

ACKNOWLEDGMENTS

ANOTHER ROUND OF THANKS TO ALL THOSE PRODUCERS, production executives, production managers, assistant directors, production accountants and production office coordinators with whom I have worked and who have helped me throughout the years.

A special thanks to Francis Coppola who gave me a story which after 20 plus years hasn't lost its magic and brilliance; [the late] Clark Paylow, who organized the original script breakdown and budget and was there for me and my many questions about how it was done; Alain Silver whose production experience helped greatly in the editing process; David Gaines for his knowledge and contributions to the post-production sections; Michael Wiese and Bob Koster for their continued encouragement and support; Stanley Neufeld for his expertise in the area of the completion bond business; Walter Hill for showing me that someone starting out in production can eventually direct and do it well; and to fellow production animals: Larry Albucher, Ira Halberstadt, Barrie Osborne, Bert Bluestein, Marty Hornstein, Lindsley Parsons, Jr., Ed Morey, Ira Halberstadt, Wolfgang Glattes, Sam Goldrich, George Goodman, Jonathan Sanger, Larry Kostroff, Bob Relyea, Jeff Coleman, Ted Zachary, Mike Hill, Steve Dawson, Jeffrey Wetzel, Nora O'Brien, Barbara Hoke, my continued thanks for being such good friends and answering my repeated questions as we were getting ready to go to press.

Thanks to all Lone Eagle staffers who kept encouraging me . . . especially Blake Busby for his amazing redesign of the forms and for getting all my changes in print, to Bethann Wetzel for her thoughtful editing throughout this process and to Jordan Posell for assuring me that I actually could actually finish this book and produce a movie at the same time.

Writing a book on budgeting was, to say the least, a big undertaking. From the very first day that I mentioned writing it my fate was sealed because I had the bad judgment of saying this to Joan Vietor. That was awhile ago. The book is now complete and only because of her vision and hard work. As I said in *Film Scheduling* there is no one I can give more thanks to than Joan. She is an excellent editor and outstanding publisher. Oh, and, by the way, also now my wife and the mother of our two great kids. She also runs the Space program in her spare time . . . My luck has tripled.

Ralph S. Singleton

AUTHOR'S NOTE

Welcome to budgeting or what might be more accurately called estimating. It has been said that movies are time and money. In the companion book, *Film Scheduling,* we discussed just how much time would be needed to schedule a film project. Here the question is how much money will be needed to produce the same project (*The Conversation*) and why that much will be required. As you become more proficient in budgeting/estimating, you will soon discover that arriving at the bottom line figure does not come instantly. A budget is a well thought-out blueprint which will be your financial plan for your project.

One of the first mistakes you can make is to try to short-cut the process. Using completed budgets from other projects can be helpful, but never forget that each project is unique and so is each budget. Your project's growth, development, and potential success are directly dependent upon how much time and care you give it, and budgeting is one of the most important steps in the entire process.

I'd love to have your comments—praise or criticism when you're finished. I am also looking forward to seeing your name on the screen when future production credits roll.

R. S. S.

HOW TO USE THIS BOOK

THIS BOOK IS INTENDED AS A GUIDE TO BUDGETING everything from major feature films and movies for television to industrial films and smaller projects.

The salaries included here are mostly *union scale wages* for the Los Angeles area. On normal Union productions, the department heads, wages are somewhat above contractual scale rates. As the crew members drop and lower on the ladder, rates come closer to scale rates. Furthermore, there are many individuals who earn higher rates than those given here.

Nonunion production rates vary tremendously. At the upper range, they are almost the same as union rates for the department heads, but as the people in each department have less and less responsibility their wages drop further and further below union rates for the various categories. On extremely low-budget productions, where the total funds available may be significantly less than $1 million, rates are entirely negotiable and sometimes complicated by deferments or other, nonmonetary inducements. This book is designed for a union crew shoot. There is a difference between union and nonunion positions on a film. The basic tasks on a film union or nonunion are the same. Keep in mind that most qualified technicians are in unions because they have, (especially the key technicians more work experience. This area of interchange has been a negotiation point for some time between the unions and the producers and studios.

As new contracts with the guilds and unions go into effect, those scale rates will increase, the fringe benefits will change, and other factors will enter into the mix. Readers should keep up to date with the current rates by using current rate source books such as the *IDC Labor Guide*. Local film commissions in areas where you intend to film either in the United States or abroad can provide you not only with rates, but also with lists of crew members whom you can contact.

Film Budgeting will guide you through the many levels of estimating details contained in any budget and give you a thorough understanding of the budgeting process. It helps you remember obscure estimating items you may overlook and guides you towards making consistent and intelligent choices in your estimates.

When doing your first budget, it is a good idea to include everything which you think could conceivably be needed during your production. Think of all the related things you will need when listing a particular budget item. For example, when listing a horse, don't forget to budget for feed, stable, and transportation, as well as for a wrangler or trainer. It is wiser to have slightly more money than you need for a project than too little.

Most producers and production managers working today created their first budgets using pencils and hand calculators. Now we use computers and the estimating process is largely automated. But when an estimate is in progress it is always a good idea to keep pencil, paper, and a hand-held calculator close at hand even if the majority of your work will by done by data entry. You will always need to figure some things out by yourself, without the help of a sophisticated program or spreadsheet. It is also a good idea to force your computer to recalculate the budget thoroughly from time to time, to check for math errors.

As with scheduling, no matter how sophisticated the computer program is, it cannot make up for one of the most important human elements: experience. Take the time to review a hard copy of your budget. Proofread each line item and spot check. Many embarrassing errors or typos can be caught that a computer might miss.

At the end of this book you will find a list of the popular computer programs available for film scheduling and budgeting at the time of publication. Programs change rapidly and competition between software designers is intense. If you are looking for a good program be sure to try them all out before purchasing one. You may find that you are more comfortable with one than another. A little research will save you hours of scheduling and budgeting time later.

In this book is the budget created for the Academy Award-winning film, *The Conversation*. I owe a debt of gratitude to Francis Coppola for permitting me to use such an excellent film project. The rates reflect current rates and standards. I have also included comments on many elements which were not factors in *The Conversation* but which might figure in your project. This form was designed to remind you of almost any element you may need in the course of production. However, just because an item is mentioned does not mean that you must use it. Use your best judgment and you should come out all right.

Good luck!

Tools

TOOLS

Let's begin with the tools you will need to complete the task of budgeting. You created several of these when you scheduled your project. If you haven't yet broken down the script and created a shooting schedule, you cannot begin to do a proper budget. The more you know about the elements (e.g., the number of days for stunts) the more accurate your budget will be.

You will need the following:

1) Script

This document is your primary source upon which your BREAKDOWN SHEETS, PRODUCTION BOARD and SHOOTING SCHEDULE were derived. Keep it nearby as you begin to fill in the numbers in each budget category.

2) Script Breakdown Sheets

Your breakdown sheets will provide the necessary detail information regarding your script.

3) Production Board (Strip Board)

The production board which you prepared for your project will give you the necessary information on who and what you will need, and for how long. If you haven't prepared a production board for your project and are attempting to budget without one, that's cheating! Take the time to do a board.

4) Shooting Schedule

This typewritten composite of all the information which is contained on your production breakdown sheets, It is easy to read in its format and provides one more cross-check for your information.

5) Calculator

Use a calculator with a paper tape as well as a visual readout. You will always want to check your calculations.

6) Pencils

If you are doing your budget by hand, you will be making too many changes to write in ink. Pencils are easy to write with and reproduce on a copy machine. And when your pencils lose their edge, you will need a pencil sharpener. An electric one saves time.

7) Scratch Paper

Any lined or unlined pad or notebook paper will work. You will find that some of your math concerning a budget area is best worked out in note form before you type it onto the budget. Also, as you are working in one area, a thought may come to you concerning something in a completely different area. Make notes. Don't try to commit everything to memory. Also, *keep the notes!* Two days from now you'll wonder what you were thinking when you wrote that figure.

8) Computer (Optional)

You can greatly cut your budgeting time by using one of the many computer programs on the market to assist in the budget process. (*Refer to the chapter on computer budgeting for a list of available programs as well as a brief discussion of computer use in budgeting.*) If you are planning to schedule and budget projects for a living, it is probably a wise investment to purchase one of the programs.

Where you work is important. You will want a quiet place with few distractions. This process you are beginning will take concentration. Everything you have learned from reading and breaking down the script will now be translated into another form—*numbers* and *money*. Since your first budget, even if prepared on a computer, will not be done in a single day, your work place should allow you the freedom to leave your materials undisturbed until the next day. This will save you a great deal of set-up time.

Budget Structure

Above-the Line and Below-the-Line

FILM PRODUCTION BUDGET

			DATE
The Directors Company	The Conversation		
PRODUCTION COMPANY	PRODUCTION TITLE		PRODUCTION NUMBER
Fred Roos	Francis Coppola	Francis Coppola	Clark Paylow
EXECUTIVE PRODUCER	PRODUCER	DIRECTOR	PRODUCTION MANAGER

11/26/72	1/30/73	11/22/72	157	14
START DATE	FINISH DATE	SCRIPT DATED	SCRIPT PAGES	CREW DAILY PAY HRS.

ACCT NO.	DESCRIPTION	PAGE NO.	BUDGET	TOTALS
0000	Development	3	58,334	
1000	Story and Screenplay	4	76,987	
1100	Producers Unit	5	656,950	
1200	Directors Unit	6	2,107,100	
1300	Cast Unit	7	3,036,899	
1400	Travel and Living	8	135,074	
1900	Fringe Benefits and Payroll Taxes	9	207,716	
	TOTAL ABOVE THE LINE		6,279,060	
2000	Production Department	10	496,472	
2100	Extra Talent	11	127,593	
2200	Art Department	12	178,071	
2300	Set Construction	13	221,645	
2400	Set Dressing	14	397,099	
2500	Property	15	236,405	
2600	Picture Vehicles	16	18,500	
2700	Special Effects	17	104,861	
2800	Camera	18	248,036	
3000	Special Equipment	19	-	
3100	Sound	20	93,201	
3200	Grip	21	178,259	
3300	Lighting	22	218,270	
3400	Wardrobe	23	199,887	
3500	Makeup and Hair	24	104,990	
3600	Set Operations	25, 26	299,785	
3700	Site Rental	27	439,050	
3800	Stage Rental and Expense	28	160,699	
4000	Location Expense	29, 30	5,500	
4100	Second Unit	31, 32	-	
4200	Tests	33	25,000	
4300	Miniatures	34	-	
4400	Process	35	-	
4500	Animals	36	4,506	
4600	Transportation	37	793,723	
4700	Raw Stock and Laboratory	38	279,549	
4900	Fringe Benefits and Payroll Taxes	39	892,605	
	TOTAL BELOW THE LINE		5,723,706	5,723,706

FILM PRODUCTION BUDGET (CONT'D)

		DATE
The Directors Company	The Conversation	
PRODUCTION COMPANY	PRODUCTION TITLE	PRODUCTION NUMBER

ACCT NO.	DESCRIPTION	PAGE NO.	BUDGET	TOTALS
5000	Film Editing	40, 41	554,758	
5100	Music	42	388,000	
5200	Film Effects	43	30,000	
5300	Titles	44	45,000	
5400	Post Production Sound	45	393,500	
5500	Post Production Film	46	124,496	
5900	Fringe Benefits and Payroll Taxes	47	268,250	
	TOTAL POST PRODUCTION		1,804,004	1,804,004
6000	Publicity	48	39,025	
6100	Insurance	49	231,929	
6200	General Expense	50	348,000	
6900	Fringe Benefits and Payroll Taxes	51	10,285	
	TOTAL OTHER COSTS		629,239	629,239
	TOTAL DIRECT COSTS		14,436,009	
7500	Contingency 10%	52	572,371	
7600	Completion Bond 3% x 14,365,082	52	430,952	
7700	Overhead (less w+Fringe)	52		
7800	Interest	52		
	TOTAL NEGATIVE COSTS		15,439,332	
8000	Deferments	52		
	TOTAL NEGATIVE COSTS (Incl. Deferments)			

PRODUCTION DAYS	
Rehearsal	10 dys
Studio	4
Loc. Location	37
Distant Location	-
Holidays	2
Travel	-
Prod. Co. Shutdown Fri. 12/23 - 1/3	
Total Production Days	53

BUDGET APPROVALS

Ralph Singleton*	
ESTIMATOR	EXEC. IN CHARGE OF PROD.
Fred Roos	Clark Paylow
PRODUCER	PRODUCTION MANAGER

June 1996*
DATE

[*Note: These refer to the production of this budget only.]

BUDGET STRUCTURE
Above-the-Line and Below-the-Line

ALL FEATURE BUDGETS, WHETHER OR NOT THEY USE the exact account numbers of a particular studio, retain the style of *the studio system*, in which a line is drawn across the top sheet. Above that line (Above-the-Line) are all the so-called artistic or creative components. Below (Below-the-Line) are all the technical and mechanical components. Of course, many of the crafts people whose departments fall below-the-line make major creative contributions. But in the studio system where each of those crew members and the equipment they used was assigned to a production by a department head, the concepts were simpler. The unit producer oversaw the above-the-line; the unit manager and department heads supervised those below. The hierarchy today hasn't changed much since then, however you will find more and more line producers taking over the functions of the producer of old, as today's producers tend more toward deal making than actually overseeing the day-to-day operations of a production.

In longer form budgets including this one, the editing or post-production costs, the overhead and ancillary costs are grouped together in third and fourth major subsections. While the account numbers and the exact order of the accounts may vary from company to company, the long form budget used by most of the industry is surprisingly uniform.

A budget structure consists of three layers:

1) Top Sheet

This is the *first* sheet you see and the *last* sheet you fill out. It is a one- or two-page summary of the total cost of your project, depending upon degree of detail and the literal size of your budget form: one legal size page or two letter size pages. The top sheet lists the totals from the 50 categories which make up this budget form.

Some producers submit only the top sheet to potential backers of their projects, because many backers are interested only in the broad strokes and bottom line (total) of a budget. The numbers on the top sheet will be generated by figures calculated on the detail level.

2) Account Level

This is the second layer of a budget. A list of the major accounts and their subaccounts comprises the *chart of accounts*. Each account is assigned a number, and each subaccount is assigned another number under the major account. For example, the *Camera Department* is known as Account 2800. Under that are sub-accounts for the *director of photography*, the *operator*, *camera rentals*, and so forth. Each of those has its own number, which relates to the major account. For instance, the operator subaccount in our budget is 2802. All the items in the budget relating to the camera operator will be placed in this subaccount.

3) Detail Lines

This is the lowest level of a budget. Any figure entered into the detail sub-accounts appears at the account level and on the top sheet, as an increment of a larger account figure. The detail level, therefore, is the only level on which figures for individual units should be entered. In this instance, the number of prep, shoot, and wrap weeks for the camera operator are multiplied by the weekly rate and yield a line item total. All the line item totals for 2802 are then added to provide the subaccount totals. Next all the subaccount totals will be combined into the total for the entire account, which will appear at the end of the account detail and on the topsheet. Computer budgets will perform this math for you automatically. As we proceed with the budget you will see how this structure is used efficiently to build up an economic picture of the project you are estimating.

Subtotal Columns
There are three columns on the budget form. "A" covers any person who is fringeable (union/guild member) andtaxable. "B" covers non-fringeable (nonunion) and taxable. "C" covers anyone exempt from fringes (such as loan-out companies), purchases and nontaxable (items on which you will pay taxes after the film is complete).

FIRST STEPS

Begin by filling in the project information requested on the summary sheet or top sheet. Do not fill in the date until the entire budget is complete. Such items as *script dated* and *script pages* can be obtained from the screenplay. The breakdown of *production days* comes from your shooting schedule as do your *start date* and *finish date.*

This is the first of several budgets which will be done before you start principal photography. Why several budgets? Your initial estimates may be too high and you may need to make cuts before the project can be financed. Script changes may also cause costs to vary. Or as actors are cast or locations are chosen, their availabilities may alter the schedule and, in turn, the budget. As the planned start date for principal photography draws closer, the deals and decisions made by the production team will further refine your cost estimates. For example, your script may call for a scene which occurs at the base of the Statue of Liberty. You budget up-to-date information on going to New York to film on location. After your first estimate, your production designer suggests to you that it can be done more easily with a mock-up of the base of the statue on a grass area in Griffith Park. So you budget more for set construction and less for location expenses. Then you find that it will be even easier to do it with a **BLUE SCREEN PROCESS** and a computer-generated Statue of Liberty. Now your set construction estimate is adjusted downwards and your electronic photography bill goes up. Until a film is in the can, the estimate can vary in interesting and unusual ways.

Next fill in the names for the project: *Executive Producer, Producer, Director,* and *Production Manager*. You should find these names also entered on the *header* of the production board.

Production Company
This is the name of the company producing the film: major studio, independent production company, your own production company, etc.

Production Title
This is the name, or working title, of the film.

Production Number
The major film companies or production companies that have more than one project in production usually assign an identifying number to a film so that correspondence can be easily identified and all bills charged to the correct production.

Independent productions can use any number, but it would be useful if it contained the year and at least one other digit unique to that production, e.g. 96-003 suggests the third production of 1996.

Crew Daily Pay Hours
The number of hours of straight time compensation you will pay the crew for a day's work are the *daily pay hours*. Suppose the crew is budgeted for a 12 hour day (a normal work day in film and television.) You will pay the crew for eight hours at straight time, and four hours at time-and-a-half. The four, time and one-half hours, will be paid as if they were six standard pay hours. So your actual work hours for the day will be 12, but your pay hours will be eight plus six, or 14. If the company works more than 12 hours almost every shooting day, it is very likely that the film will go over budget. When *The Conversation* was scheduled, each day's work was weighed keeping an average 12 hour work day in mind. The exception to the pay-hour rule is the technician who is paid on a *weekly* flat or **ON CALL SALARY** (*e.g., set decorator.*)

Rehearsal

Fill in the number of days needed for rehearsal, based on what your project can afford. If you are doing an *average* feature film ($10-12 million independent average, now over $30 million for studios), estimate your director and cast for ten *working* days (Monday through Friday.) This gives the director time to work with the cast and explore the characters and scenes in the screenplay. Rehearsal time is important. Without it the shooting period is used to answer many of the cast's questions and problems while 85 plus technicians wait around on the set. Unfortunately in most television shows (especially episodic) money is in short supply and little, if any rehearsal time is made available. You basically rehearse on the set on the day you're shooting the scene(s).

Production Days

Go to the end of the top sheet and locate the section entitled *production days*. You will be able to complete this information based on the production strip board. Production days are divided into three types: *Studio, Local Location* and *Distant Location.*

Studio Days are those days on which the company does its filming within a studio. The production office is also considered the studio and, therefore, no travel time is figured into the day's work schedule.

Local Location Days are those days where your film company is performing its work near home base, without necessitating an overnight stay. If you choose to bus your crew to a local location from the studio, they are paid for the travel time. If you ask them to drive-to or **REPORT TO** a location then studio conditions apply and they are on the clock from when they arrive. *[Note: This might seem simple enough, but there are several hidden costs involved in a drive-to. More than likely you will have to pay for a secured parking area and give each crew member a mileage allowance. On a union shoot where most technicians will be working under I.A.T.S.E. (Interna-*

tional Alliance of Theatrical Stage Employees) conditions, they will qualify for **GOLDEN HOURS** *(aka* **GOLDEN TIME***) or enhanced overtime two hours earlier then when they are bused to a location. It should also be noted that, whether it is a full union or nonunion show, you may elect to drive certain people, such as stars or the director, to location while asking the rest of the cast and crew to drive.]*

Distant Location Days are shoot days which take place outside the **STUDIO ZONE**, or are far enough for your crew to need lodging arrangements. Certain cities have specified areas within which are considered local locations, and outside of which are considered distant locations. (See following page for more detailed explanation.)

Holidays

These are legal days off. There are nine days recognized by the unions in California: *New Year's Day, Presidents' Day, Good Friday, Memorial Day, Independence Day, Labor Day, Thanksgiving Day, the day after Thanksgiving*, and *Christmas Day*. If a holiday falls on a Saturday, the previous Friday is considered the holiday. If the holiday falls on a Sunday, the following Monday is the day off.

Travel Days

Those days on which the company is transported to an overnight location. The rule of thumb is that "travel time is work time," so avoid the common mistake of budgeting for only one-way transportation. Later on when you are figuring wages, don't forget that your cast and Union crew are paid a minimum day or eight hours at regular time for any travel day no matter how much time is actually spent in traveling. If the trip is a short one, however, it is permitted to travel and work (i.e., shoot scenes) or work and travel on the same day.

Special Days
These are any circumstances which might require you to shut down or delay the completion of principal photography. For example, the crew of *The Conversation* agreed to accept a week off without pay between Christmas and New Year's. This gave them a much-needed rest and allowed the company a breather to recoup for the final weeks of filming.

IMPORTANT TERMS

Although the following terms are defined in the *Glossary* in the back of the book, their definitions are repeated here. Get to know the definitions of these terms, as they are used frequently in production:

Studio Zone
Many cities have specified areas of a certain radius from a central point. In Los Angeles, it is a radius of 30 miles from the old AMPTP (Alliance of Motion Picture and Television Producers) headquarters at La Cienega and Fairfax. In New York City it is wherever the subway goes. Anything outside of that area is considered to be a distant location. More precisely, any location where cast and crew are required to spend the night is considered a *distant location*, and anything else is considered to be within the *studio zone*.

Location
Any locale used for shooting away from the studio. Location shooting provides special problems for production managers who must arrange for food, shelter, toilet facilities, transportation to and from for cast and crew plus generators and any other special equipment.

Report To
An instruction written on the **CALL SHEET** to indicate that crew members are working at a studio or at a local location, that they are expected to transport themselves to the set, and that their work time can begin upon their arrival at the **SET**.

Bus To

As opposed to *report to*, this signifies a location day for the crew. Their work (pay) time begins when they report to the bus for the ride to the location and ends when the bus returns them to their point of origin after the day's work. On IATSE shows, overtime conditions change on a *bus to*, specifically **GOLDEN TIME** does not begin until after 14 hours as opposed 12 hours of work in the *studio location* or on a *report to location*.

Drive To

Money paid to an employee for furnishing his own transportation to and from location. The usual sum is $.30 per mile. [*Note: Remember that the IRS allows $.28 per mile, and taxes will be charged not for the $.02 difference, but for the whole $.30. Some companies pay for the gasoline used avoiding the $.30 per mile charge. Most companies consider mileage money, kit/box rental and other items outside of the basic salary to be taxable income. These payments are reported on a 1099-MISC form to the government.*]

Wage Scale

There are union locals which deal with theatrical and television films throughout the United States. The major centers are Los Angeles, New York and Chicago. The rates vary (with the exception of WGA, DGA and SAG) from place to place. Some quote hourly minimums and others quote daily minimums. Again we are using the union locals in Los Angeles for *The Conversation*. Check your local area for the current rates.

Five-Out-Of-Seven Day Rule

The most recent guild and union contracts now permit that a workweek, while in a *studio zone*, may be any five out of the seven week days. For instance, you might be using a location, such as a courthouse, which is only available during the weekend. To take advantage of this location on the weekend you may define your workweek as Wednesday through Sunday, with each Monday and Tuesday off. Once you define this work week, however, you must stay with it for the entire show.

Account 0000

Development Costs

PAGE NO. 3

PRODUCTION NUMBER	PRODUCTION TITLE	DATE

0000 DEVELOPMENT COSTS		SUBTOTALS		
ACCT NO.	DESCRIPTION	A	B	C
	Story and Screenplay			
	Rights and Options ALLOW			6,234
	Drafts and Treatments			
	Typing ALLOW			1,000
	Script Duplication ALLOW			500
	Producer's Unit			
	Producer			
	Assoc. Producer			
	Secretary 12 weeks @ 500		6,000	
	Additional Hire 12 weeks @ 300		3,600	
	Director's Unit			
	Director			
	Secretary			
	Additional Hire			
	Budget Preparation FLAT			3,000
	Script Breakdown, Production Board and			
	Budget Preparation Fee			
	Accounting			
	Legal			
	Incorporation			1,500
	Contracts			1,000
	Business License ALLOW			12,712
	Other ALLOW			5,000
	Office Overhead			
	Telephone and Telex ALLOW			3,000
	Answering Service			300
	Telephone Installation Charge			
	Office Rent 750/mo. X 6 mos.			4,500
	Equipment/Furniture ALLOW			1,000
	Rental			
	Purchase			
	Data Processing ALLOW			1,500
	Supplies			500
	Stationery			250
	Postage 100/mo. X 6 mos.			600
	Transportation			
	Car Allowance .28□ per mile X 100 per wk. X 6 mos		728	
	Gas, Oil			
	Additional Expenses			500
	RESEARCH/TRAVEL ALLOW			2,000
	Miscellaneous			1,000
	Fringe Benefits Allow 18.5% "B" Column (10,328)		1,910	
	SUBTOTALS		12,238	46,196
	TOTAL ACCT 0000			58,334

A = Fringeable/Taxable
B = Non-Fringeable/Taxable
C = Non-Taxable

SEC. 21.109. MOTION PICTURE, TELEVISION AND RADIO PRODUCERS:
(Title amended by Ord. No. 167,416, Eff. 12/27/91, Oper. 1/1/84.)

(a) (Amended by Ord. No. 167,416, Eff. 12/27/91, Oper. 1/1/84.) For the purposes of this section a motion picture, television, or radio producer is a person who engages in the business of producing motion pictures, television programs, radio programs or advertising material for such media, including pictures or programs in which animation is used. Said businesses include, but are not limited to, the development of a story, whether based on fact or fiction, the photographing of the story or program, whether by means of photographic film, magnetic tape, or other device, the recording of the program, and the cutting, scoring, editing, and final preparation of the picture, program or commercial for release or viewing, and when performed by a person engaged in the foregoing activities also includes either or both of the following:

1. The lending by a motion picture, television or radio producer of the services of employees for which the producer has contracted to one or more other producers; and

2. The furnishing of motion picture, television or radio studio facilities to other such media producers where the facilities include, in addition to physical equipment, the services of technicians such as cameramen, soundman, carpenters, electricians and set decorators.

Every person engaged in the business of being a motion picture, television, or radio producer shall pay a tax in the amount provided in subsection (c). The measure of the tax in each instance shall be the total of the following sums: the gross cost of production of motion pictures, television programs, radio programs and advertising materials; the gross receipts received by the producer in return for the lending of the services of employees as described herein; and the gross receipts received by the producer in return for the furnishing of studio facilities in the manner described herein.

(b) (Amended by Ord. No. 167,416, Eff. 12/27/91, Oper. 1/1/84.) Every person engaged in the business of reconstructing motion pictures, television programs or commercials by synchronizing pictures with sound, or making or producing sound scores, other than a sound score made or produced by a motion picture, television or radio producer in the preparation for release of a production, shall pay a tax measured by the gross cost of the work done in the amount provided in subsection (c).

(c) (Amended by Ord. Nos. 159,384, Eff. 11/8/84, Oper. 1/1/85 and 166,204, Eff. 10/11/90, Oper. 1/1/91.) The taxes charged for the privilege of engaging in the businesses described in this section are as follows:

Where the measure of the tax is less than $50,000.00, the tax shall be $147.80 per year;

Where the measure of the tax is $50,000.00 or more, and less than $100,000.00, the tax shall be $295.65 per year;

Where the measure of the tax is $100,000.00 or more, and less than $200,000.00, the tax shall be $591.25 per year;

Where the measure of the tax is $200,000.00 or more, and less than $300,000.00, the tax shall be $886.90 per year;

1

ACCOUNT #: NAME: Effective Jan 1, 1992

L.A.M.C. Section 21.109 MOTION PICTURE, TELEVISION and RADIO PRODUCERS

The tax rate for this business classification is based upon certain gross cost of production and other associated activities in the City of Los Angeles. For purposes of this ordinance, gross cost of production include, but are not limited to, the cost of:

(1) Producing motion pictures or photoplays, whether using actors or animated characters;
(2) Developing of screen play;
(3) Photographing or taping said picture;
(4) Cutting, scoring, editing and final preparation.

In addition to the above costs, income from the following activities is included in the basis for tax when performed by the producer:

(1) Lending by the producer of the services of contract players to other producers.
(2) Furnishing of studio facilities to other producers, where the facilities include, in addition to the physical equipment, the services of technicians,(cameramen, soundmen, electricians, carpenters, decorators,etc.)

TAX SCHEDULE

BASIS FOR TAX IF GROSS COSTS OF PRODUCTION IS:

				TAX
		not more than	$ 49,999	$ 147.80
at least	$ 50,000	but less than	$ 100,000	$ 295.65
at least	$ 100,000	but less than	$ 200,000	$ 591.25
at least	$ 200,000	but less than	$ 300,000	$ 886.90
at least	$ 300,000	but less than	$ 400,000	$ 1,182.50
at least	$ 400,000	but less than	$ 500,000	$ 1,478.15
at least	$ 500,000	but less than	$ 600,000	$ 1,773.75
at least	$ 600,000	but less than	$ 700,000	$ 2,069.40
at least	$ 700,000	but less than	$ 800,000	$ 2,365.00
at least	$ 800,000	but less than	$ 900,000	$ 2,660.65
at least	$ 900,000	but less than	$ 1,000,000	$ 2,956.25
at least	$ 1,000,000	but less than	$ 1,100,000	$ 3,251.90
at least	$ 1,100,000	but less than	$ 1,200,000	$ 3,547.50
at least	$ 1,200,000	but less than	$ 1,300,000	$ 3,843.15
at least	$ 1,300,000	but less than	$ 1,400,000	$ 4,138.75
at least	$ 1,400,000	but less than	$ 1,500,000	$ 4,434.40
at least	$ 1,500,000	but less than	$ 1,600,000	$ 4,730.00
at least	$ 1,600,000	but less than	$ 1,700,000	$ 5,025.65
at least	$ 1,700,000	but less than	$ 1,800,000	$ 5,321.25
at least	$ 1,800,000	but less than	$ 1,900,000	$ 5,616.90
at least	$ 1,900,000	but less than	$ 2,000,000	$ 5,912.50
at least	$ 2,000,000	but less than	$ 2,100,000	$ 6,208.15
at least	$ 2,100,000	but less than	$ 2,200,000	$ 6,503.75
at least	$ 2,200,000	but less than	$ 2,300,000	$ 6,799.40
at least	$ 2,300,000	but less than	$ 2,400,000	$ 7,095.00
at least	$ 2,400,000	but less than	$ 2,500,000	$ 7,390.65
at least	$ 2,500,000	but less than	$ 2,600,000	$ 7,686.25
at least	$ 2,600,000	but less than	$ 2,700,000	$ 7,981.90
at least	$ 2,700,000	but less than	$ 2,800,000	$ 8,277.50
at least	$ 2,800,000	but less than	$ 2,900,000	$ 8,573.15
at least	$ 2,900,000	but less than	$ 3,000,000	$ 8,868.75
at least	$ 3,000,000	but less than	$ 3,100,000	$ 9,164.40
at least	$ 3,100,000	but less than	$ 3,200,000	$ 9,460.00
at least	$ 3,200,000	but less than	$ 3,300,000	$ 9,755.65
at least	$ 3,300,000	but less than	$ 3,400,000	$ 10,051.25
at least	$ 3,400,000	but less than	$ 3,500,000	$ 10,346.90
at least	$ 3,500,000	but less than	$ 3,600,000	$ 10,642.50
at least	$ 3,600,000	but less than	$ 3,700,000	$ 10,938.15
at least	$ 3,700,000	but less than	$ 3,800,000	$ 11,233.75
at least	$ 3,800,000	but less than	$ 3,900,000	$ 11,529.40
at least	$ 3,900,000	but less than	$ 4,000,000	$ 11,825.00
at least	$ 4,000,000	but less than	$ 4,100,000	$ 12,120.65
at least	$ 4,100,000	but less than	$ 4,200,000	$ 12,416.25
	$ 4,200,000	or more	the tax is	$ 12,711.90

On your worksheet (page 2), enter the gross cost of production in **Column A**, **"Basis For Tax"** adjacent to **Fund L, Class Code 109.** Find your tax from the schedule above and enter the tax in **Column C, "Tax Computation"**, and in **Column E.**

IF THIS BUSINESS ACTIVITY WAS NEW LAST YEAR, after entering the amount of your tax in **Column "E"**, take that amount, and from it, subtract $147.80. Enter the resulting amount in **Column "F", "Back Tax"**. Now, enter the total of the amounts from **Column E** and **Column F** to **Column G** of the worksheet and in the **"Tax Due"** column adjacent to **Fund L, Class Code 109** of your renewal form (pages 4 & 6).

IF THIS BUSINESS ACTIVITY WAS NOT NEW LAST YEAR, enter the amount from **Column E** to **Column G** of the worksheet and in the **"Tax Due"** column adjacent to **Fund L, Clase Code 109** of your renewal form (pages 4 & 6).

rev 12/94 -2D- RETAIN FOR YOUR RECORDS

CITY OF LOS ANGELES

TAX WORKSHEET

retain for your records

Account No.: NAME:

(*) indicates an activity that was new last year and may be subject to BACK TAX. See page 8. (* *) See page 8. BUSINESS ACTIVITY DESCRIPTION	FUND	CLASS	Column A BASIS FOR TAX See page 1 ENTER HERE AND ON ANNUAL TAX REPORTING FORM RENEWAL	Col. B TAX RATE	Column C TAX COMPUTATION see inst. (4) below	Col. D MINIMUM TAX	Column E Amount from Col. C or Col. D whichever is larger	Column F *BACK TAX If activity new last year: Col. E minus Col. D	Column G TAX DUE Col. E Plus Col. F ENTER HERE AND ON ANNUAL TAX REPORTING FORM RENEWAL
I PAYROLL EXPENSE ①			(1) .00						
II BUSINESS CLASSIFICATION ②			(2) .00	$ (3)	(4)	$ (5)	(6)	(7)	(8)
③			.00	$		$			
④			.00	$		$			
⑤			.00	$		$			
⑥			.00	$		$			
⑦			.00	$		$			
⑧			.00	$		$			
⑨			.00	$		$			

(1) Column A. Line 1: Enter payroll expense. If zero, enter 0. Also enter payroll expense or zero (0) if no payroll expense. on line 1. in Column A. pages 4 and 6 of the renewal form.

(2) Column A. Lines 2-9: Enter BASIS FOR TAX (gross receipts, alleys, tables, etc.); see page 1.

(3) Column B: This is the tax rate for this business activity.

(4) Column C: The tax computation is based on the rate shown per one thousand dollars ($1,000) of gross receipts or fractional part thereof. **Round up total** gross receipts in Column A to the next highest $1,000. Enter the result of the rounded amount of Column A multiplied by the tax rate in Column B.

EXAMPLE: Gross receipts of $237,461 would be calculated as 238 x TAX RATE = TAX. However, in Column A of the Reporting Form your gross receipts would be shown as $237,461.

(5) Column D: This is the minimum tax for this business activity.

(6) Column E: Enter the larger amount of Column C or D. If zero, enter 0.

(7) Column F: Subtract Column D from Column E for all activities with an asterisk (*) and enter the result. If no BACK TAX enter zero (0) in Column F.

(8) Column G: Enter the total of Columns E and F.

(9) Columns A and G (shaded areas): Transfer all information from these columns of the TAX WORKSHEET to lines 1-9 of the Annual Tax Reporting Form Renewal.

(10) Complete the Annual Tax Reporting Form Renewal (pages 4 and 6).

0103-03-000527745

CITY OF LOS ANGELES
OFFICE OF THE CITY CLERK
Tax and Permit Division

ANNUAL TAX REPORTING FORM
1996 RENEWAL

RETURN THIS COPY

P.O. BOX 54770 LOS ANGELES, CA 90054-0770

ACCOUNT NO.	MC	O.B. DATE	OFFICE USE ONLY Pd. Dt.	PC	PERIOD	HATER FLD REC'T #

COMPLETE THE WORKSHEET BEFORE MAKING ENTRIES ON THIS FORM.

	BUSINESS ACTIVITY DESCRIPTION		FUND	CLASS CODE	ENTER FROM WORKSHEET (COL. A) BASIS FOR TAX	(COL. G) TAX DUE
I	PAYROLL EXPENSE	①			.00	
II	BUSINESS CLASSIFICATION	②			.00	$
		③			.00	$
		④			.00	$
		⑤			.00	$
		⑥			.00	$
		⑦			.00	$
		⑧			.00	$
		⑨			.00	$

IMPORTANT
IF ANY OF THE FOLLOWING CHANGES APPLY TO YOUR BUSINESS OPERATION, PLEASE READ THE REVERSE SIDE OF THIS FORM, AND CHECK THE APPLICABLE STATEMENT BELOW.

- (a) ☐ Legal Name, and/or DBA
- (b) ☐ Address Changes
- (c) ☐ Building Sold
- (d) ☐ Business Sold or Discontinued
- (e) ☐ Business Activity Sold or Discontinued
- (f) ☐ Portion of Business Activity Sold or Transferred

Z 999
OFFICE USE ONLY

	ENTER TOTAL LINES ② THRU ⑨ ABOVE.	→	⑩ $
III PRINCIPAL TAX DUE	TOTAL OF TAX PLUS 3¾% SURTAX: COMPUTE AS FOLLOWS: AMOUNT ON LINE ⑩ X 1.0375 =	→	⑪ $
IV LATE PAYMENT	INTEREST (IF PAID AFTER 02-29-96)	See page 1	⑫ $
	PENALTY (IF PAID AFTER 02-29-96)	See page 1	⑬ $
V TOTAL AMOUNT DUE: TOTAL OF LINES ⑪ ⑫ & ⑬	MAKE CHECKS PAYABLE TO: City Clerk, City of Los Angeles. Your check or money order must be drawn on United States Banks only. Please write your account number on your check.		⑭ $

enf. MAIL RENEWAL TO: P.O. BOX 54770 LOS ANGELES, CA 90054-0770

I DECLARE, UNDER PENALTY OF PERJURY UNDER THE LAWS OF THE STATE OF CALIFORNIA THAT TO THE BEST OF MY KNOWLEDGE THE FOREGOING IS TRUE AND CORRECT.
0103-04-000527745

SIGNATURE ____________ DATE ________
TITLE ____________ DAYTIME PHONE ( ) ________

- 4 -

PRODUCTION CHECKLIST

DATE

PRODUCTION COMPANY | PRODUCTION TITLE | PRODUCTION NUMBER

CAST – SPEAKING	
Deal Memos	
Contracts Signed	
Wardrobe Fitted	
Special Make-up	
Hair Falls or Wigs	
Stunt/Photo Doubles	
Minors – Intent to Employ	
Welfare Worker/Teacher	
SAG – Station 12 Checked	
Musicians	
Other:	

CREW – CAMERA	
Equipment Ordered/Checked	
Film Ordered	
Dolly Needed	
Other:	

CREW – SOUND	
Equipment Ordered/Checked	
1/4" Tape Ordered	
Walkie Talkies	
PA System	
Playback	
Communication System to Set	
Other:	

CREW – OTHER	
Art Director –	
Grips – Any Special Equipment	
Electricians – Light Changes	
Special Effects – Discuss & Set	
Props – Discuss	
Make-up – Period/Special	
Body Make-up	
Hair – Period/Special	
Wardrobe – Period/Special	
Greensman – Special	
Script Supervisor – Script Timing	
Dialogue Coach	
Transportation Coordinator – Period/Special	
Set Decorator – Period/Special	
Other:	

SILENT – ATMOSPHERE	
Interviews	
Fittings	
Vouchers	
Mileage	
Minors – Intent to Employ	
Welfare Worker/Teacher	
Make-up or Hair – Period/Special	
Adjustments Necessary	
Piano Player for Music Cues	
Other:	

MISCELLANEOUS	
Technical Advisors	
First Aid	
Police	
Guards	
Fire Safety Officers & Fire Permits	
City License/Permits	
Location Permits	
Heaters	
Livestock or Animals	
Handlers or Wranglers	
Tables and Benches	
Schoolroom Facilities	
Coffee & Rolls	
Breakfast	
Lunch	
Dinner	
Call Sheets	
Set Status Reports	
Production Reports	
Transportation and Lunch Lists	
Other:	

EQUIPMENT	
Generator	
Extra Camera	
Crane	
Special Process	
Trucks	
Vehicles – Picture or Standby	
Buses	
Insert Car	
Water Wagon	
Honeywagons	
Dressing Rooms	
Motor Homes	
Other:	

0000—DEVELOPMENT COSTS

DEVELOPMENT ENCOMPASSES EVERYTHING THAT HAPPENS before a project is funded. In independent production, it is that time prior to the backers' approval of the project for production. At a major studio, it is the time when the studio advances money to explore the feasibility of production.

When a project is being developed, either by you or by a studio or production company, certain costs are incurred in that development. The 0000 account allows you to keep track of all these expenses. If the project is being developed under a **DEVELOPMENT DEAL**, these expenses will be charged against whatever money was advanced, and later incorporated into the production budget. If the project is being developed from out-of-pocket money without benefit of a development deal, then use this account to keep track of all your expenses for possible reimbursement when the project is financed. Depending on the method of accounting chosen, these costs can remain broken out in this account or can be reassigned under their respective categories.

Remember that if you are developing the project on speculation, you could very easily end up bearing the development costs yourself if financing is never completed. So use your money wisely.

STORY AND SCREENPLAY

Rights and Options

In the normal order of filmmaking, a project usually begins with something written on paper—an original script, a bestselling book, a magazine article, or a few words jotted down on a cocktail napkin. The right to use these words to create the film need to be secured and paid for. It is not unusual for the final purchase price of the story and screenplay to be upwards of six figures. It is unusual, however, to pay that entire price during the development process. More often than not, a producer secures an option—the right to buy the rights—for a fixed fee.

In the case of *The Conversation*, we are dealing with an original screenplay and a well-known screenwriter. Francis Coppola's work demands a higher price than the average writer would expect and a great deal more than the Writers Guild of America scale: $62,337. However, for development costs, we are going to include the cost of the **OPTION** on the property. For our budget, let's use 10 percent of the purchase price, or $6,234.

When negotiating this option agreement, it is customary to negotiate the entire writer's contract. If the writer is a member of the Writer's Guild of America (WGA), then certain minimums will apply as well as fringe benefits. The cost of negotiating this option should be included in development costs under Legal (*see page 28.*) The fringes, however, would be included under the Story and Screenplay Account 1000.

Typing

Whether or not you use a computer or word processor, the script will need to be typed and retyped several times until you have the draft with which you feel comfortable, so. Allow approximately $1,000.

Script Duplication

From making a few copies of the 10 page **TREATMENT** to making copies of the 110-120 page screenplay for prospective backers—the cost of duplicating pages really adds up. It is not unusual to spend in the neighborhood of $500 in script duplicating costs while you are in Development. *[Note: Once your project is given a green light—a "go" picture—then you will need to duplicate scripts for the entire crew. These costs would be included under the Story and Screenplay Account 1000—not Development.]*

PRODUCER UNIT

Producer

If you as the *producer* are personally funding your project, you will want to be reimbursed for your expenses when the project gets financed. Keep records and document all your expenses showing whom you saw and how you spent the money to secure the go ahead for your project. If you are operating under a **DEVELOPMENT DEAL** with a major studio or independent that permits an advance against your fees, this amount can be drawn in increments or on a weekly basis, but expect to charge it back (i.e., reduce) the fees you are paid when pre-production actually begins.

Associate Producer

When your project is in development, you will find it is useful and necessary to get some assistance. Although money is usually tight during this period, it is a good idea to negotiate a **STEP DEAL** whereby your *associate producer* receives a small amount in the beginning to be increased when the money for the budget is funded. Also your associate producer could be paid a portion of the weekly rate now and with the other portion deferred until the project is funded. Since there are no rules, it depends upon what the project can afford.

Secretary

The key to getting a project off the ground is communication. All your correspondence must be typed. If you are proficient on a personal computer, you may be able to handle this by yourself for a while. Eventually, you will need to hire a *secretary* to type, answer the phones and set up your office. You will probably spend at least $500 per week for a secretary in a major city, slightly less in smaller towns.

Additional Hire(s)

If you find yourself spending more time personally dropping off scripts or, are using a messenger service which is getting costly, you might want to consider hiring a **RUNNER** or **GOFER** to take care of this for you. Many students are looking to break in by doing "anything in the motion picture business," so you should be able to find a willing runner for not too much money. Figure around $200 to $300 per week including payment for automobile usage and fuel. Independent productions often use **INTERNS** or unpaid persons who agree to work for expenses only. A temporary secretary might also be needed for a few days to mail out your proposal to prospective money sources. Figure at least $5-$6 per hour. If the temp is hired through a temporary agency you can expect to pay more from $7.50 to $12.50 per hour.

DIRECTOR UNIT

Director

You may have a *director* working with you developing the project. If you are working as an independent producer, having a marketable director attached to your project can help you raise the money for production. There are times when the director comes with the project, as when a director has written or co-written the script. If a director is working with you in the development stage, the director will want to be paid or reimbursed for at least expenses he has paid to help you fund the project. If the director is a member of the Directors Guild of America and is actually "supervising the development of a screenplay (as distinguished from reviewing or commenting upon a completed or substantially-completed screenplay)," then per the DGA Basic Agreement the fee for these "development services" is $26,634 (effective July 1, 1994).

BUDGET PREPARATION, SCRIPT BREAKDOWN, PRODUCTION BOARD & BUDGET PREPARATION FEE

The cost of breaking down your film project varies upon whom you get to do it. It takes approximately two weeks by hand or one week on computer to break your script down and complete a budget. A typical fee is between $2,500 and $5,000. The basis for this is Directors Guild scale for unit production managers since they usually do this type of work. Scale for a unit production manager is $2,705 per week (effective July 1, 1994). If you do your own breakdown and budget and have limited experience doing so, it is highly recommended that you have a professional who does film budgets look your work over before you submit it.

Accounting
It is wise to retain an accountant or bookkeeper. If you form a corporation for your production company and/or project, there will be reports which have to be submitted to the state agency of the state in which you are incorporated. Failure to comply costs could result in decertification and/or fines (and other problems discussed immediately below under Legal) which can be avoided if you have an accountant. Keep your accountant informed of anything to do with finance. Begin with weekly reports to the accountant. As your project develops and costs increase you may wish to switch to daily reporting of what you have spent and what you have committed to down the road. Waiting too long to get all the facts together will always cost you money. The financiers will need to see a detailed report of how much has been spent to date and may want to have a *cash flow*, a detailed document based on the budget and showing exactly when and how much money will be needed in order to produce the project.

LEGAL

Incorporation/Limited Liability
Incorporating, or forming LLPs or LLCs (Limited Liability Partnerships or Limited Liability Corporations), will limit your personal liability to some extent. When outside investors or partners are involved, you should discuss forming such an entity to protect yourself and your partners from certain liabilities. Incorporating, or forming an LLC or LLP, is moderately expensive, however, and should be done when your attorney advises to. Allow at least $1,500 for incorporation costs.

Contracts
As your project progresses, you will need to have contracts with the writer, director, and various other individuals and companies who have decided to be in business with you. Your attorney should read them before you sign. Speak to your attorney about your project and try to set some guidelines ahead of time. Most entertainment attorneys charge between $150 to $400 per hour. That may seem

high to you now, but will seem a small price to have paid if you find yourself in litigation later due to poorly prepared contracts.

Business License

Depending on the rules and regulations of the city in which you are working, you may have to obtain a business license. It also depends upon what business you're in. If you are set up in the city of Los Angeles, your license fee will depend upon certain gross costs of production and other associated activities in the city of Los Angeles. (*See Appendix.*) If *The Conversation* had been done in Los Angeles, the business license would be $12,711.90 since the gross cost of production is in the upper scale ($4.2 million or more).

Other

Any other legal expense not covered under the above goes in this account. For instance, this account could cover the cost of negotiations for the screenplay and with the distributor.

Office Overhead

You may need to rent an office for the development period. Since it obviously is less expensive to use your own home or office, you can cut down your development expenses by doing so. If you have a development deal with a major studio they will probably give you office space on their lot, although they will charge it to your production and repay themselves as soon as your project is given a *green light*. You may also negotiate a secretary as part of your studio deal.

Telephone and Fax

A call to the local business office will give you the costs. Your phone bill will depend upon where your project takes place, how many people are using the phone, and how many calls are made. If you have several domestic and/or overseas locations, using a fax is less expensive and highly recommended. If your project, has key personnel in one city scouting and the production office in another, you may find that a great deal of time and expense can be saved by sending faxes rather than sending everything by an overnight delivery service. Allow a minimum of $3,000. This fee will be slightly higher if you need to pay setup charges for your phone, or phone system.

Answering Service/Answering Machine/ Pager/Cellular Phone

When your project is just beginning, you don't ever want to miss a phone call. When your project is a "go" and you are in production, you sometimes wish you could permanently silence the phones! In any event, it is always important to be reachable by telephone. Until you can afford someone to answer your phones on a permanent basis, either an answering service, answering machine, or custom features from your local phone company is a good idea. A custom features package includes *call waiting*, *call forwarding*, and *voice mail* with a personalized message. These are available in most localities for a onetime installation fee and a small monthly charge. Some custom packages, high-end answering machines, and, of course, an answering service, can page you when a message is received. Many people today use cellular phones making you instantly available. Discount rates and package deals are available.

If you are using a personal computer, than look into using e-mail or another telecommunications systems available from several companies.

Pagers can be leased for pennies a month or purchased for under $100 and are quite sophisticated. Newer models not only beep you or vibrate on your belt (if you are on the set and wish to be silent) with the caller's number, but can also display alphanumeric information that gives you a new time for dailies or the appointment you have coming up. At press time, new combination pages/ phones were being released. They are about the size of an average pager and cost about $300.

Office Rent

This will vary depending upon what part of the country you live in, what section of town you want your office located, and what amenities you require. As an example, the cost of warehouse property in one part of the Los Angeles costs as little as $.55 per square foot. The cost runs around $2.25 per square foot in a suburb which is twenty minutes away. Your budget should include $500 to $1,000 per month for rent during the development period. If you are supporting the development costs yourself, try not to commit to an office until you have a firm commitment for financing. Rent mounts up, and until you have a "go," most of your meetings will likely take place in other people's offices.

Equipment/Furniture

At the beginning it is advisable to rent as little as possible. If you know that your development period is going to be long, then buying a file cabinet, a desk, or even a small copying machine will quite possibly be cheaper. Try to keep this figure under $1,000.

Data Processing

Almost everyone has a computer these days, and you will be using yours for all your office work, from letter typing to check reconciliation. Since more than likely you already own a computer, you should allot some money in this account for supplies such as toner cartridges for the printer, paper, disks, etc. Fifteen hundred dollars ($1,500) is what we've put in here. The cost of a program for breakdowns and budgeting can also be included here and may be amortized over several projects. (*See Computer Budgeting chapter for more details.*)

Supplies

This covers staples, pens, ribbons, labels, pencils, etc. Try to keep this figure within reason. Five hundred dollars ($500) should be adequate.

Stationery

Stationery companies, like script services, have built large businesses on production companies that never got to the first day of filming. Stationery is important, but sinking a large amount of money into custom designed letterhead at the expense of some other more critical need is a mistake. Your word processor and a laser printer can create a very professional letterhead for you, and print it on bond paper and envelopes. There will be plenty of time for the mailing labels, personalized memo pads and the like when you are funded and into pre-production. If possible keep this under $250.

Postage

A postage meter is recommended if you really plan to send a great deal of mail. It costs a minimum of $15 per month to rent plus the postage used. You must figure the value of time lost by the person waiting in long postal lines to mail urgent contracts. Figure about $100 per month for letters, scripts, and contracts.

Transportation

You will need some means of getting around to show and sell your project. Renting your car to the project is no longer legally possible. However, you have the choice of charging off the operating costs (gasoline, oil, maintenance to the production) or charging the production with a fee of per mile, but not both. The government allows you to write off $.28 per mile. Allow 100 miles per week for six months.

Miscellaneous

Anything which does not fit into any of the above categories will be labeled miscellaneous. Allow $1,000.

Fringe Benefits

Some budget forms place *fringe benefits,* or *fringes* into a single account. Most long form budgets such as this one place the aggregate production fringes for all personnel into separate accounts above-the-line and below-the-line.

There are two types of fringe benefits. Government fringes which refers to the employer's share of various payroll taxes are a complete alphabet soup which includes FICA, FUI, SUI, SDI, and any other contributions which may be required by local laws. Worker's Compensation is actually insurance against on-the-job injury suffered by anyone on the producer's payroll. It involves payment of a statutory minimum premium which varies from state to state that is based on a percentage of the total payroll and is usually adjusted upwards after the film is completed and the payroll is audited. It can be included in the insurance account; but since it is a percentage of payroll, many budget preparers include it in the total percentage of government fringes.

For people working under guild or union contract, there are also union fringes. These are the employer contributions stipulated in the applicable basic agreement and that are paid into the pension, health, and welfare funds of the guild or union members. There are also employee contributions to both government and union accounts, and the employer is responsible for making certain that these are withheld; but since these are deducted from the person's base pay, they do not figure in the budget.

If a payroll service is used, include that fee in the fringes account. A payroll service is a company that, for a fee, becomes the *employer of record* for the producer. The producer hires the payroll service to pay the picture's personnel, to make the withholdings, forward the money to the appropriate government agency or trust fund, file all reports to the IRS, state and local tax boards, and guild and unions, send W2s and 1099s to the employees, and have unemployment claims filed against them.

Whether or not a payroll service is used, government fringe rates may vary based on the unemployment and worker's comp claims previously made. Union fringes depend on the contract. You should research all of the appropriate fringes before entering specific amounts.

During the development period, government fringes must be paid on salaried personnel. People working as *independent contractors*, including producers receiving fees for services, may be subject to withholding on these fees in anticipation of their income being reported on a 1099-MISC form. In addition, benefits must be paid to any union or guild to which you or anyone else belongs. Such benefits as pension contributions, vacation and holiday pay must be paid. The rate of payment depends upon the union basic agreement.

Only fringes associated with Development should be entered here. Production fringes will also be discussed in Account 1900. If the production company is not a signatory to the guild or union in question, then the benefits do not have to be paid since the individual is working outside the basic agreement

Add up all the entries under either subtotals "A" or "B" and you have the fringed development costs. Total all the columns and you have the *development costs.*

Account 1000

Story
and
Screenplay

PAGE NO. 4

PRODUCTION NUMBER | PRODUCTION TITLE | DATE

1000 STORY AND SCREENPLAY

ACCT. NO.	DESCRIPTION	LOCAL/ On Loc.	PREP	SHOOT	WRAP	TOTAL	RATE	SUBTOTALS A	B	C
10	Rights & Expenses	Local								
		On Loc.								
		Local								
		On Loc.								
20	Writers Screenplay with Treatment	Local			ALLOW		62,337	62,337		
		On Loc.								
		Local								
		On Loc.								
30	Script Writing	Local								
		On Loc.								
		Local								
		On Loc.								
40	Script Duplication	Local								2,500
		On Loc.								
		Local								
		On Loc.								
50	Script Timing	Local				ALLOW	500			500
		On Loc.								
		Local								
		On Loc.								
60	Secretary(ies)	Local		8.2			750		6,150	
		On Loc.								
		Local								
		On Loc.								
		Local								
		On Loc.								
70	Research, Technical, Screenings									
						ALLOW				5,000
85	Additional Expenses									
95	Miscellaneous		ALLOW							500
							SUBTOTALS	62,337	6,150	8,500
							TOTAL ACCT 1000	76,987		

A = Fringeable/Taxable
B = Non-Fringeable/Taxable
C = Non-Taxable

1000—STORY AND SCREENPLAY

THE UNDERLYING RIGHTS OF EVERY MOTION PICTURE refers to the concept or story line. In the case of an original screenplay, i.e., one whose author has conceived of both the plot and then written the detailed script, these rights are embodied within the script and purchased with it (this would be *The Conversation.*) If the author has adapted some historical event, such as the Chicago Fire or the Battle of Waterloo, or used a public domain literary source, such as a Shakespearean play or a novel by Nathaniel Hawthorne, the public owns these ideas and there are no rights to buy. But a contemporary play, a newspaper article, or even an anecdote told at a party, are the property of others—either explicitly by formal copyright or implicitly by inferred copyright. The producer will have to acquire the rights to adapt the material for the screen from the individual or corporate third party who owns them. To insure that the *conveyance* or transfer of rights cannot be deemed *gratis* and revert to the original owner, so consideration should be paid. Anything from one dollar up is acceptable.

After you have purchased the rights to make a movie out of the original story a workable screenplay must be written. In theatrical ventures this will consist of scene descriptions and dialogue.

10: Rights & Expenses

This account refers to the separate cost involved in buying the rights to any material which is *not embodied* in the screenplay.

20: Writers

Writers here represents the people who write the actual screenplay, not the original story. (*See Account 1010.*) In cases where the same person has written the story and the screenplay, two separate fees are usually negotiated: one for the story and the other for the screenplay. This can cover fees for additional writers, rewrites, etc. There is no rule about what the total cost of rights and screenwriter(s) should be, but on an average picture, the range usually falls between two and one-half percent (2.5%) and five percent (5%) of the total direct costs. On a $10 million budget, this account would total between $250,000 and $500,000. If this is to be a Writers Guild script, be sure you follow the WGA guidelines. Put in the present Writers Guild minimum of $62,337.

Story Consultant/Editor

A *story consultant* or *story editor* works with the writer to help fashion the most dramatically effective screenplay. Some novelists such as William Goldman might be quite capable of adapting his own book; but many novelists, playwrights, or journalists are neither interested in nor experienced enough to adapt their own material into script form.

In television, the story editor is the person who heads up the story department. Many television producers are former writers and story editors, who have demonstrated the ability to keep the flow of new scripts going. The story editor could also be the person who is in charge of a group of contract writers who provide weekly scripts.

40: Script Duplication

You should plan a complete distribution of the script to all the principal cast members and the crew. You will need 150 copies. To be more precise, you can divide your script duplication into *local costs* and *on location costs*. Your allowance for costs should be $2,500.

You may also need to allow for script duplication during the casting period, which can entail several hundred more copies that will be sent out to actors, agents, etc., while the picture is being cast. You can detail that here or as a subaccount item under Cast/Casting Fees (Account 1309).

50: Script Timing

Script timing is the process of determining how long the finished picture will run on the screen. The purpose is to ensure that the final draft of the script is neither too long nor too short, although the former is an acceptable situation when the understanding is that scenes are likely to be cut down or cut out altogether during the editing process.

In low and medium budget pictures, where there is often a deal with a distributor that calls for delivery of a finished picture ranging from 95 to 110 minutes in length, timing a script and then removing unneeded scenes *and* unneeded days from the schedule before production starts may be a critical part of the budgeting process. The fee is from $500 to $1,000. It should take one to three days depending upon the script and the timer. The individual doing the timing should be a script supervisor, ideally one who has worked with the director on other projects and/or may be set to do your picture. In this way the methods used by the director (e.g., action sequences run long for this director) are known and a more accurate time of the script's length will be achieved.

60: Secretary

You should allot some time for someone to type the screenplay and revisions. I'd recommend eight weeks overall (prep/shoot.)

70: Research

Any project takes a certain amount of research. In the case of *The Conversation*, the screenwriter learned about the various methods employed by the companies involved in private investigation. The main character, *HARRY CAUL* is a specialist in audio intelligence gathering. You might begin your inquiry with the Yellow Pages, at your local library or with a company or individual who specializes in researching projects for people. Many researchers advertise in the WGA and DGA monthly magazines.

The fee depends upon how much is being asked for and how quickly the information is needed. Using a *technical advisor* in developing a screenplay is quite common. Again in the case of *HARRY CAUL*, it would be advisable to find a specialist in the area of private investigation using state of the art methods. There is no set fee for this individual's services as a technical advisor, but you may find that the producer and/or director would need an advisor during the actual production period. The actors can have firsthand knowledge of how and what an investigator goes through in a day. From my experience, advice and guidance from a professional only adds to the quality of your production. If the producer feels that using the technical advisor beyond the screenplay is valid, then a step deal can be worked out. In this way the cost of the individual's services can be spread into the time where you will have more money.

Screenings as a form of research are helpful to the writer. The producer can show the writer a film such as *The Magnificent Seven* to exemplify a style used to develop seven characters and still keep the plot moving along. Today most people use video cassettes, and save the time and trouble of paying for a screening room and projectionist. Screening material by or for the writer can save time in conveying the point you are trying to make and aid in the research on your subject or type of character.

This is an account for which you may end up budgeting an allowance as you are not quite sure of the exact amounts.

If research is needed for other than the dramatic purposes of the script, e.g., to provide information on period clothes for the *costume designer* or customized motorcycles for the *transportation coordinator*, this may be budgeted here and the screenwriter or researcher paid or reimbursed out of this account. Normally, the individual departments would do this research themselves as part of their preparation.

85: Additional Expenses (Travel & Living Expenses)

If you have brought a writer from another city or sent him or her somewhere else to scout a location used in the script, work with a director who is out of town, etc., list all the costs of airfare, hotels, and per diem (an allowance for meals and sometimes other incidentals for each day someone is away from his or her home) here. [*Note: Until shooting begins, I prefer to pay the actual costs and not pay an agreed upon fee (per diem).*] In this case the writer and director are the same person. He lived in San Francisco and traveled to Los Angeles to cast the film. The writer's travel and living expenses are found, therefore, under Account 1400—Travel and Living.

95: Miscellaneous
You should allow a sum of money to cover anything that doesn't fit under any of the other categories.

LEGAL CLEARANCES

Although you may have contracts with all the owners of rights, writers, and researchers that permits you to use their property and the results of their hired labor in making your picture, you may still need to *clear* certain details in the script. You may in fact be required to do so by the insurance carrier that is issuing you the *Errors and Omissions policy*. There are additional details about this coverage under the Insurance account, but one of the acts which this policy insures against is the unintentional invasion of the privacy to others. For instance, suppose your picture has a psychopathic character who teaches chemistry at Berkeley and kidnaps and murders the occasional traveler as in *The Vanishing*. Suppose that your writer has unwittingly described an actual chemistry professor somewhere in the United States, a person who may, when the movie is released, sue you for defamation.

There are researchers and services who will go through you script, isolate potential problems with any proper names and places, and check to see if you have inadvertently depicted an actual person, place, or thing that is not public or generally known. If you have, they can provide a list of cleared alternative proper names which you may substitute. The same is true for telephone numbers, license plates—prop houses rent cleared cardboard plates to tape over the real ones on picture cars—street addresses, etc. An alternative often used with proper names of secondary charaters or references is to use an actual person who is working on the film or known to someone working. Many prop persons and set decorators have immortalized their offspring and relatives by putting their names on moving vans, office buildings, or billboards visible in the background of scenes.

—— *Notes* ——

Account 1100
Producers Unit

PAGE NO. 5

PRODUCTION NUMBER | PRODUCTION TITLE | DATE

1100 PRODUCERS UNIT

ACCT. NO.	DESCRIPTION	LOCAL/ On Loc.	DAYS/WEEKS PREP	SHOOT	WRAP	TOTAL	RATE	SUBTOTALS A	B	C
01	Executive Producer(s)	Local								0
		On Loc.								
		Local								
		On Loc.								
02	Producer(s)	Local					ALLOW			450,000
		On Loc.								
	Co-Producer	Local					ALLOW			100,000
		On Loc.								
03	Associate Producer(s)	Local	13	10	26	49	1,020		50,000	
		On Loc.								
04	Line Producer	Local								0
		On Loc.								
08	Secretary(ies) ALLOW	Local				20 dys	$10 hr.		1,600	
		On Loc.								
	Co-Producer's Secretary	Local	13	10	26	49	650		31,850	
		On Loc.								
	Assoc. Producer's Secretary ALLOW	Local	4	10	4	18	500		9,000	
		On Loc.								
	Production Executive	Local								0
		On Loc.								
	Production Supervisor	Local								0
		On Loc.								
		Local								
		On Loc.								
		Local								
		On Loc.								
70	Research, Technical, Screenings									
	ALLOW									10,000
80	Packaging Fee									0
85	Additional Expenses									
95	Miscellaneous									3,500
99	Loss, Damage, Repair ALLOW									1,000
	SUBTOTALS								92,450	564,500
	TOTAL ACCT 1100							656,950		

A = Fringeable/Taxable
B = Non-Fringeable/Taxable
C = Non-Taxable

1100—PRODUCERS UNIT

OBVIOUSLY "PRODUCER" IS A TERM WHICH HAS MANY possible meanings. I have included the most obvious here. Pick and choose which best fits your project.

01: Executive Producer(s)

The title usually given to the person responsible for either financing the film or securing the financing for the film. An *executive producer* can be brought in at any time. In some cases, the executive producer credit can be given to the unit production manager or some other person associated with the production. It can even be the star's agent. The executive producer usually receives a fee; therefore, breaking down by days or weeks would not be correct. Divide the fee into payments from the preparation period to the wrap (or post production) period. The fee is wide open. There are no rules about amount or payment schedule! You must evaluate the services and arrive at a mutually agreed upon sum.

Payment Schedule:

There is a traditional method of paying fees. The fee is usually paid in three segments: first third on signing the contract, second third on the beginning of principal photography, and third when the finished film (or tape) is delivered. It can also be paid in four segments: First quarter on signing of contract, second quarter on beginning of principal photography, third quarter on beginning of post production, and fourth quarter on delivery of the answer print.

What you will budget usually depends upon how important this individual's contribution is to the project. If the person receiving the executive producer's title is working on the production in another category, the salary range could be determined by what that position demands monetarily. The best person to ask is the producer. Since *The Conversation* did not have an executive producer, we are putting in a fee of zero.

02: Producer(s)
The responsibility for the project's success or failure rests here. The producer puts together the package, the various parts of the project which allow for a green light The importance of this individual cannot be overstated. The producer makes the final decisions on the creative and economic elements of the project. As with the writer and the executive producer, the producer is usually paid a fee for services rendered. Since there is no scale rate for a producer, the amount is negotiated. To determine the position's value is difficult. It really depends upon the individual's experiences, track record and who is making the deal.

There is a general axiom in the film industry which states that the entire complement of producers (Executive, Producer, Associate, etc.) should not earn more than five percent (5%) of the total budget, but this is certainly not definitive. Once you arrive at a total budget, go back and set salaries for your producing team. This means that the contingency, completion bond, overhead, interest, and deferments are not counted (*See the Top Sheet, second page.*) When this unit is included in the finished budget, you can see if it is in line with the accepted norm. The producer will spend a long time on a project (usually over a year) and should be compensated for that time. A fee of $450,000 is included in the total. There can be a co-producer (more than one). In the case of *The Conversation,* Francis Coppola was the writer/producer, and he had his long time associate, Fred Roos, assume many of the producer's responsibilities under the title of co-producer. Again there is no set amount. Here we have allowed $100,000. Today the average total production fee for a major studio feature with a budget over $20 million is between $1 million and $1.5 million dollars or five to seven and one-half percent (5%–7%.)

The producer is primarily a gatherer who finds a workable script and matches it with the proper combination of director, stars, and other aesthetic elements. Then he finds the money, either through backers or through a major studio, or combination, to produce the picture. Ideally, the producer is the first person on a project and the last person off. (In episodic television this is person who is called the executive producer.) Also, the producer may be involved in the release and **EXPLOITATION** of the film. Many directors and actors who initiate their own projects act as their own producer.

It is an idiosyncrasy of the Academy of Motion Picture Arts and Sciences that when a picture is voted Best Picture of the Year, only the producer may accept the award—not the executive producer, not the co-producer, just the producer. This was originally intended to accord the honor to the person most responsible for bringing the project to fruition.

04: Line Producer

In the traditional studio system, many of the creative approvals and decisions on all projects were reserved for the studio head. Producers and directors were assigned to units, and the producer, in particular, was responsible for implementing the creative decisions and making sure that all the production departments adhered to the budget.

Now with producers working side-by-side with directors on such creative issues of script development and casting, many projects engage a *line producer* to address all the budgetary concerns both above-the-line and below-the-line. Often, the production manager will perform this function and receive a line producer credit rather than executive producer: (or, as noted below, associate producer or supervising producer or co-producer or co-executive producer.) Fees vary with a maximum of about $400,000.

03: Associate Producer(s)

On feature films the significance of this title varies from production to production. It may be given as an additional credit to the production manager, the editor, the writer, an agent, et al. Some people in the industry consider this a worthless credit. However, as stated in the development section, associate producers are very important to the production. They receive fees for their services which are usually allocated during the entire production. No rules apply to the amount.

The title can also be part of the financial package and be given to someone designated by the financiers to oversee expenditures. Or, it can be given to someone instrumental in securing a key element in the package, such as a lead actor. If your project warrants it, especially if you are developing other projects, then an associate producer is a good idea, especially if he or she aids in getting all the information which speeds your project along.

In television, the credit for associate producer often goes to the person in charge of post production. This person usually coordinates the efforts of the editors, the lab, the post-production sound personnel, titles, opticals, etc. On episodic television, this can be a key job with immense responsibilities relative to air dates.

The amount of compensation depends upon what you have to spend and how much assistance you need. Usually a step deal can be arranged where the associate producer receives a small amount in the beginning to be increased when the money for the budget is funded. Or, the associate producer could be paid half the amount now, with payments spread over a certain number of weeks, and half deferred until the money is available. Since there are no rules, it depends upon what the project can afford and what is negotiated.

We will use $50,000 for the associate producer of *The Conversation.* The payments begin during the preparation period which in feature films is usually three months. This comes to approximately 13 weeks (12.9 actual) and the shooting period runs 9.4 weeks including the Christmas week hiatus. The production company paid the associate producer for the Christmas week. An average post production period is six months (26 weeks.) Since the film was shot entirely in San Francisco, all filming was local. If it is agreed that the fee of $50,000 is to be divided equally over the length of the production then simply add preparation time (13 weeks) plus shooting time (ten weeks), again allowing for the closed Christmas week and the remainder of the last shooting week which concludes on Tuesday, plus 26 weeks of post production (or wrap), for a total of 49 weeks. By dividing 49 weeks into the $50,000 fee, you get a weekly salary of $1,020.41. If you fall behind in any of the production periods and do not make it up, you will obviously go over budget in this area. A good idea is to negotiate a few "free weeks" in the deal in the event you do run over schedule. [*Note: On The Conversation, Mona Skager was the associate producer. She also went to Los Angeles for casting.*]

08: Secretary (ies)

The producer and associate producer may need the services of a secretary. You must evaluate this. In most cases the producer will have someone who is invaluable whom he or she likes to employ. The chosen secretary will have a great bearing on the salary level which is anywhere from $500 to $1,000 per week for this special assistant to the producer.

We will budget $650 per five day week for the co-producer's secretary. Weekend work will require additional payment. The associate producer's secretary will be paid $500 per week.

Additional secretaries will be brought in on an as needed basis. Your best bet is to allow for what is called additional *work days* meaning the number of days needed to complete a task. Over the course of the 49 weeks of production, we will require approximately 20 days at an hourly wage of $10. This $1,600 gives you protection for unforeseen expenses such as script page changes, reports, schedules, etc., which suddenly arise.

Production Executive

We are including this account here because more and more companies are assigning a *production executive* or *an executive in charge of production* to projects and charging the projects for their work. In television, production executives usually oversee more than one show; feature production executives are typically exclusive to that project. This credit is sometimes given to the production manager. You also may find this individual called *production supervisor*. Most who do this work are non-DGA (who seek membership as a unit production manager). Many have either strong production (nonunion) or accounting backgrounds. The fee varies between $1,000 to $3,000 per week.

70: Research, Technical, Screenings

As with the story and screenplay units, you need to allot a sum of money to cover these costs. The producer and his team will be doing a great deal of research for the project. The writer, cast, director and locations will have to be found. A *technical advisor* may be necessary as was the case with the screenplay (Account 1000). In addition to script advice, *The Conversation* required professional assistance in determining the type and cost of electronic surveillance equipment needed. Producer research and meetings are charged here under the producer account.

Screenings are sometimes held to review the past work of prospective directors and some below-the-line personnel, such as production designer, director of photography, costume designer, whose work will be critical to the look of the picture. As was previously mentioned most of this is now done with videocassettes. Sometimes this can be misleading when making a decision about a cinematographer (director of photography–DP) or a production designer (art director). Colors on tape can often shift and the viewer sees something other than the original textures and lighting. Improper tuning and faulty equipment add to this distortion, in short, where look is a critical concern, there is no substitute for screenings of an actual film. Amounts budgeted in this category are determined by the scope of your project. Each production is unique. For *The Conversation* we used $10,000 for all research, technical and screenings.

80: Packaging Fee

There are some executive producers who are specialists in packaging film projects and are paid a fee for this service. Dino De Laurentiis, who purchased the rights to the book, *Six Days of the Condor,* and brought Robert Redford, Faye Dunaway and Sidney Pollack into the project, is an example. Since six days was too long to sustain suspense, the film became *Three Days of the Condor.* For *The Conversation* there was no packaging fee. More commonly today, agencies are paid packaging fees. CAA, ICM and William

Morris Agency, the Big Three, are in the position formerly occupied by the major studios. They have the writers, producers, directors and stars, can package projects in-house, and then go to a studio for financing. To arrive at a figure for such a service, an agreement is made during the development period. The experience and success of the packager determines the size of the fee, which can be as much as ten percent (10%) of the budget.

95: Miscellaneous

Use this area for items which do not fit into any of the above categories. I'm allowing $3,500 here.

99: Loss, Damage, Repair

This is the first time we've seen this category. Unfortunately during the course of a production something will be lost or damaged and costs will arise. Most insurance policies have a high deductible and these items won't be covered unless they are among a long list of things either lost or damaged at the same time. A simple allowance of $1,000 for such unforeseen problems should suffice.

Notes

Account 1200
Directors
Unit

PAGE NO. 6

PRODUCTION NUMBER | PRODUCTION TITLE | DATE

ACCT. NO.	1200 DIRECTORS UNIT DESCRIPTION	LOCAL/ On Loc.	PREP	SHOOT	WRAP	TOTAL	RATE	SUBTOTALS A	B	C
01	Director	Local	12	9.2	26	47.2	ALLOW	2,000,000		
		On Loc.								
		Local								
		On Loc.								
02	Second Unit	Local						0		
	Director	On Loc.								
		Local								
		On Loc.								
03	Choreographer	Local						0		
		On Loc.								
		Local								
		On Loc.								
04	Dialogue Director	Local						0		
		On Loc.								
		Local								
		On Loc.								
60	Secretary(ies)	Local	12	10	26	48	750		36,000	
		On Loc.								
	Assistant	Local	12	10	26	48	650		31,200	
	to Director	On Loc.								
		Local								
		On Loc.								
		Local								
		On Loc.								
		Local								
		On Loc.								
70	Research, Technical, Screenings									
				ALLOW						1,000
85	Additional Expenses									
	Storyboard artist: 16.2 wks (prep/shoot) x 2000							32,400		
95	Miscellaneous		ALLOW							1,500
	Director's Entertainment					ALLOW				5,000
							SUBTOTALS	2,032,400	67,200	7,500
							TOTAL ACCT 1200	2,107,100		

A = Fringeable/Taxable
B = Non-Fringeable/Taxable
C = Non-Taxable

1200–DIRECTORS UNIT

01: Director

THE DIRECTOR IS EXPECTED TO BE THE PRIMARY CREATIVE decision-maker. Final approval of all aspects of the production, from performances to camera placements to set design and the choice of locations, resides with the director. After production, the director supervises the cutting done by the editor(s) and delivers a cut which is his version of the finished film. On most major productions, directors do not contractually have the right to **FINAL CUT.** In most cases, the studio, producer, or some other third party will have the right to make changes to the director's cut before releasing the picture.

A director can be a member of a guild (Directors Guild of America, Directors Guild of Canada, etc.) or not. There is no rule stating that the director *must* belong to any organization. However, if the film company is not signatory to the Directors Guild of America (i.e., does not have a current contract with them) then members of the Directors Guild cannot work on this project. The vast majority of pictures in major release are made by DGA members.

For *The Conversation* we will enter 12 weeks of preparation. The film commences shooting on a Sunday and continues for a total of 41 days. With the exception of that first Sunday, all filming is done on a five day work week. The time period including the production hiatus from December 25th until January 2nd is calculated to be 9-2/5 weeks. The wrap and post production period begins immediately after filming concludes and continues for 26 weeks. Depending on the total budget, the DGA has established a minimum feature salary, or scale compensation, based on 11 or 13 weeks. In practice, particularly on lower budget features, as long as the director is paid for at least 11 or 13 weeks, the DGA will not prevent him or her from rendering services over a longer period without additional compensation. You may budget scale as either 11 or

13 times the minimum weekly ($9,848 until 6/30/96) or simply as the total figure. The DGA also requires that a feature director be allowed at least ten weeks to deliver *director's cut*. This provision actually has a greater bearing on the amount of time which you will budget for the editor(s), as the minimum editorial period must take this ten weeks into account. You should figure 22 weeks for a base on your project.

As with all work covered by guild or union basic agreements, scale increases at given points within the term of the agreement. If you are budgeting scale now for a project to shoot in six months, make certain that the minimum rates for directors, actors, etc., will not have automatically increased by that time. If you know that they will increase, budget the amount that will be in effect at the time of your proposed shoot date. Since Coppola is the producer as well as the director of *The Conversation*, he will work in all phases of post production until the picture is released. With a director of his calibre you should budget $2 million.

As discussed in the development section, if the director is involved in developing the screenplay, there will be an additional payment depending on the magnitude of the director's involvement.

If the company is signatory to the DGA contract, only two people outside of the Directors Guild are permitted to have the word *director* in their titles: the director of photography and the art director. What we used to call the casting director is now given the credit, *Casting By . . .*

02: Second Unit Director

On some films, sequences not involving the principal performers are shot by *second unit directors*. If the production company is a signatory to the DGA agreement, this work must be done by a DGA member.

Some films require an additional director for special areas (e.g., animals, underwater.) Such employment is usually for a finite period of time, and often this job will be performed by a member of the film's production staff (the unit production manager or the first assistant director.) Often the stunt coordinator will direct a second unit consisting mainly of stunt work. However, on DGA projects, the coordinator must be a DGA member in good standing—or be willing to join—when hired to direct the second unit. Often a second unit director is hired to help bring in a project which has fallen behind schedule and must finish on time. The presence of a second unit gives the principal unit more flexibility in meeting stop dates.

Your project's script requirements and schedule will determine the need of a second unit director. *The Conversation* did not require the services of a second unit director to film a small car chase and a static scene of a burning car.

03: Choreographer

The work of a *choreographer* may or not be covered in the Screen Actors Guild (SAG) Basic greement, depending on the deal. This category is included in this unit as the choreographer works with the director. A professional choreographer usually choreographs all the dance numbers. If the dance number is choreographed, the dancers will, more than likely, be professionals and therefore also be covered by SAG. This is a specialized area and requires certain special working conditions (dance or rehearsal floors, proper room temperature, footwear, rest periods, etc.) Check the SAG contract for there may be additional costs which you will need to put into your budget.

The Conversation had a small dance number in *Harry's Warehouse* but it did not require a choreographer.

The length of work will be based on your shooting schedule. Usually no wrap time is needed, but definite preparation time is needed for rehearsal. The amount of time required is based on the difficulty and number of dances in your project.

The rate range for major studio productions is between $1,500 to $2,500 per week. For lower budget productions it can be considerably less and negotiated as a flat fee.

04: Dialogue Director/Coach

A *dialogue coach* runs lines or rehearses actors on the set. Not all productions have dialogue coaches. Typically, one is engaged to help a particular actor who may have trouble memorizing lines and/or have a role which is a unusually long or complex. In multi-camera television where the entire cast performs in the show in continuity before a live audience every week, the dialogue coach helps all the actors alone or in groups. A different type of dialogue coach is used to help non-English proficient or heavily-accented performers working in the U.S. or, conversely, to coach English-speaking actors whose role calls for an accent other than his or her normal one, for example Irish-born Liam Neeson to master a German accent for *Schindler's List* or for Mel Gibson to sound less Australian.

Some actors have personal dialogue coaches to make up cue cards, rehearse with them, etc., and might make employment of a particular dialogue coach a contractual requirement.

The rate range here is $1,000 to $2,500 per week.

05: Secretary/Personal Assistant

Since directing is often more than a five days a week, eighteen hours a day job, the DGA Basic Agreement calls for feature directors to be given a *secretary* or *personal assistant*. Even on non-DGA shows such a person is hired for the director. Many established directors bring their own special assistant who fields the many requests which can be distracting to the director. This saves the loss of valuable creative time on the project. Salaries vary, but figure a minimum of $750 per week. The start date will coincide with the director's start of preparation. For *The Conversation* we required 12 weeks of preparation, 10 weeks of shooting, and 26 weeks of post production. In many cases the director's secretary will not be needed for this entire period. This should be checked with your producer. Whatever the time period, it should be less than the 26 weeks of post production. But note, a director who is accustomed to working with a particular secretary may include as part of his deal that the assistant is to be paid until the end of post production. In this case, his secretary will be with the director through post. I would also add in an assistant for the whole period on this film. Use $650 as a floor. Your film may not need this additional person—ask your producer.

70: Research, Technical, Screenings

Your director may wish to see footage from a picture or ask for technical assistance. Any of these areas which are directly attributed to the director should be placed here. We will allow $1,000.

85: Additional Expenses (Directors Buy-Out)

If a director is paid more than a fixed amount over scale, the DGA Agreement permits some of this amount to be deemed a prepayment of residual obligations. A *buy out* is the sum paid to a director specifically to offset all liabilities for any future payments. This is not a common deal point.

85: Additional Expenses (Storyboard Artist)

Some directors, particularly on films with complicated action sequences, may want to use storyboards or a series of line drawings of what shots they would like to get. The director may keep these for his or her own reference only, or may use them to illustrate to the director of photography, production designer, second unit director, producer, or anyone else how he or she sees the scene. Mickey Moore's second unit work for Steven Spielberg, for example, involved extensive communication between the two directors via storyboards.

Any of the crew members listed above (or stunt coordinators or choreographers) may produce a storyboard for their own use. When a director needs assistance in preparing a storyboard, a *storyboard artist* who has no other function on the project may be hired. The rate range here is $750 per week for lower budget pictures up to $2,500 for studio features.

95: Miscellaneous

Your director will to take people to lunch/dinner on business for the film. Over the entire length of the director's contract (47.2 weeks), you must allow for entertainment expenses. I'm figuring $5,000 on this film.

Account 1300

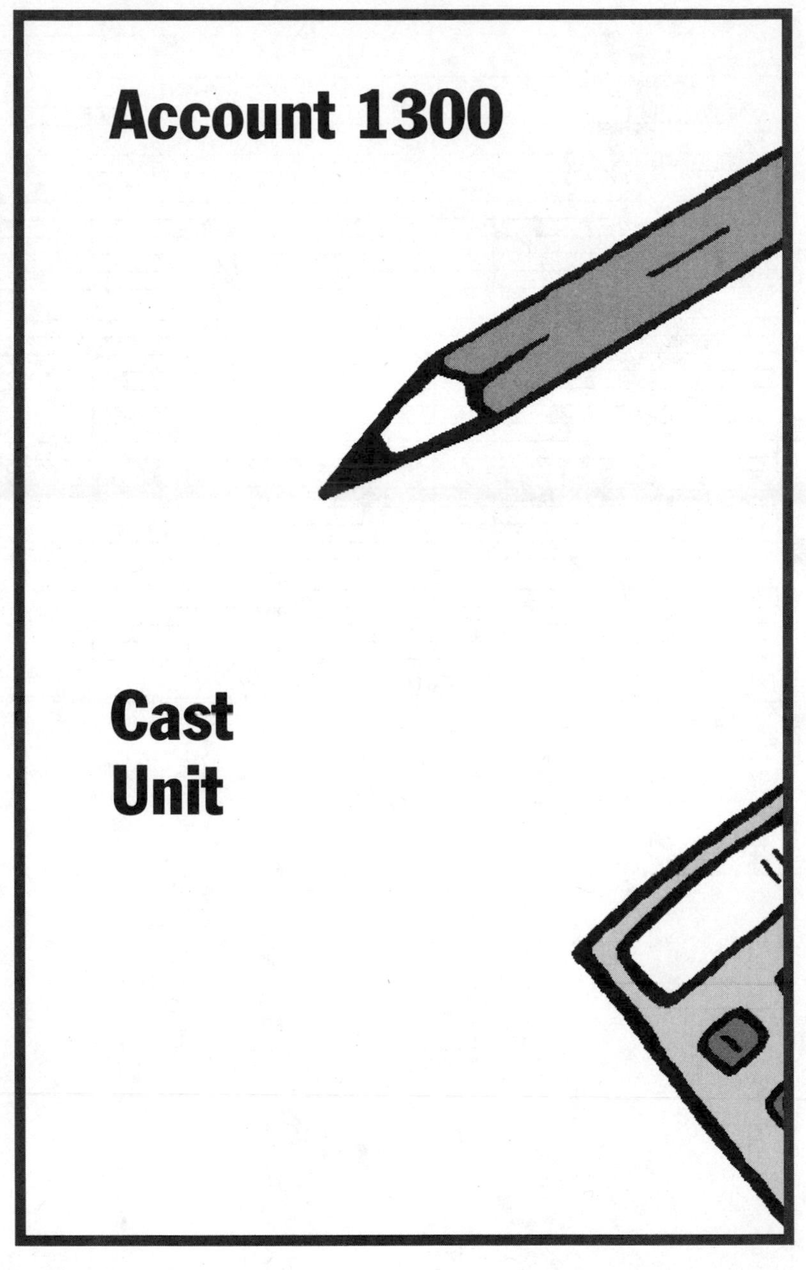

Cast Unit

PAGE NO. 7

PRODUCTION NOUMBER | PRODUCTION TITLE | DATE

1300 CAST UNIT					SUBTOTALS		
ACCT NO	DESCRIPTION	TIME	RATE	AMOUNT	A	B	C
01	Principal Players						
	(See Detail Page 7A; 7AA Day Out of Days)				2,500,000		
02	Supporting Players						
	(See Detail Page 7B)				72,701		
03	Day Players						
	(See Detail Page 7C, 7CC)				58,645		
04	Stunt Coordinator ALLOW			5,000	5,000		
05	Stunts (See Detail Page 7D; 7DD detail pg)				8,788		
06	Looping – Actor's Fee		ALLOW		31,349		
	29 Day Players x $1081						
07	Overtime: 30% of 58,645		ALLOW		17,594		
08	Cast Fees		ALLOW	50,000			50,000
	Cast Assistant ALLOW	15 WK	1,000	15,000		15,000	
09	Casting Expenses Incl. Video Sys. ($500) Computer Rental ($250)		ALLOW	20,000			20,000
10	Welfare Worker/Teacher	1 WK	1,322	1,322	1,322		
11	Rehearsal Expenses	2 WK	2,500				5,000
12	Musicians (See Accts. 2143, 2145)						
85	Additional Expenses						
	Cast Contractuals		ALLOW	250,000			250,000
95	Miscellaneous		ALLOW	1,500			1,500
				SUBTOTALS	2,695,399	15,000	326,500
				TOTAL ACCT 1300	3,036,899		

A = Fringeable/Taxable
B = Non-Fringeable/Taxable
C = Non-Taxable

ACCOUNT 1300—Cast Unit

PAGE NO. 7A

PRODUCTION NOUMBER	PRODUCTION TITLE	DATE

1301 PRINCIPAL PLAYERS						SUBTOTALS		
		DAYS / WEEKS						
CAST NO.	CHARACTER	WORK	HOLD	TOTAL	RATE	A	B	C
1	HARRY CAUL - (*) Schedule F Player	37	4	41	ALLOW	2,000,000		
2	*A ANN - (*A) Schedule F Player	13	2	15	ALLOW	250,000		
3	MARK - (*A) SCHEDULE F PLAYER	10	3	13	ALLOW	250,000		
*	Add'l 10 rehearsal days, 4 travel days							
*A	Add'l 1.5 rehears days 4 travel days							
					SUBTOTALS	2,500,000		
		TOTAL DETAIL ACCT. 1301				2,500,000		

A = Fringeable/Taxable
B = Non-Fringeable/Taxable
C = Non-Taxable

ACTORS DAY OUT OF DAYS

PAGE NO. 7AA

PRODUCTION COMPANY:
PRODUCTION NUMBER:
PRODUCTION TITLE/NUMBER: The Conversation
PRODUCTION TITLE: Francis Coppola
DATE:
SCRIPT DATE:
DATE:

Rehearsal–R Hold–H Started–S Travel–T Worked–W Finish–F On Call–C

	NO.	CHARACTER	LAST	1	2	3	4	5	6	7	8	9	10	11	12	13	14	15	16	17	18	19	20	21
				Week 1						Week 2					Week 3					Week 4				
		Day Number		1	2	3	4	5	6	7	8	9	10	11	12	13	14	15	16	17	18	19	20	21
		Date																						
		Day of the Week		Su	M	Tu	W	Th	F	M	Tu	W	Th	F	M	Tu	W	Th	F	M	Tu	W	Th	F
	1	Harry Caul		SW	W	W	W	W	W	H	H	H	W	W	W	W	W	W	W	W	W	W	W	W
	2	Ann					SW	W	W	W	W	W	W	H	W	W	W	W	W	H	H	H	H	H
	3	Mark						SW	W	W	W	W	W	H	W	H	W	W	W	H	H	H	W	H
*	4	Mr. C				SWF													SW	H	H	H	H	H
*	5	Stanley		SW	H	H	H	H	H	H	H	H	WF											
*	6	Paul Meyers						SW	W	W	W	W	WF											
*	7	Martin															SW	W	WF					
	8	Wm. P. Moran																						
	9	Meredith																						
	10	Millard																						
	11	Mrs. Goetner																			SW	WF		
	12	Ron Keller																				SW	WF	
	13	Mrs. Corsito																				SWF		
	14	Bob																				SW	WF	
	15	Bob's Wife																				SWF		
	16	Amy												SWF										
	17	Lurleen																						
	18	Male Sec'y																					SW	WF
	19	Tony																		SWF				
	20	Male Recept.															SW	WF						
	21	Mime						SW	W	W	W	WF												
	22	Young Man						SW	WF															
	23	Young Woman						SW	WF															
	24	Shopper #1								SWF														
	25	Shopper #2								SWF														
	26	Shopper #3								SWF														
	27	Laundry Lady																						SWF
	28	#27's Little Boy																						SWF
	29	Woman #1 - Elev.														SWF								
	30	Woman #2 - Elev.														SWF								

Continued on next page

ACTORS DAY OUT OF DAYS

PAGE NO. 7AA

PRODUCTION COMPANY:
PRODUCTION TITLE/NUMBER: The Conversation
PRODUCTION TITLE: Francis Coppola
PRODUCTION NUMBER:
DATE:
SCRIPT DATE:
DATE:

Rehearsal–R Hold–H Started–S Travel–T Worked–W Finish–F On Call–C

			Week 5					Week 6					Week 7					Week 8				
	Day Number				22	23	24	25	26	27	28	29	30	31	32	33	34	35	36	37	38	39
	Date																					
	Day of the Week		M	Tu	W	Th	F	M	Tu	W	Th	F	M	Tu	W	Th	F	M	Tu	W	Th	F
NO.	CHARACTER	LAST	HOLIDAY BREAK	CHRISTMAS & NEW YEARS																		
1	Harry Caul				W	W	W	H	W	W	W	W	W	W	W	W	W	W	W	W	W	W
2	Ann				H	W	W	W	W	W	W	H	W	W	W	W	W	W	W	WF		
3	Mark				H	W	H	W	H	H	H	H	W	W	H	H	H	W	W	WF		
* 4	Mr. C				H	H	H	WF														
* 5	Stanley												SW	W	W	W	W	H	H	H	W	W
* 6	Paul Meyers														SW	W	W	H	H	H	W	W
* 7	Martin																					SW
8	Wm. P. Moran														SW	W	W	H	H	H	W	W
9	Meredith														SW	W	W	W	W	H	W	W
10	Millard																					
11	Mrs. Goetner																					
12	Ron Keller																					
13	Mrs. Corsito																					
14	Bob																					
15	Bob's Wife																					
16	Amy																					
17	Lurleen														SW	W	W	H	H	H	W	WF
18	Male Sec'y																					
19	Tony																					
20	Male Recept.																					
21	Mime																					
22	Young Man																					
23	Young Woman																					
24	Shopper #1																					
25	Shopper #2																					
26	Shopper #3																					
27	Laundry Lady																					
28	#27's Little Boy																					
29	Woman #1 - Elev.																					
30	Woman #2 - Elev.																					

Continued on next page

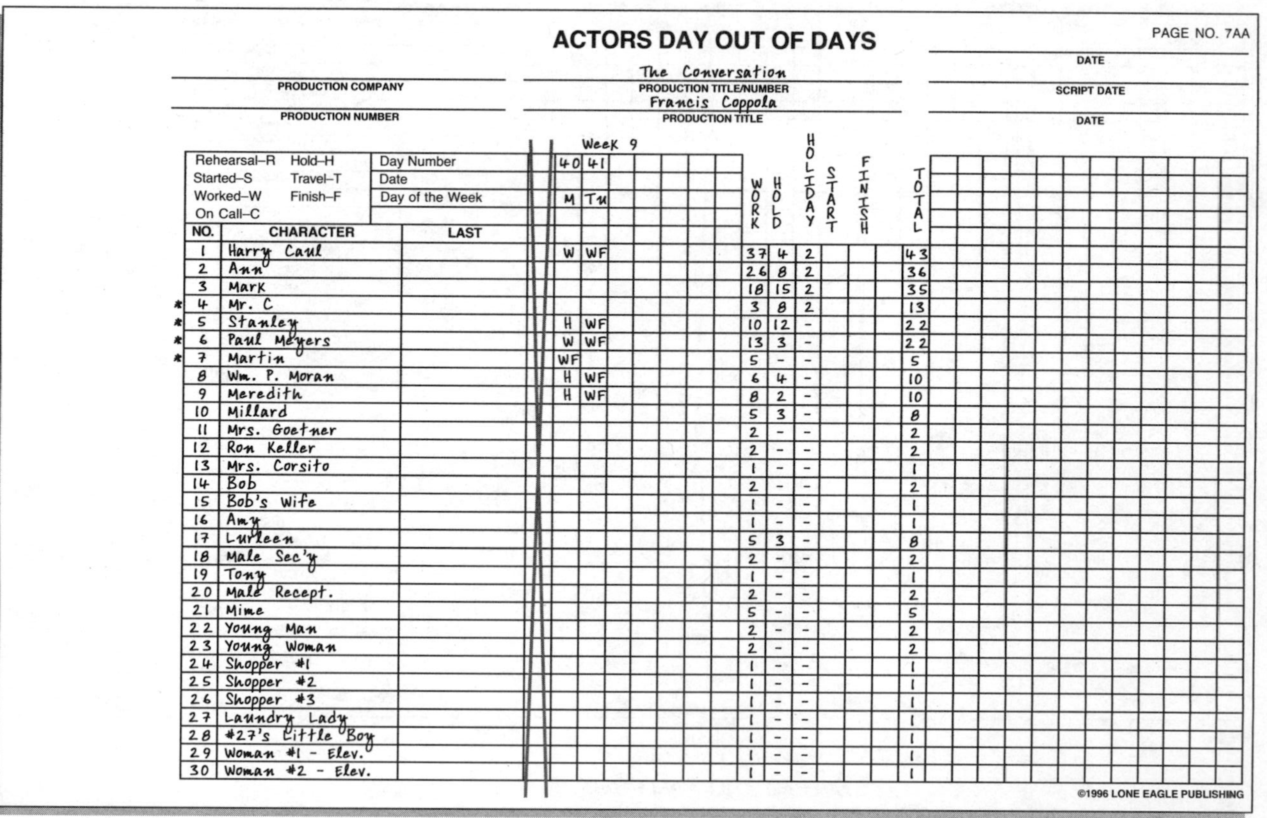

ACTORS DAY OUT OF DAYS

PAGE NO. 7AA

PRODUCTION COMPANY:
PRODUCTION NUMBER:
PRODUCTION TITLE/NUMBER: The Conversation
PRODUCTION TITLE: Francis Coppola
DATE:
SCRIPT DATE:
DATE:

Rehearsal–R Hold–H Started–S Travel–T Worked–W Finish–F On Call–C

Week 9

	NO.	CHARACTER	LAST	Day Number 40 / Day of the Week M	Day Number 41 / Day of the Week Tu	WORK	HOLD	HOLIDAY	START	FINISH	TOTAL
	1	Harry Caul		W	WF	37	4	2			43
	2	Ann				26	8	2			36
	3	Mark				18	15	2			35
*	4	Mr. C				3	8	2			13
*	5	Stanley		H	WF	10	12	-			22
*	6	Paul Meyers		W	WF	13	3	-			22
*	7	Martin		WF		5	-	-			5
	8	Wm. P. Moran		H	WF	6	4	-			10
	9	Meredith		H	WF	8	2	-			10
	10	Millard				5	3	-			8
	11	Mrs. Goetner				2	-	-			2
	12	Ron Keller				2	-	-			2
	13	Mrs. Corsito				1	-	-			1
	14	Bob				2	-	-			2
	15	Bob's Wife				1	-	-			1
	16	Amy				1	-	-			1
	17	Lurleen				5	3	-			8
	18	Male Sec'y				2	-	-			2
	19	Tony				1	-	-			1
	20	Male Recept.				2	-	-			2
	21	Mime				5	-	-			5
	22	Young Man				2	-	-			2
	23	Young Woman				2	-	-			2
	24	Shopper #1				1	-	-			1
	25	Shopper #2				1	-	-			1
	26	Shopper #3				1	-	-			1
	27	Laundry Lady				1	-	-			1
	28	#27's Little Boy				1	-	-			1
	29	Woman #1 - Elev.				1	-	-			1
	30	Woman #2 - Elev.				1	-	-			1

ACTORS DAY OUT OF DAYS

PAGE NO. 7AA

PRODUCTION COMPANY: ________ | PRODUCTION TITLE/NUMBER: The Conversation | DATE: ________

PRODUCTION NUMBER: ________ | PRODUCTION TITLE: Francis Coppola | SCRIPT DATE: ________

DATE: ________

Rehearsal–R Hold–H
Started–S Travel–T
Worked–W Finish–F
On Call–C

		Week 1						Week 2					Week 3					Week 4				
	Day Number	1	2	3	4	5	6	7	8	9	10	11	12	13	14	15	16	17	18	19	20	21
	Date																					
	Day of the Week	Su	M	Tu	W	Th	F	M	Tu	W	Th	F	M	Tu	W	Th	F	M	Tu	W	Th	F
NO.	CHARACTER / LAST																					
31	Man in Elevator													SWF								
32	Demo Man																					
33	Speaker																					
34	Man in Booth																					
35	Young Driver																					
36	Motel Clerk																					
* 37	Bus Driver #1				SWF																	
* 38	Bus Driver #2				SWF																	
39	McNaught																	SWF				
40	Anncer./P.A. Syst.																				SWF	
41	Tel. Oper. #1																					SWF
42	Chrome Dome V.O.																					
43	Woman in R-Room																					
44	Tel. Oper #2																					
45	Man #2 in Booth																					
46	Male Voice (V.O.)																					
47	Female Voice (V.O.)																					

Continued on next page

ACTORS DAY OUT OF DAYS

PAGE NO. 7AA

PRODUCTION COMPANY:
PRODUCTION NUMBER:
PRODUCTION TITLE/NUMBER: The Conversation
PRODUCTION TITLE: Francis Coppola
DATE:
SCRIPT DATE:
DATE:

Rehearsal–R Hold–H
Started–S Travel–T
Worked–W Finish–F
On Call–C

NO.	CHARACTER	LAST	Week 5 M	Tu	W 22	Th 23	F 24	Week 6 M 25	Tu 26	W 27	Th 28	F 29	Week 7 M 30	Tu 31	W 32	Th 33	F 34	Week 8 M 35	Tu 36	W 37	Th 38	F 39
31	Man in Elevator																					
32	Demo Man																					
33	Speaker																					
34	Man in Booth																					
35	Young Driver																				SWF	
36	Motel Clerk				SWF																	
* 37	Bus Driver #1								SW	WF												
* 38	Bus Driver #2								SW	WF												
39	McNaught																					
40	Anncer./P.A. Syst.																					
41	Tel. Oper. #1																					
42	Chrome Dome V.O.																					
43	Woman in R-Room																					SWF
44	Tel. Oper #2																					
45	Man #2 in Booth																					
46	Male Voice (V.O.)																					
47	Female Voice (V.O.)																					

(Week 5 M column: HOLIDAY BREAK; Tu column: CHRISTMAS & NEW YEARS)

Continued on next page

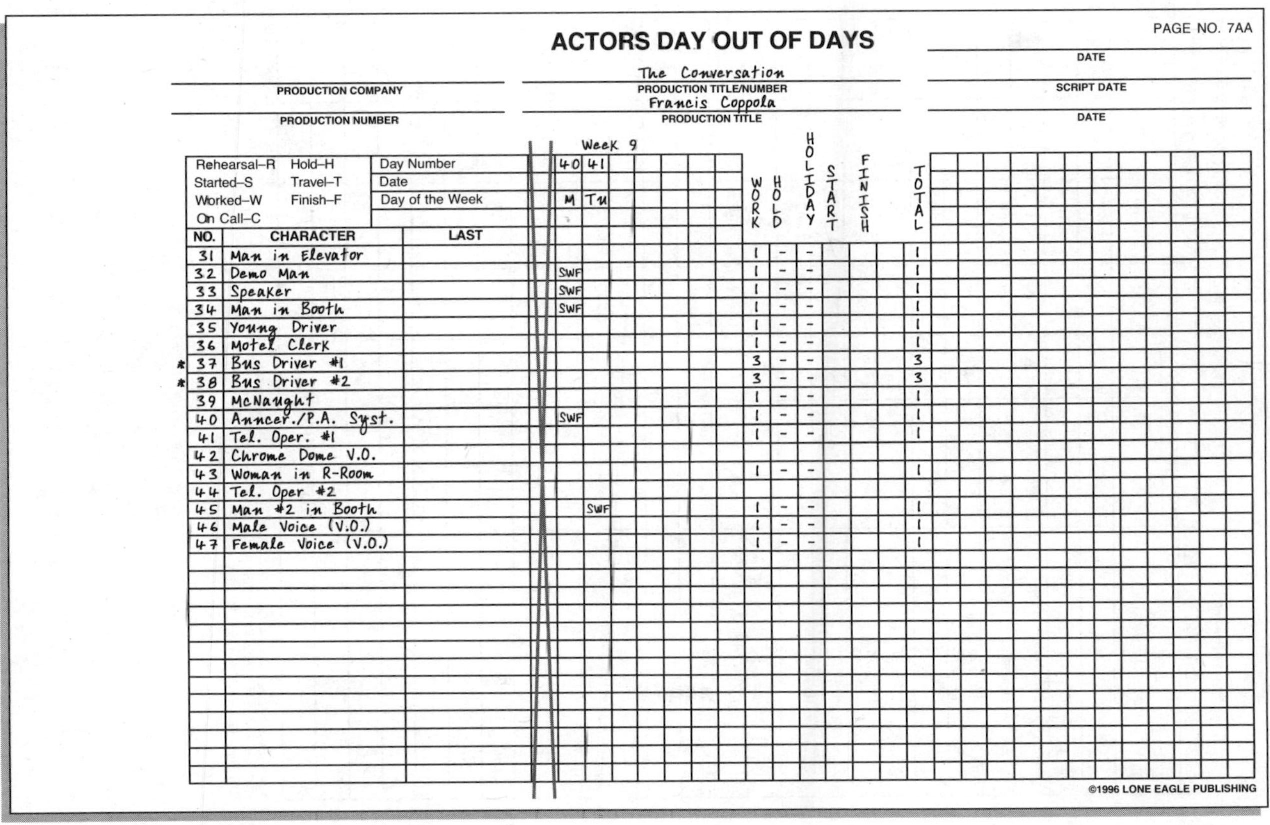

ACTORS DAY OUT OF DAYS

PAGE NO. 7AA

PRODUCTION COMPANY: ____ PRODUCTION NUMBER: ____

PRODUCTION TITLE/NUMBER: The Conversation

PRODUCTION TITLE: Francis Coppola

DATE: ____ SCRIPT DATE: ____ DATE: ____

Rehearsal–R Hold–H Started–S Travel–T Worked–W Finish–F On Call–C

Week 9

	NO.	CHARACTER	LAST	Day Number: 40 Day of the Week: M	Day Number: 41 Day of the Week: Tu	WORK	HOLD	HOLIDAY	START	FINISH	TOTAL
	31	Man in Elevator				1	-	-			1
	32	Demo Man		SWF		1	-	-			1
	33	Speaker		SWF		1	-	-			1
	34	Man in Booth		SWF		1	-	-			1
	35	Young Driver				1	-	-			1
	36	Motel Clerk				1	-	-			1
*	37	Bus Driver #1				3	-	-			3
*	38	Bus Driver #2				3	-	-			3
	39	McNaught				1	-	-			1
	40	Anncer./P.A. Syst.		SWF		1	-	-			1
	41	Tel. Oper. #1				1	-	-			1
	42	Chrome Dome V.O.									
	43	Woman in R-Room				1	-	-			1
	44	Tel. Oper #2									
	45	Man #2 in Booth			SWF	1	-	-			1
	46	Male Voice (V.O.)				1	-	-			1
	47	Female Voice (V.O.)				1	-	-			1

PAGE NO. 7B

PRODUCTION NOUMBER | PRODUCTION TITLE | DATE

1302 SUPPORTING PLAYERS						SUBTOTALS		
		DAYS / WEEKS						
CAST NO.	CHARACTER R T	WORK	HOLD	TOTAL	RATE	A	B	C
4	Mr. C - Drop	1 dy			1081	1081		
	Pick-Up	3 wks			2500	7500		
	SW 11/29 3 4		11	21				
5	STANLEY - Drop	2 wks			2500	5000		
	Pick-Up	3 wks			2500	7500		
	SW 11/26 WF 1/30 5 4	8	12	29				
6	PAUL MEYERS - Drop	7 dys			1081	7567		
	Pick-Up	3 wks			2500	7500		
	SW 11/29 WF 1/30 5 4	13	3	25				
7	MARTIN - Drop	3 dys			1081	3243		
	Pick-Up	1 wk			2500	2500		
	SW 12/13 WF 1/29 3 4	5	0	12				
8	WILLIAM P. MORAN	3 wks			2500	7500		
	SW 1/17 WF 1/30 3 2	6	4	15				
9	MEREDITH	3 wks			2500	7500		
	SW 1/17 WF 1/30 3 2	8	2	15				
10	MILLARD	2 wks			2500	5000		
	SW 1/17 WF 1/30 3 2	8	2	15				
16	AMY	5 dys			1081	5405		
	SWF 12/8 2 1	1		5	1081	5405		
					SUBTOTALS	72,701		
		TOTAL DETAIL ACCT. 1302				72,701		

A = Fringeable/Taxable B = Non-Fringeable/Taxable C = Non-Taxable
SAG Weekly Scale: $1822; With O.T. = 12 hrs. Pay = $2,500
SAG Daily: Scale + 10% = $576 for 8 hrs. worked

PAGE NO. 7C

PRODUCTION NOUMBER	PRODUCTION TITLE	DATE

1303 DAY PLAYERS						SUBTOTALS		
		DAYS						
CAST NO.	CHARACTER	WORK	HOLD	TOTAL	RATE	A	B	C
11	Mrs. Goetner	2 dy		2	1081	2162		
12	Ron Keller	2 dy		2	1081	2162		
13	Mrs. Corsitto	1 dy		1	1081	1081		
14	Bob	2 dy		2	1081	1081		
15	Bob's Wife	1 dy		1	1081	1081		
17	Lurleen	2 wk		2 wk	2500	5000		
18	Male Secretary	2 dy		2	1081	2162		
19	Tony	1 dy		1	1081	1081		
20	Male Receptionist	2 dy		2	1081	2162		
21	Mime	5 dy		5	1081	5405		
22	Young Man	2 dy		2	1081	2162		
23	Young Woman	2 dy		2	1081	2162		
24	Shopper #1	1 dy		1	1081	1081		
25	Shopper #2	1 dy		1	1081	1081		
26	Shopper #3	1 dy		1	1081	1081		
27	Laundry Lady	1 dy		1	1081	1081		
28	# 27's Little Boy	1 dy		1	1081	1081		
29	Woman #1 in Elevator	1 dy		1	1081	1081		
30	Woman #2 in Elevator	1 dy		1	1081	1081		
31	Man in Elevator	1 dy		1	1081	1081		
32	Demo Man	1 dy		1	1081	1081		
33	Speaker	1 dy		1	1081	1081		
34	Man in Booth	1 dy		1	1081	1081		
35	Young Driver	1 dy		1	1081	1081		
					SUBTOTALS	40,673		
		TOTAL DETAIL ACCT. 1303				see 7CC		

A = Fringeable/Taxable
B = Non-Fringeable/Taxable
C = Non-Taxable

PAGE NO. 7CC

PRODUCTION NOUMBER | PRODUCTION TITLE | DATE

1303 DAY PLAYERS						SUBTOTALS		
		DAYS						
CAST NO.	CHARACTER	WORK	HOLD	TOTAL	RATE	A	B	C
36	Motel Clerk	1 dy		1	1081	1081		
37	Bus Driver #1	1 dy		1	1081	1081		
	(Drop/Pick-Up)	1 wk		1	2500	2500		
38	Bus Driver #2	1 dy		1	1081	1081		
	(Drop/Pick-Up)	1 wk		1	2500	2500		
39	McNaught	1 dy		1	1081	1081		
40	Anncr./P.A. System (vo)	1 dy		1	1081	1081		
41	Tel. Operator #1 (vo)	1 dy		1	1081	1081		
42	Crome Dome (vo)	1 dy		1	1081	1081		
43	Woman in Bathroom (vo)	1 dy		1	1081	1081		
44	Tel. Operator #2 (vo)	1 dy		1	1081	1081		
45	Man #2 in Booth (vo)	1 dy		1	1081	1081		
	(Day #41, Scn. 128)							
46	Male Voice (vo)	1 dy		1	1081	1081		
47	Female Voice (vo)	1 dy		1	1081	1081		
					SUBTOTALS	17,972		
					TOTAL DETAIL ACCT. 1303	58,645		

A = Fringeable/Taxable
B = Non-Fringeable/Taxable
C = Non-Taxable

PAGE NO. 7D

PRODUCTION NOUMBER | PRODUCTION TITLE | DATE

1305 STUNTS						SUBTOTALS		
	SCENE	DAYS / WEEKS						
CAST NO.	DESCRIPTION / NOS.	WORK	HOLD	TOTAL	RATE	A	B	C
	Stunt Players	12 dys			524 dy	6288		
	Adjustments				ALLOW	2500		
	FOR:							
Day 3	EXT. STREET Scn. 365							
Day 27	EXT. STREET 7 HARRY'S							
	BUS Scn 297							
Day 38	INT / EXT CAR Scn. 150							
	7 doubles (7)	1 dy		7				
	(a) 1 driver need prep	1 dy	Prep 1 dy	1				
	3 Stunt men in Mustang	3 dy		3				
	(a) driver need prep		Prep 1 dy	1				
					SUBTOTALS	8,788		
					TOTAL DETAIL ACCT. 1305	8,788		

A = Fringeable/Taxable
B = Non-Fringeable/Taxable
C = Non-Taxable

PAGE NO. 7DD

STUNT BREAKDOWN FORM

Francis Ford Coppola Prods.	The Conversation	
PRODUCTION COMPANY	PRODUCTION TITLE	PRODUCTION NO.
Francis Coppola	Francis Coppola	Clark Paylow
PRODUCER	DIRECTOR	PRODUCTION MGR.
Vic Stuntman	Nov. 22, 1996	Nov. 24, 1995
STUNT COORDINATOR	SCRIPT DATE	DATE

SCENE NAME(S) Ext. Street - Burning Car

SCENE NO.(S) 365

SCENE DESCRIPTION Mr. C and his Mercedes Benz go up in Flames

CAST/STUNT PERSON Robert Duvall / Sandy Stuntman

EQUIPMENT DESCRIPTION	PROVIDED BY
1. Used Mercedes (1)	- Transportation
2. Rubber Cement	- Effects
3. Propane Gas w/Fantail Burners	- Special Effects
4. Dummy	- Props
5. Water Tanker	- City
6. Uniformed Safety Officer	- City
7. Special Effects Person - class one card	- Crew

RIGGING

Fantail burners require several hours to set up.

1300—CAST UNIT

"Speaking," or more particularly, "the utterance of a meaningful sound," is what separates the *actor* from the *extra*. While extras in New York, Los Angeles, and many other cities are also members of the Screen Actors Guild (SAG) and covered by its *basic agreement*, the utterance of that meaningful sound that changes an extra into an actor currently multiplies the scale compensation by a factor of eight.

The speaking parts of your film fall into three categories: *principals*, *supporting players* and *day players*. These categories are divided by the importance of the individual actor to the project. In principal, this importance also has a direct relation to the amount of compensation each actor receives. The least important category is the day player. Keep in mind that certain small parts (cameos) may be cast with well-known actors, so that some day players may earn more in eight hours than an unknown, scale supporting player earns in eight weeks.

Although stunt players and stunt coordinators are hired under the Screen Actors Guild agreement and appear before the cameras, they usually do not speak.

The first step in doing your cost estimate is to fill out what is called the actors *day out of days* form. Look at the filled out form in the beginning of this chapter. If you want to try filling out your own form, use the blank one on page 89 in *Movie Production and Budget Forms* (Lone Eagle Publishing.) There are 47 speaking parts in *The Conversation*, therefore you will need six pages. Note that the back of the form on page 90 is a continuation of page 89, giving you room for more days. If your overall production time is under six weeks and you have fewer than 30 cast members, then one copy is fine.

After you have determined the number of days and/or weeks each player works times the rate each is to be paid, transfer your subtotal to the *Cast Unit* page. Attach the actors day-out-of-days as backup to the budget.

01: Principal Players

While there is no strict rule of thumb for how much stars should be paid, consider the overall budget of your picture. If your total budget is $12 million, then, unless you are a close, personal friend, it is extremely unlikely that either Demi Moore or Arnold Schwarzenegger will be participating in the project as their current fees are higher than yur total budget. Depending on the physical requirements of your script and the other above-the-line salaries, you might, however, be able to pay an actor $500,000 or even a $1 million.

Budget realistically. If this is a *serious* film with only $2 million available for the entire production, you might reasonably expect even known actors to come aboard for scale. Don't expect them to do that, however, if you are paying yourself or anyone else a disproportionately hefty fee. Conversely, if this is *Sorority Babes in the Slimeball Bowl-O-Rama, Part 4,* don't expect an actor to cut his or her rate because the part is so challenging.

In *The Conversation*, the principal players are HARRY, ANN and MARK. Usually, the actor's name (e.g., Gene Hackman) and/or the number of days will tell you that you are dealing with a principal player, not a supporting player. Fill in *Cast Number*: (1), *Character*: HARRY CAUL; *Rehearsal*: 10 days; *Start Work*: November 26; *Work*: 37 days; *Hold*: four days; *Travel*: four days; and *Work Finish*: January 30, for a total of 55 days. To make it easy, you can use the cast numbers from the day-out-of-days for the subaccounts and place them in front of these category totals.

02: Supporting Cast

Supporting Players have featured parts. Some may work for only a few days; others, a few weeks. Some may work only two days in two weeks and be paid for the full two weeks because of other scheduling constraints as well as SAG's requirement that actors be paid for all intervening days. The *drop and pickup* rule applies here (See Account 1303–Day Players.)

Begin with the supporting players: MR. C., STANLEY, PAUL MEYERS, MARTIN, WILLIAM P. MORAN, MEREDITH, MILLARD and AMY. From your day-out-of-days fill in days worked, holds, etc. The amount you pay is open-ended with no fixed amount. Try to find out what the player made on his last job. The casting office can be helpful here. What you pay for an actor will depend upon how well you make the deal and how badly the actor wants to play the part.

03: Day Players

Day players are actors who work on a daily basis and must be notified by the end of the day if they are to work the next day. SAG does permit day players to be dropped and picked up or taken off salary and rehired (either on a daily or weekly basis), if there are at least ten days intervening between the first and second employment. An actor may be dropped and picked up only once. Keep in mind that you can go from a daily deal to a weekly but not a weekly deal to a daily.

MRS. GOETNER (11) is the first day player on your list. Day players work only a few days on a few scenes. All the rest of the actors through character 47 (except for AMY, number 16) will go on your day player list.

04: Stunt Coordinator

Stunt coordinators are members of the Screen Actors Guild. They responsible for the organization and coordination of all stunts on a production. There is no special rate for a stunt coordinator in SAG but all stunt personnel are covered in the Stunts Budget—Account 1305. On lower budget features, coordinators work for scale. On higher budgeted films they earn $5,000 to $7,500 per week.

While it is not a legal or union requirement, if your show has *any* stunts in it, whether it's a five car collision or an actor tripping over a garden hose, it is extremely ill-advised to think that you can get by without a qualified person to coordinate your stunts. There *are* both laws and union rules which detail the procedures that must be followed before any stunt is attempted. Although your director and production staff should know the rules for their own protection as well as yours, placing that burden entirely on them can have disastrous consequences. Most coordinators will gladly review a screenplay and give you an opinion of whether all the scripted stunts can be accomplished safely, and how many people and prep days will be needed. Since the stunts happen over such a long period of time (November 28–January 25), make an allowance for the time the coordinator is needed. I'd recommend $5,000.

05: Stunts

The Conversation had three sequences where a stunt coordinator could possibly be used: Scenes 144-158 (Day 38, January 25)—the encounter with the Ford Mustang); Scene 297 (Day 27, January 10)—where HARRY stumbles out the doors of the electric bus while the bus is still moving; and Scene 365 (Day 3, November 28)—"a mangled automobile where we close on the body of MR. C. slumped bleeding over the wheel of the crushed Mercedes. The automobile bursts into flames." On page 73 (page 7D of the budget form) is a stunt breakdown form for this scene as an example. You will know your show better if you do the same for your project. It was the producer's and director's choice not to have a full time stunt coordinator for the show. Why? The picture and the picture's budget didn't warrant it.

Let's begin with the car chase. Only once in the sequence, Scene 150, while the Mustang was careening around a corner did the driver almost go out of control. An experienced stunt driver with coordinating experience was hired to coordinate this sequence, as well as to review the entire script for any other possible exposure to hazards. The director elected to stage Scene 297 so that no danger could come to HARRY (Gene Hackman) as he left the bus. For Scene 365, the director and producers did not want to use a stunt double for MR. C. in the burning car. The emphasis here was to create an illusion through special effects that MR. C. was burning in the car.

Since this film is a dramatic piece and not an action movie, one week of preparation is adequate for a stunt coordinator. Sometimes the coordinator will perform some of the stunts. If so, pay the coordinator a salary *and* an adjustment for the stunt. The adjustment is based upon the difficulty of the stunt and how many times the stunt coordinator needs to perform it. The rate for the adjustment should be negotiated *before* the stunt is performed. The stunt coordinator is on payroll every day a stunt performer is, so budget accordingly.

If you have many stunts, determine the amount of time necessary to prepare each stunt. A *gag* such as the James Bond skiing off a mountain and then releasing a giant Union Jack parachute took several months to prepare—from finding the location, to rigging, to shooting. Most of the cars you see in stunt movies are not street cars. Most have been purchased in duplicate or triplicate, taken into a special effects garage and rigged with heavy duty shocks, reinforced steel, roll bars, and other safety devices to minimize the risk. Allow prep time for the stunt coordinator to advise regarding the stunt cars.

Utility Stunt Players

Utility stunt players are those stunt people who participate, and sometimes get knocked over, in scripted scenes—be it the bar fight in *48 HRS.* or the huge shoot-out scene in the streets of Mexico City in *Clear and Present Danger*. Allow a certain number of work days in either case.

Stunt Doubles

When actors would possibly be placed in a dangerous situation, they are replaced by *stunt doubles*. These doubles resemble the actor and, when dressed in costume, makeup, and shot performing the action in a long shot, are almost impossible to spot.

In *The Conversation*, there are three days which could require stunt personnel. The producers decided that Scene 297 could be done without a stunt double and HARRY could safely leave the bus. The coordinator would be there to show HARRY how to leave the bus without hurting himself.

In Scene 365, the stunt coordinator would help to lay out the sequence so that MR. C. (Robert Duvall) would be able to leave the vehicle if it were necessary. Scenes 144-158—the car sequence—required the most planning. For safety reasons, all the involved cast members: HARRY (1), STANLEY (5), PAUL (6), MORAN (8), MEREDITH (9), MILLARD (10), LURLEEN (17), except for the YOUNG DRIVER (35), have to be doubled.

So we know that you are doubling seven people in the staff car. What about the Mustang? This is the car doing most of the action in this sequence. In Scene 144 it reads, "Some young guys in a souped-up Mustang zip by them." We discover in Scene 158 that the young man driving the Mustang is WILLIE SANCHEZ. The driver sees a young Hispanic male. For now, figure a minimum of three people in the Mustang, counting the driver. The driver and the other occupants are stunt personnel. If the director sees more than three, then add the additional stunt person. Remind yourself to ask the director. On page 7D of your budget (see page 73), list the Cast Number, Scene Description/Nos., etc., for each stunt. List your stunts as they appear in the production board. They fall on days 3, 27 and 38.

Note that on day 38 the two drivers of the vehicles are given a day of preparation with the stunt coordinator. They will check course, check their equipment and have a wardrobe fitting. The passengers in the two cars are each given a day for a wardrobe fitting.

The drivers for the two vehicles will probably receive additional compensation (an *adjustment*) for their driving skills and any stunts which are created for the chase. These adjustments are agreed upon before they perform the stunt. In most cases, you will schedule multi-cameras for a stunt so that you will see the stunt from more than one angle. A project involving action sequences increases the costs for additional cameras (equipment) and camera crews (labor.)

If your production needs a helicopter, or any other special equipment, to perform a stunt or action sequence, note that under Special Equipment (Account 3000.)

To better understand all the costs of a stunt scene or sequence, break down the sequence into its necessary elements: *labor* and *materials*. Turn to page 74 and review the sample. List actor Robert Duvall under *Cast*. Since he will not be doubled, no stunt man is listed. The stunt coordinator, however, will be standing by. A dummy will be there if the decision is made to go without the actor or photograph the dummy in a separate cut.

The equipment and personnel needed comes next. Here you determine who is responsible for each item and each specialized individual. The cost of all of these requirements will fall under each specific category (e.g., *picture vehicle* for the Mercedes Benz).

After completing a stunt breakdown form for each stunt performed, make a note to put each item in the correct category as you come to it (picture vehicles, special effects, props, etc.)

Stunt Adjustments

Most stunt players work for scale. *Stunt adjustments* are additional pay for performing hazardous or complex stunts. Allow a total amount for all the stunts contained in your project. Remember that the adjustment is combined with the stunt player's basic rate, and that it can also increase the overtime rate.

06: Looping

Looping involves replacing previously recorded dialogue with newly recorded sounds or speech. Some reasons for looping are: unwanted noise in the background, unintelligible speech, changing certain words for a television release, or changing the scripted words in post production. The principal actors are called back during post production to rerecord those lines that need looping. The looping process is also referred to as Automatic Dialogue Replacement (*ADR*.) Actors watch a *loop* of the designated scene and, guided by a countdown or *click track*, mouth the replacement.

Actors is are paid a full day's work for looping no matter how short a time he is needed. *[Note: This applies to day players and scale players. Actors working for over scale or for more than a certain period may be required to return for a specific number of loop days without added compensation or, if for less than four hours, be paid a half day only. In their contracts, such days are termed "nonconsecutive loop days". This means that the producer can call the actor in at a convenient time in post-production without further payment. If the actor is out of town on another project or because he lives there, the Producer is responsible for airfare, etc.]* Since *The Conversation* deals extensively with tape recorded voices, it will be necessary to loop ANN's and MARK's voices. Allow two days of looping time for ANN and MARK. Build this into the budget and schedule it now. The conversation scheduled to take place between ANN and MARKfrom Day 5 to Day 10 is the same that HARRY listens to in his warehouse from Day 30 to Day 37. This is not much time to get the recording in good enough shape to use in HARRY's scenes. If everything isn't crystal clear during the shooting days in Union Square and the post production department can't pull the dialogue from the master audio recordings of their speeches, then all or part of their speeches will have to be looped. Usually, the director will want to be present during the looping session. You will need to work this out without affecting your shooting schedule by looping in post production after principal photography. We will also need time to loop lines that were lost due to poor sound recording conditions.

There are 29 day players, not counting the seven players who are **VOICE-OVERS**. Let's figure the worst case and put in one day of looping for all day players, i.e., 29 looping days.

07: Overtime

Actors are contractually entitled to a minimum rest period or *turnaround.* While occasional reductions of this turnaround time between location days are permitted on features, the minimum is twelve hours between each work day, thirty six hours between six day weeks, and fifty-six hours between five day weeks. If an actor is required to return before the minimum rest period, then you will have to **FORCED** the call and ask the actor return before completing the contractual minimum rest period. The penalty for this is $950 per incident or one day's pay, whichever is less. If it means keeping an actor and crew in sync with the hours of daylight, it can sometimes be money well spent. For budgeting purposes, don't anticipate any forced calls, but do allow for *overtime*. This is where you put your best estimate for such costs.

Overtime on principal actors and supporting players is usually a negotiated item. SAG Schedule F performers or those whose total guaranteed compensation is above a certain amount are paid penalties but not overtime. All players are usually paid based on an eight hour day. For the ninth and tenth hours, they are paid at the rate of time-and-a-half. After ten hours, the rate is double time. For day players who make considerably more than scale, contracts can be negotiated so that their overtime allowance does not become astronomical.

If the actor works more days than you scheduled, he will be paid for each additional day worked. An example that has become legendary occurred on David Lean's *Ryan's Daughter*. Robert Mitchum spent several *months* on location instead of the originally scheduled few *weeks*. The cost ran into many hundreds of thousands of dollars. You do not have to budget for such an extreme eventuality, but you do allow for some problems. A normal 12 hour work day is actually 14 straight time pay hours (plus a minimum 1/2 hour lunch break) for an actor. If an actor's rate is $600 per day, figure 1/8 or $75 per hour x 14 hours = $1,050 a day per day player.

We are budgeting 12 hour days. Any thing above the 12 hours per day will be considered overtime. With 29 day players involved, we shall allow 2 hours of overtime per day. There are 45 work days worked by these 29 players. How did we arrive at this number? We got it from the DAY-OUT-OF-DAYS form we did. Add up all the day player days worked, not including those who are doing voice overs If you allow two hours of overtime per person, per day at $150 per hour for 45 days, the overtime allowance total is $13,500. If you have day players at different rates, calculate the average of two hours of overtime as a percentage of the total. Four work hours, or straight time pay hours, is approximately 30 percent (30%) of the 14 hours budgeted. Include 30 percent (30%) of the total compensation to all day players as the overtime allowance.

Weekly players who are not Schedule F performers may also earn overtime. Their work week is defined as 44 hours over five days. They will likely have hold days on which no overtime is earned, so the percentage can be lower. Ten to 20 percent (10-20%) is reasonable.

08: Cast Fees

As with all above-the-line people, rates for casting persons vary widely. For a major feature film $40,000 to $100,000 would be appropriate. The average is $50,000. For a lower budget picture the fee would range from $10,000 to $20,000. This fee applies to one casting person and, depending on the deal, may include assistant(s), office, etc. Add in a casting assistant for 15 weeks for $1,000 per week. This can be divided up into other labor used in office as well. It will certainly not include duplication, messenger service, toll calls and the like. If you are filming outside of the New York or Los Angeles areas you might have to allow for an additional, local casting person.

09: Casting Expenses (Videotape System)

A simple v*ideotape system*a VHS playback unit and monito—will allow you to view videotapes of prospective actors, saving hours of interviewing time. It also lets you see the work of people who are not in town. You will pay for the equipment. Allow $500.

09: Casting Expenses (Computer/Copying)

Any equipment rented should be at market rates. If a computer is used, $250 should cover this expense. Count the principal cast and estimate the number of scripts that you are likely to send out (between 200 and 1,000 is typical) then multiply by $5 a piece. Figure an average of 600 copies x $5 or $3,000.

09: Casting Expenses(Office/Phone/Miscellaneous)

If you are covering all the casting department's expenses, allow $20,000 which should also cover the above-mentioned videotape and computers.

10: Welfare Worker/Teacher

On Day 17, HARRY's niece, TOREY, is in McNAUGHTON's office. If the actress playing the niece is under eighteen, she will require the services of a *Welfare Worker/Teacher* as will the LITTLE BOY (28) who works on day 21. The Office of Social Services has jurisdiction over welfare workers/teachers. Their work day begins when the minor arrives and ends when the minor is dismissed. Welfare workers must uphold the rules and regulations which govern the use of minors while employed, and provide education for the minor.

There are extremely strict guidelines regarding the length of time the child actors may work. [*Note: If you have read Film Scheduling, you will remember this as Parameter Factor No. 6.*] You will build your schedule and work day around the rules that govern the child. No prep or wrap time is required unless there is rehearsal and/or costume fitting time involved. *The Conversation* required the services of a welfare worker/teacher for two days on the schedule. There are no scenes requiring the use of children in the background as atmosphere (extras). Therefore, budget only two eight hour shooting days plus rehearsal/costume fittings. One week should work here.

Some budgets place welfare worker/teachers who work with actors or extras in the production account

11: Rehearsal Expenses

Rehearsal expenses for space rental will vary widely. The local film commission should be able to give you names and addresses of schools, churches, legitimate theaters which can be used as rehearsal space. Don't forget to check the local yellow pages.

This expense covers the cost of the physical space you will rent if you have rehearsal prior to principal photography. When possible, the cast should rehearse in the actual locations. If not, use a large rehearsal hall. Ten days of rehearsal prior to the start of principal photography is usually enough time to allow the actors and the director to get to know each other and work out any problems with the material.

Rehearsal space should have a large wooden floor (easier on the feet) which allows the art department to mark with white tape the approximate sizes of the principal sets to be used. The director, writer, cast, first assistant director, script supervisor and director of photography—with possible visits from the gaffer (head electrician), art director and key grip—can finalize the shooting plan and smooth out any rough edges before the first day of principal photography. This can save a great deal of time during the shooting period as well as a great deal of money. For *The Conversation* we are planning to use space for two weeks, working Monday through Friday.

The range here is $250 to $500 per day. Figure $2,500 per week for two weeks.

[*Note: Some directors do not like rehearsals. They feel that actors lose too much spontaneity and are given too much information.*]

12: Musicians

Budget sideline *musicians* who work in the picture here or under Extras—Account 2145.

85: Additional Expenses (Cast Contractuals)

Cast contractual expenses can include anything from flowers, a manicurist, a security guard, to a personal secretary. Contractually agreed to special expenses would be itemized here. Such items could be costs for a helicopter for special transportation, a wheelchair, special hair dressing over and above the costs for daily hair and make up. Discuss these items and costs with your producer so there are no surprises. There will be expenses involved in traveling (buses, taxis, etc.) in addition to what has been budgeted in Account 1400–Travel and Living. For *The Conversation* we will allow $250,000. This figure varies on the contractual arrangements with the stars. On a big budget picture with big-name stars, this cost can exceed $1,000,000. Lower budget pictures may pay little or nothing.

98: Miscellaneous

This line item provides a cushion to cover expenses which belong to the casting area but can't be defined anywhere else in the category. Let's make it a $1,500 allowance. As with the Additional Expenses category, if you find your budget to be too high, then cut down on these allowances.

[*Note: When actors are employed by other than major studios or major independent producers, SAG may require that a bond be posted with them as a guarantee that its members will be paid. While this is not an additional fee and is refunded after production has wrapped and all the fringe payments have been received by SAG, if your company is not yet a signatory, keep in mind for cash flow purposes that you may be required to post up to 40 percent (40%) of the total salary and fringes in your cast budget as a performance guarantee.*]

Account 1400

Travel and Living

LOCATION EXPENSE – DETAIL | PAGE NO. 8

PRODUCTION NUMBER | PRODUCTION TITLE | DATE

1400 TRAVEL AND LIVING – ABOVE-THE-LINE

		AIRFARES			LODGING (PER DIEM)			MEALS (PER DIEM)				
POSITION / NAME	DESTINATION (RT)	NO. FLIGHTS	RATE	SUB-TOTAL	NO. DAYS	RATE	SUB-TOTAL	NO. DAYS		RATE	SUB-TOTAL	TOTALS
Writer/Director Francis F. Coppola	S.F. - L.A.	3	280/rt	840	21	200/dy	4,200	21	B	157/dy	3,297	8,337
									L			
									D			
Co-Producer Fred Roos	S.F. - L.A.	3	280/rt	840	21	200/dy	4,200	21	B	157/dy	3,297	8,337
									L			
									D			
Associate Prod. Mona Skager	S.F. - L.A.	3	280/rt	840	21	125/dy	2,625	21	B	100/dy	2,100	5,565
									L			
									D			
Director's Secretary	S.F. - L.A.	3	280/rt	840	21	125/dy	2,625	21	B	60/dy	1,260	4,725
									L			
									D			
Co-Producer's Secretary	S.F. - L.A.	3	280/rt	840	21	125/dy	2,625	21	B	60/dy	1,260	4,725
									L			
									D			
									B			
									L			
									D			
									B			
									L			
									D			
									B			
									L			
									D			
									B			
									L			
									D			
									B			
									L			
									D			
	SUBTOTALS 1401		4,200		1402	16,275		1403		11,214		31,689
			TOTAL DETAIL ACCT 1400							see BB		

A = Fringeable/Taxable B = Non-Fringeable/Taxable C = Non-Taxable

LOCATION EXPENSE – DETAIL

PAGE NO. 8A

PRODUCTION NUMBER | PRODUCTION TITLE | DATE

1400 TRAVEL AND LIVING – ABOVE-THE-LINE

		AIRFARES			LODGING (PER DIEM)			MEALS (PER DIEM)				
POSITION / NAME	DESTINATION (RT)	No. Flights	rate	subtotal	no. days	rate	subtotal	no. days		rate	subtotal	totals
ACTOR: H. Caul Gene Hackman	L.A. - S.F.	5	280/rt	1,400	80	243.75 dy	19,500	10.5 wK (80 dys)	B L D	1,000/wK 150/dy	31,500 12,000	32,900
ACTOR: ANN Cindy Williams	L.A. - S.F. Drop & P/up	4	280/rt	1,120	32	125/dy	4,000	4.5 wK (32 dys)	B L D	100/dy	3,200	8,320
ACTOR: Mark Frederic Forrest	L.A. - S.F. Drop & P/up	4	280/rt	1,120	32	125/dy	4,000	4.5 wK (32 dys)	B L D	100/dy	3,200	8,320
ACTOR: Mr. C Robert DuVall	L.A. - S.F. Drop & P/up	4	280/rt	1,120	28	125/dy	3,500	4 wK (28 dys)	B L D	100/dy	2,800	7,420
ACTOR: Stanley John Cazalet	L.A. - S.F. Drop & P/up	4	280/rt	1,120	42	125/dy	5,250	6 wK (42 dys)	B L D	100/dy	4,200	10,570
ACTOR: Paul Michael Higgins	L.A. - S.F. Drop & P/up	4	280/rt	1,120	42	125/dy	5,250	6 wK (42 dys)	B L D	100/dy	4,200	10,570
ACTOR: Martin Harrison Ford	L.A. - S.F. Drop & P/up	4	280/rt	1,120	21	125/dy	2,625	3 wK (21 dys)	B L D	100/dy	2,100	5,845
ACTOR: Moran Allen Garfield	L.A. - S.F.	2	280/rt	560	21	125/dy	2,625	3 wK (21 dys)	B L D	100/dy	2,100	5,285
ACTOR: Meredith Elizabeth Macroe	L.A. - S.F.	2	280/rt	560	21	125/dy	2,625	3 wK (21 dys)	B L D	100/dy	2,100	5,285
ACTOR: Millard	L.A. - S.F.	2	280/rt	560	21	125/dy	2,625	3 wK (21 dys)	B L D	100/dy	2,100	5,285
		SUBTOTALS 1401		9,800	1402		52,000	1403		38,000		99,800
					TOTAL DETAIL ACCT 1400					see 8B		

A = Fringeable/Taxable
B = Non-Fringeable/Taxable
C = Non-Taxable

LOCATION EXPENSE – DETAIL

PAGE NO. 8B

PRODUCTION NUMBER — PRODUCTION TITLE — DATE

1400 TRAVEL AND LIVING – ABOVE-THE-LINE												
		AIRFARES			LODGING (PER DIEM)			MEALS (PER DIEM)				
POSITION / NAME	DESTINATION (RT)	No. Flights	rate	subtotal	no. days	rate	subtotal	no. days		rate	subtotal	totals
ACTOR: Amy Teri Garr	L.A. - S.F.	2	280/rt	560	11	125/dy	1,375	1.5 wk (11 dys)	B L D	150/dy	1,650	3,585
									B L D			
									B L D			
									B L D			
									B L D			
									B L D			
									B L D			
									B L D			
									B L D			
									B L D			
		SUBTOTALS 1401		560	1402		1,375	1403		1,650		3,585
			TOTAL DETAIL ACCT 1400					135,074				

A = Fringeable/Taxable
B = Non-Fringeable/Taxable
C = Non-Taxable

1400—TRAVEL AND LIVING

THIS ACCOUNT CONTAINS THE ANCILLARY COSTS FOR above-the-line personnel only. If you are shooting on local locations and in the studio only, allow a nominal amount here. If you know that one or more of your cast members will be brought in from out of town, budget for airfare, local housing, and per diem. SAG has a table of minimum per diems depending on the city to which its member has been transported. Also, if such seating is available on the flight, all DGA members and SAG Actors in groups of fewer than ten must be flown First Class. Producers can travel coach.

If all or part of your shooting schedule is on distant location, budget airfare, housing, and per diem for everyone who will work out of town. Some stars are contractually granted extra airline tickets for family or assistants, hotel suites or other enhanced accommodations, and per diems much higher than the SAG minimums. Remember also that minors must be accompanied by a guardian who will also need an airline ticket, per diem, and, depending on the relationship to the minor, separate housing.

On this production there is a breakdown of travel and living for cast members since many will come from Los Angeles and travel to San Francisco.

The director and his secretary, the co-producer and his secretary and the associate producer went to Los Angeles for casting during the prep period. There is time and money for this in the budget.

Account 1900

Fringe Benefits and Payroll Taxes

PAGE NO. 9

PRODUCTION NUMBER	PRODUCTION TITLE	DATE

1900 FRINGE BENEFITS AND PAYROLL TAXES – ABOVE-THE-LINE

ACCT NO.	DESCRIPTION	PAYROLL	PENSION	HEALTH & WELFARE	TOTALS
01	Loanout-Max. Fringe on $200,000 Ceilings: $250,000 (H&W) DGA $ 200,000 (Pension)	%	% 5.5	% 7	28,500
02	PGA $	%	%	%	
03	WGA $	% 12.5	% inc.	% inc.	7,792
04	SAG CORP. $600,000	12.8%	%	%	76,800
	(Loanouts/Fringe at $200,000) SAG $ 194,077	% 27	% inc.	% inc.	52,401
05	IATSE $ 33,722	% 29	% inc.	% inc.	9,779
06	NABET $	%	%	%	
07	OTHER $ 180,800	% 18	%	%	32,544
10	or Allow				

SUBTOTALS				207,816
TOTAL ACCT 1900				207,816
TOTAL COST ABOVE-THE-LINE				6,279,260

1900—FRINGE BENEFITS AND PAYROLL TAXES

THE AMOUNTS ENTERED HERE PERTAIN TO ABOVE-THE-LINE people only. Use Account 4900 for the below-the-line fringes. The development area has already accounted for fringes/taxes.

Union Payroll

As mentioned before, the government portion of fringes are FICA, FUI, et al, as defined below. They currently average 18.5 percent (18%.) You can use that as a reasonable estimate until you have exact numbers. Some companies allot more or less money to this account depending on their own experiences. Below are some key definitions to help you understand the lingo of fringe benefits and taxes.

FICA

Federal Insurance Contribution Act (FICA) or the employer and employee contributions to Social Security.

There is a maximum annual amount on which this tax is levied. This amount, currently $57,600, is increased periodically by statute. Other government fringes have lower cutoffs. Many computerized budget programs will permit you to adjust individually. If you are doing your budget by hand, you can reasonably use the FICA cutoff for all government fringes. However, remember not to apply the 18.5 percent (18.5%) to any individual's once it exceeds the maximum. If your production takes place later in the year and you use a payroll service, your company may reap an unexpected fringe benefit if any of your employees has worked on other shows using the same payroll service. As the payroll service is considered the employer of record, those people may already have exceeded the annual cutoff and your production will not be responsible for paying any additional fees.

FUI
Federal Unemployment Insurance, sometimes called FUTA (Federal Unemployment Tax Act).

SUI
State Unemployment Insurance.

Worker's Compensation
A benefit paid to an employee in the event of a work-related injury. The employer pays a certain rate based on an employee's salary and their job category (clerical, executive, etc.)

SDI
State Disability Insurance.

Medicare
The employee contribution to government sponsored medical insurance fund.

Union Fringes
Writers, directors, actors and any other guild or union members whose salaries are detailed above-the-line also have pension, health, and welfare contributions made on their behalf. As an example, DGA fringes for directors are 12.5 percent (12.5%), five and one-half percent (5.5%) pension and seven percent (7%) health and welfare. An additional two and one-half percent (2.5%) is deducted directly from the director's salary as the employee's contribution. These fringes are also subject to a cutoff or maximum amount. The current cutoff rate for a DGA director is $200,000 annually.

Many actors, directors, writers, and other highly-paid employees have formed their own corporations. Technically, these people are employed by their own corporations which loan out their services to the producer or production company. Technically this also means that the personal **LOAN OUT CORPORATION** is responsible for the payment of that employee's fringes. Many contracts stipulate that the producer will pay both the corporation both a fee for the services of (f/s/o) the individual and repay the corporation for any costs (i.e., fringes) that it may incur as a result of this employment. Because some loan-out corporations have regularly neglected to pay the guild fringes, both SAG and the DGA hold the employer or producer directly responsible for the payment of these fringes.

Nonunion Payroll

The *nonunion payroll* part of this is for secretaries and other nonunion employees. It includes only their FICA, FUI, SUI, SDI, Medicare, and Worker's Compensation payments.

State Sales Tax

While this mostly applies to goods and services that are budgeted below-the-line, some items such a script duplication may be subject to a sales tax. It is easier to assume that your budgeted allowance for a certain item, e.g., $1,000 includes the sales tax, rather than breaking it out as a separate line item here.

Below-the-Line

BELOW-THE-LINE

THIS IS THE MAJOR PORTION OF YOUR BUDGET FORM. This area reflects the costs of technicians (labor) and materials (rentals and purchases). Labor costs are usually calculated on a daily basis. On larger projects that daily rate is estimated on a weekly basis. Also included in below-the-line costs are raw stock, processing and equipment.

It is important that as soon as the department heads have been hired, read their scripts, and begun their breakdowns, they meet with the director individually to discuss what is expected from each department. This should be done as early as practical in the pre-production period so that the departments have the maximum possible time to carry out the director's wishes. Each department head should have the opportunity during prep to meet regularly with the director to show the items requested and be sure it is what the director had in mind.

All the departments may be involved but most significantly *Property, Set Dressing, Wardrobe, Locations, Transportation*, and sometimes *Makeup.*

As these department heads make decisions in consultation with the director, there will be a direct impact on your budget estimates. You will need to meet regularly with all these departments in order to verify that your projected costs will be your actual costs.

Account 2000

Production Department

PAGE NO. 10

PRODUCTION NUMBER | PRODUCTION TITLE | DATE

2000 PRODUCTION DEPARTMENT

ACCT. NO.	DESCRIPTION	LOCAL/ On Loc.	DAYS/WEEKS PREP	SHOOT	WRAP	TOTAL	RATE	SUBTOTALS A	B	C
01	Production	Local	12	8.2	4	24.2	2,705	65,461		
	Manager	On Loc.								
	Prod. Fee	Local		8.2		8.2	585	4,797		
	Comp. of Assign.	On Loc.								
02	First Assistant	Local	6	8.2	1	15.2	2,569	39,049		
	Director O.T.	Local	.6	1		1.6	2,569	4,110		
	Prod. Fee	Local		8.2		8.2	475	3,895		
	Comp. of Assign	On Loc.								
03	Second Assistant	Local	3	8.2	1	12.2	1,722	21,008		
	Director O.T.	Local	7 dys	41 dys		48 dys	344	16,512		
	Prod. Fee	Local		8.2		8.2	363	2,977		
	Comp. of Assign.	On Loc.								
05	Location Manager	Local	10	8.2	3	21.2	1,756	37,227		
	O.T.	Local	10	8.2		91 dys	351	31,959		
	Asst. Location	Local	4	8.2	1	13.2	678	8,950		
	Manager O.T.	Local	4	8.2		61 dys	136	8,296		
10	Production	Local	10	8.2	6	24.2	1,781	43,100		
	Accountant	On Loc.								
15	Asst. to Production	Local	10	8.2	6	24.2	988	47,822		
	Accountant 2X	On Loc.								
20	D.G.A. Trainee	Local	1	8.2		9.2	482		4,434	
	O.T.		.1	1.3		1.4	482		675	
25	Production Assts.	Local	8	8.2	3	19.2	450		8,640	
	2 X	On Loc.	3	8.2	1	12.2	450		10,980	
26	Accounting P.A.	Local	6	9	5	20	500		10,000	
	Post Prod. Asst.	On Loc.			20	20	1,781		35,620	
48	Interpreters	Local								
		On Loc.								
50	Script	Local	3	8.2	1	12.2	2,265	27,633		
	Supervisor O.T.	Local								
55	Production Office	Local	10	8.2	2	20.2	1,035		20,907	
	Coordinator	On Loc.								
60	Production	Local	10	8.2	2	20.2	602		12,170	
	Secretary	On Loc.								
	Additional Hire	Local		10 dys		10 dys	75		750	
	2nd 2nd A.D.	Local		15 dys			338	5,820		
80	Technical Advisor's	Local	4			4	1,000		4,000	
	1 & 2	On Loc.		16 dys		16 dys	500		8,000	
85	Additional Expenses						ALLOW		6,000	500
	(including computers)	computer								
95	Script Box Rent / Misc. /		2	8.2	1	11.2	150			1,680
	Script Timing / Polaroid						ALLOW			3,500
97	Production Board/ Budget Prep.	SEE DEVELOPMENT ACCOUNT								
							SUBTOTALS	368,616	122,176	5,680
							TOTAL ACCT 2000	496,472		

A = Fringeable/Taxable
B = Non-Fringeable/Taxable
C = Non-Taxable

2000–PRODUCTION DEPARTMENT

THE PRIME RESPONSIBILITY OF THE PRODUCTION DEPARTMENT is to supervise the project under the authority of the producer. If the film company is a signatory to the Directors Guild contract, there are staffing requirements. In addition to the director, you must hire a unit production manager, a first assistant director, and a second assistant director. A second second assistant director and/or Directors Guild trainee may also be recommended. In New York, the location manager is also a member of the Directors Guild and paid either as a second assistant director or second second assistant director.

01: Production Manager

Production manager and unit production manager, or UPM, are equivalent terms for the Directors Guild of America. The production manager not only manages the production phase of a project but also in a larger sense runs the company business. This is the most important production person below the line. The production manager is the person to whom the producer usually turns for a budget. If a studio is involved, it uses its Estimating Department to create a budget; but the producer can and often does ask the production manager to make a budget. If your project calls for many locations inside or outside the United States, you may need additional unit production managers from the areas in which you are shooting.

In the United States, the Directors Guild and the Alliance of Motion Picture and Television Producers (AMPTP) maintain **QUALIFICATIONS LISTS** of unit production managers and assistant directors (ADs.) In theory, a DGA UPM has qualified to be a UPM by working a certain numbers of days as a first assistant director and as a second assistant director. *[Note: A person may become qualified for UPM work by beginning as a second AD, working 520 days in that capacity, and qualifying to be a first AD, then working 260* *more days as a first and qualifying to be a UPM. In practice, many people who have worked as nonunion UPM for the prescribed numbers of days may qualify for direct placement on a qualification list in that category.]* A production manager is, therefore, as qualified as a first assistant director in breaking down and scheduling a script as well as budgeting it. Whether working for a studio or independent producer, the UPM can and will rework these before beginning official pre-production or until his or her employer is comfortable with it. When pre-production formally begins, the UPM will set up production offices, hire the crew, negotiate contracts with vendors and deals with agents of below-the-line personnel as well as handle the myriad of other essential things necessary for production. Some UPMs also supervise all or part of the post-production. Usually the UPM will remain with the show until all the production costs are settled and accounted for and then be released.

Theatrical productions typically needs to prepare for at least one or 1-1/2 times the shooting period. Let's figure 12 weeks for *The Conversation. We* shall assuming that the unit production manager was from San Francisco. Figure the 12 weeks of prep. The shooting period is eight and two fifths weeks. We figured this out when we broke down the script and created a production board. In most cases four weeks is sufficient to pay the production vendors and get post-production on track.

Since the director of *The Conversation*, Francis Coppola, belongs to the DGA, the project was required to hire a DGA unit production manager—Clark Paylow.

Production Fee/Severance

The *production fee* is an additional minimum compensation paid to DGA UPM, first AD, and key second AD for every production (shooting) day. In multi-camera television, the fee is paid on the day the show is blocked, or whenever cameras are used even if no scenes are actually filmed. As with most scale compensation, the contractual weekly can be prorated after the first week to reflect actual days worked or planned to be worked. For estimating purposes here, we will only allot it to the actual production period.

Severance refers to **COMPLETION OF ASSIGNMENT PAY**, the contractual amount paid to certain crew members to allow them to finish up all their paperwork before leaving the job. The unit production manager will receive one week's pay for completion of assignment. This is normally paid at the studio rate, as opposed to the distant-location rate. The same applies to the first AD and the key second.

Computer Rental

With most below-the-line departments, some of the personnel will own some of the equipment they use, and the production staff is no exception. The UPM, ADs, production coordinator, and production accountant are all likely to use computers. Renting their own machines from them will be less expensive than a commercial supplier. Although on long-term productions or the first of several projects, it may be most cost effective to buy and amortize the cost. *(See more detailed note on computers on pages 123-124.)*

Many major studios and independents are paying a flat fee of $1,500 for the run of the picture for *computer rental* and the use of the production software which it may need.

Underwater Work Allowance/Aircraft Flight Pay

All DGA members are entitled to *hazard pay* when working under ten feet of water or per flight when working in the air. If the individual(s) in question is being paid above scale, the additional compensation cannot be used to offset these allowances. Currently, the allowance is $146 per dive or flight. If there are more than one dives or flights during a single day, the fees become negotiable. There were no flights or dives in *The Conversation*, so this does not apply to this budget.

Incidental Allowance

On distant location a UPM or AD will receive a daily *incidental allowance* in addition to their regular per diem. This should cover dry cleaning bills and such. Currently, this figure is $14 per day and is covered in Account 4005.

Clothing for Hazardous Work
It is the employer's responsibility to provide suitable clothing if a unit production manager or assistant director has to engage in work where the conditions are wet or cold. After the show is over it is traditional for the production company to offer the clothes to the crew and cast at half-price.

Dinner Allowance
On local location, if a UPM and/or AD starts work on or before 9:00 AM and works after 7:30 P.M., they shall be paid a dinner allowance unless the employer furnishes a dinner beginning no later than 9:00 P.M.

Overtime
Allow a couple of days to cover *overtime* and weekend work. Use the distant location rate with the production fee if your picture is on distant location.

Unit Manager
The terms production manager, unit production manager, and *unit manager* have virtually become synonymous. Many times in a busy television or theatrical production company, you will sometimes find an executive production manager who is responsible for overseeing all the productions at the company. The UPMs for each production would then report directly to this executive production manager.

Starting with the unit manager we have budgeted DGA minimum wages.

02: First Assistant Director (First AD)
Whether in feature or television production, the DGA Basic Agreement sets a minimum preparation time for the *first assistant director* and second key assistant directors. Before a production begins, the first AD breaks down the script and schedules the show, paying particular attention to the availabilities of actors and locations. The first AD scouts all the location, and, with the director, calculates the

amount to time that will be spent at each one. The first AD directly administers the extras budget by setting the number of extras needed for each scene and with the director's and production manager's approval, working with the Extras Casting people to hire them. The first AD has an assistant called a *second assistant director*, or second AD. (*See page 110.*)

The first assistant director is the liaison between the director and production manager. During production, the assistant director is primarily responsible for setting the **CALL TIME**—making sure that everyone and everything is in the right place at the right time. He is also responsible for maintaining open lines of communication so that all the departments can know and be prepared for whatever scene is next. The first AD physically runs the set. He announces a take and calls, "Quiet on the set!" He asks the mixer to *roll sound* and the camera operator to *roll camera* when they are ready. Between *action* and *cut*, the first AD silently turns the set over to the director. The first and second will stage movements of any required extras and will cue them to start their background action before the director cues the actors.

The assistant directors led by the first are also the safety officers on the set. They are the primary liaison between the director, stunt coordinator, and special effects crew on any stunt or other dangerous work. They are responsible for holding regular safety meetings with cast and crew, particularly when working on a **PRACTICAL** location, i.e., one that is normally what the movie depicts it to be from a restaurant to a construction site. Locations like the latter may have other ongoing activities and/or unexpected hazards.

Except in episodic television, the director has the contractual right to designate the first assistant director, subject only to salary negotiations.

On *The Conversation* we are bringing in the first AD for preparation six weeks prior to the beginning of principal photography. At the end of the show, the first AD will also receive one week's completion of assignment pay figured at normal studio rates. Again, this is part of the basic agreement of the DGA.

03: Second Assistant Director (Second AD)

The *key second assistant director* is the first AD's principal assistant. While the first AD remains on the set with the director, the key second physically prepares and distributes the *call sheet* according to the first AD's instructions. The call sheet lists the next day's work, which cast and crew members are needed, and when they are asked, or "called" to report.

The key second is also responsible for preparing and/or collecting all the following daily paperwork:

Production report: a detailed listing of what scenes were shot, which cast and crew were used and for how long, and other specific details on many lunches were eaten to how many feet of film were used.

Screen Actors Guild sign-out sheet: a written record of how many hours they worked that day, including notes about being on hold, stunt adjustments, meal periods, etc. Each actor signs this sheet at the end of their working day.

Script supervisor's report: a summary of scenes and setups accomplished

Cutter's log for the editor

Camera reports for each roll of film

Sound logs for each reel of tape

Vouchers for each extra

Contracts for day players, and

Time cards, daily and weekly, on the crew.

Besides assisting in the placement and cueing of extras as well as helping to maintain crowd control, the second AD is the main conduit of information to the cast and crew about the daily schedule. The second AD is responsible for telling each actor how much time remains until he is needed on the set. At the appropriate time, the second AD escorts the actor from his trailer or room to the set.

Both on features and television (other than multi-camera television), the key second usual has a group of assistants headed up by the *second second assistant director* and/or a *DGA trainee.* On guild productions, the second is a member of the DGA or some equivalent union covering production personnel (e.g., Directors Guild of Canada, Directors Guild of Great Britain). We will bring the key second in three weeks before principal photography begins. This will put at least one of the assistant directors at the rehearsal of the actors to take place just prior the start of principal photography. The second AD will also contractually receive one week of completion of assignment pay.

Traditionally, the first AD selects the key second AD.

04: Second Second Assistant Director (Second Second AD)

When a show is large enough to warrant hiring a *second second AD*, some of the work of the second AD, such as being responsible for preparing the production report and maintaining regular liaison with the production office, then goes to the second second AD. Besides having their own computers, ADs may also have their own cellular telephones and pagers, which may be packaged with their services for a rental fee. On certain DGA shows, second seconds may also act as location managers (see below). When *The Conversation* was made, most shows didn't use second second ADs. (They usually hired non-DGA production assistants instead.)

Let's analyze how we would be utilizing second second ADs on *The Conversation.* On Day One we are shooting in the Financial District and a city park. The park will present the major problem with crowd control, traffic control and extras. On Day Two, we are scheduling 45 extras for the day to work in Harry's neighborhood. There is also the bus scene and then we move to the market. The day has a number of extras, crowd control possibilities since you are shooting exteriors, and a possible move. Days 1, 2, 4, 5, 6, 7, 8, 9, 14, 26, 27, 38, 39, 40 and 41 are days on which you might need an additional second assistant director. Look over those days in the shooting schedule. Just because you have budgeted for an additional second doesn't mean you will automatically hire someone. The final decision as to whom should be hired rests with the assistant director, with the production manager's approval. Weigh each day individually for your recommendation.

05: Location Manager

A *location manager* helps find, secure, and supervise work on practical locations. Many location managers also arrange sound stage rentals. On a practical location, the location manager will arrange for filming permits, hiring police and fire personnel as needed, posting parking signs, and even finding a place for the caterer to set up lunch. In Southern California, location managers are members of Teamsters Local 399; in New York, they are members of the DGA.

The location manager begins work by reading the script and making a complete list of all locations necessary for filming. Then the location manager, meets with the director, producer and UPM to determine what the locations should look like, how upscale or not, what the surrounding countryside should be, etc. If the script calls for a *mansion*, it is up to the location manager to narrow the choices down by asking appropriate questions such as: "What kind of a mansion do you need?" "Is it in a wealthy neighborhood surrounded by lush greenery and perhaps other mansions?" "Is it isolated on top of a mountain with a view of a lake?" "What kinds of *city streets* are needed?" "Ghetto areas?"

Armed with this information, the location manager then begins to whittle down the possible locations to areas within easy driving distance for the crew. After this, the location manager will take the director (and possibly the producer, and UPM) to see the two or three most likely choices for each location. This gives the director a chance to tell the location manager which locations suit the picture well or not and why. The "why" is important because it gives the location manager further guidance in finding better locations. If money is tight, you might consider hiring a less expensive location scout, who merely finds locations but does not manage them during production.

You should bring the location manager in as early as possible. Much depends upon the number and difficult of your locations. If you are dealing with government controlled locations such as federal, state, or city owned parks, or with distant locations in another state or country, the time can be longer than anyone anticipates. Be sure to give your location manager enough time to finish the job. Overtime will be necessary, since property owners are not usually at home during the day. After going over our shooting schedule, we are going to start our location manager on *The Conversation* ten weeks before the start of principal photography. This amount of time is normal for a movie on which almost all filming will be on location. (If the filming had taken place in another location other than Southern California, e.g., San Francisco, Atlanta, Georgia, or Canada, we would have hired a separate location manager to handle each separate area.) Our location manager is from San Francisco. There are 45 locations to be surveyed and secured. After discussing the show with the director (Francis Coppola), the production manager knew that only one set would have to be constructed (INT. HARRY'S APT.), and that would be done on location. This is not to say other construction would not be necessary, but a sound stage would not be rented where sets would be built.

After the shooting is over, the location manager requires time to finish all necessary paperwork—thank you letters to locations, contracts, payments, and such. We are going to allow three weeks for wrap.

On many features with a variety of locations and other complexities, it is normal to hire one or more assistant location managers. As was the case with additional second assistant directors you should weigh the needs of your location department. The location manager may need an assistant. The assistant location manager does not have to work the entire show. Such a person can be called in on an as-needed basis. We are not going to add an assistant location manager since the location manager was able to handle this show alone.

Car Allowance and Mileage

This situation is unique in the film business. The location managers working under a Teamsters contract are entitled to have both $175 per week car allowance and $.30 per mile for mileage. Non-Teamster location managers and members of other guilds or unions are entitled to the mileage allowance or car allowance but not both. Car allowance amounts are negotiable.

10: Production Accountant

The *production accountant* (aka production auditor, location auditor, or location accountant), is always the member of the production staff. Her primary responsibility is to maintain up-to-date, accurate financial records of the costs entailed in the production of the film or television show. On a union production in Los Angeles, this position is covered by Local 717. The production auditor works directly with the production manager and the financing entity.

Major studios have systems to which individual production accounts must conform—their own production budget forms, each with its own chart of accounts. All bills for labor or materials must be coded according to the chart of accounts to enable you to track costs in each department. On any production, the chart of accounts used in the budget should be the same as that used by the accountant to produce the *Cost Report.* The cost report, in fact, should be a replication of your budget that contains five columns of totals beginning with the *Budgeted Total* continuing with *Actual Cost* to date, *Estimated Cost to Complete*, *Estimated Total Cost*, and the *Over and Under* or the amount by which the *Estimated Total Cost* is over or under the *Budgeted Cost.* This document, which the production accountant will update on a weekly basis in consultation with the production manager and other department heads as needed is one of the most important document which any production prepares.

For independent producers, most accountants will have one or more programs already on their computers. If compatibility is an issue, there are programs available from the payroll services. Normally you will lease one for a specific length of time such as the run of the project. This can cost up to $2,500 for a six-month lease. These programs will save your accountant many hours of time. They also give you the flexibility of giving daily (if required) up-to-the-minute reports for your cost-to-complete.

The production accountant will set up the books for the production. All the major studios have production accountants, who on large features earn between $1,600 and $2,500 per week for local filming or $2,000 to $3,000 for distant location. On low budget productions those figures can be lowered by a third or so.

A really effective accounting department has two assistants: one handling payroll and the other handling bills or accounts payable. As already mentioned, there are a few excellent payroll services or firms that can handle the payroll for you and become the employer of record. They charge either by the check ($8 to $15) or by a percentage of payroll—one-quarter to one-half of one percent (.25% to .5%.) By the check may seem costlier, but, in fact, for salaries above $3,000 a week, it can be less expensive. Many services will allow you to use a per check method above-the-line where salaries are larger and a percentage method below-the-line. If your company is employing free-lance accountants, the assistant's rate will range from $750 to $1,500 per week.

PAYROLL

Everyone on the show should fill out and sign a deal memo. The person's entered and agreed upon deal (hours, any rentals, etc.) are reflected on this memorandum. Most employees are on hourly deals and record their daily hours on a time card. (It is not unusual to have one person in a department fill out the time cards for the entire department.) The production manager reviews and approves the time cards, and assistant production accountant figures out the employee's wages.

More and more companies are using payroll companies. The payroll company becomes the employer of record and pays your employees under its own contracts which it has signed with the various unions. The payroll company also handles all payroll accounting. Usually these companies charge a very small percentage of the work which filters through their offices. Since many production companies are formed to film one project, they may not be around in several years to deal with any accounting problems. More than likely, the payroll company will.

ACCOUNTS PAYABLE

A good accounting department uses a purchase order (PO) system. Almost all purchases are placed on individual purchase orders which are then approved by the production manager. When the bills come in, the accounts payable person attaches a copy of the purchase order to each bill, sends it to the department head for approval and then to the production manager for final approval. The invoice is then sent back to the accounting department for coding and to have a check drawn. The checks (usually requiring two signatures) are then sent to the production manager for final approval and signature. All this is done by an individual in the accounting department. Using this system, the production company can accurately track the daily costs of the film project from pre-production to its release.

DGA TRAINEES

In 1965 the DGA and AMPTP established a *Training Program for Assistant Directors* to answer the ongoing need for qualified second ADs. There are programs for the East and West Coasts based out of New York and Los Angeles in which trainees spend the industry-standard number of days to become qualified second ADs (i.e., 400 working days for placement on the Southern California list).

As trainees are the only people other than DGA members who are permitted to perform assistant director work on a DGA production, all union features under the jurisdiction of the Directors Guild of America are encouraged to employ a trainee, if one is available. Very few applicants are accepted each year in the DGA Training Program. The trainee candidates must pass rigorous written and oral examinations. There may be as many as 1,500 candidates in a given year applying for as few as a dozen openings. Many of the most prominent UPMs and ADs working today (not to mention a few directors, producers, and studio executives) came into the industry as DGA trainees. While the rate for trainees varies based on the individual's number of days in the program, even a trainee who has worked more than 300 days begins at less than $500 per week. The basic work week is 54 hours with overtime for anything over that, however that is considerably less than DGA scale for a second second AD.

25: Production Assistants

Originally this job was done by a relative of someone who needed a job (a college kid, younger sibling, etc.) this job has become an official entry-level position. Instead of just being called a "PA" or "gofer," there are now various jobs and job titles which fall into this category. This term may be applied to a variety of jobs distinction between *Set Production Assistants* or *PAs* and *Office PAs*, who are usually runners, or even euphemisms from *Production Associate* to *Executive Gofer*. The rate of pay varies from $250 to $500 per week. I have, at times, had a production associate who was not paid at all but who worked just for the experience. Persons working without pay in any department are usually referred to as *Interns*. Whatever the actual job title, in such a case you must be careful as to how you handle their use of vehicles, because your insurance will not cover anyone not actually on payroll. In Los Angeles on Union films you will find production associates working as runners or messengers but seldom if ever on the set. As already noted, all Guild-covered production work is done only by the ADs and/or the DGA trainee, and DGA field representatives to observe the working conditions. The production office as well as the editorial and art departments will need the assistance of these production associates.

48: Interpreter

Your project may need the services of an interpreter especially if all or part of your film is scheduled out of the country, or if an actor speaks English as a second language. The amount of time is directly dependent upon your project. You must figure in the amount of time you will be on location during the prep period. You may hire someone on your production staff (e.g., the first AD) who speaks the language in question. This person will assist in interpreting and also be able to think in production terms. The cost here varies. Your best bet is to speak to others who have filmed in the country where you are planning to shoot. Get some recommendations and some price quotes. Since *The Conversation* was filmed in San Francisco, there was no need for an interpreter.

50: Script Supervisor

The *script supervisor* (previously known as a continuity clerk) is responsible for recording detailed notes on every take, to include dialogue, gestures, action, lens used, costumes, makeup, so as to ensure that all these elements match from shot to shot and scene to scene. The script supervisor, who is usually found sitting on a low chair near the camera, also gives numbers to the coverage (the individual close-ups or other shots which the director films but which are not noted in the printed script). She also records the numbers of the takes which the director wants printed, and makes certain that the her records, the camera assistant's logs and mixer's logs all match with regard to noting the takes to print on each roll of film and audio tape. Individual departments—particularly props, wardrobe, and makeup—will have their own breakdowns and records of scene. Since films are usually shot out of sequence, the script supervisor's notes are the primary reference of what scenes have been filmed and any changes thereto. They also include the director's notes as to why a scene was not printed or which portion of a good scene is to be used. These notes are submitted at the end of each shooting day and are an essential tool for the editor and director when cutting the film together. Some people feel that after the director, the script supervisor has the second most important job on the set. Without the help of this person, the director's job would be infinitely more difficult, as there are so many details to keep track of while shooting a film.

Script supervisors are frequently called *the eyes and ears of the film editor*. It is the script supervisor's responsibility to keep the editor informed, with the script notes, of what happened on each day of shooting. Script supervisors are part of IATSE Local 871 in Los Angeles and Local 161 in New York City.

Even though the script supervisor's work should be finished by the end of principal photography (or second unit photography, if needed), it would be wise to add in three days to a week in order to clear up any questions the editing department, producer or director might have. Also, script supervisors like to turn in a clean, typed report at the end of production and this will give them time to complete it.

The selection of the script supervisor may be done by the director, producer or the production manager. The script supervisor will start employment three to four weeks before principal photography and will attend the rehearsals. Most, if not all script supervisors are paid on a daily not a weekly basis go into overtime after six hours of work. The general crew (grips, electricians, etc.) will go into overtime after eight hours work.

Polaroid Camera/Film

As a backup to written continuity notes by any department, instant photographs have become essential. Sometimes on the set there is a union jurisdiction conflict between the *unit still photographer* and the *script supervisor* as to who should take the Polaroid shots of certain items needed for continuity. Many times only the still photographer is allowed to take these shots. This conflict does not exist in the makeup or wardrobe trailers. Therefore, allow $2,000 in Miscellaneous Account 2095.

55: Production Office Coordinator

Production office coordinator (abbreviated POC) is a member of the production staff who works directly for the production manager and acts as a liaison between everyone during the production. The POC is responsible for setting up production offices and establishing all office procedures. She is also responsible for gathering all final information for the standard paperwork (i.e., contact lists, cast and crew lists, call sheets and production reports.) She makes sure that all shooting schedules, scripts and script revisions are properly formatted and distributed. The POC is in charge of coordinating all production meetings. She is also the person to turn to for all insurance matters (certificates of insurance, claims, etc.) When on distant location, the POC makes all the travel and housing arrangements in addition to setting up production offices, ordering and shipping film and equipment. When the film is finished, the POC then assists in shutting down all the departments.

On union films, production coordinators are covered by Local 161 New York City and by Local 717 in Los Angeles. Not all studios and independents are signatories to this local. Check with your producer, but use the union minimums in your budget. The stronger of the two unions is in New York which also includes the script supervisors.

The UPM usually selects the POC as they work so closely together. In order to get properly organized, we are bringing the POC in eight weeks before shooting begins. As for wrap time, there is no provision in the contract. The files must be properly finished and all those who worked with the production must have their accounts settled. The minimum wrap time I would suggest is two weeks. On *The Conversation*, we are scheduling three weeks for the POC.

When you are in production, the production office should be open one hour before the first crew call to one hour after wrap to handle the script notes and changes. It is wise to employ both a POC and a production secretary and stagger their hours. This is a smart way to maintain an efficient production office.

60: Additional Hire—Temporary Secretary

If you need any additional personnel in the production department such as a temporary secretary list those fees here. We are going to allow ten work days for additional secretarial help at a flat rate of $75 per day. This is also the place to record fees for a second second AD to cover the heavy days. I allowed 15 days at $338 per day.

60: Additional Hire—Production Office Coordinator—Location

You will need an additional coordinator if your project calls for you to go out of the country or on distant location. Using a local person who knows the local crews, sources for materials and supplies, and local rules and regulations can be a major benefit.

80: Technical Advisors

If there is an area in the script which needs to be technically accurate in areas where you don't have the expertise (e.g., police procedure, psychology), then hire *a technical advisor* .

In *The Conversation*, HARRY CAUL (Gene Hackman) needs someone to teach him how to operate the tape recorder and other surveillance equipment. He also is shown playing the saxophone. He will need an advisor who will at least teach him how to finger the instrument.

Technical advisors vary in cost. Determine your requirements, then start your research. While developing the project, your producer may have some contacts for you. In the case of *The Conversation* we are hiring a technical advisor three weeks before principal photography begins. In that time he will teach the actors the basic workings of the surveillance equipment, participate in the selection of the correct surveillance equipment, be available for the director for questions concerning procedure while conducting a surveillance case, as well as aid the production designer in sets planned for the show. A special arrangement is worked out to pay the advisor only as needed. The schedule shows us that the technical advisor will be needed in the warehouse scenes and the scenes in Union Square which we have on the schedule for five days. By blocking your material—i.e., scheduling the same location appearing more than once in the script to be shot back-to-back—you are able to bring the technical advisor in at specific times, cutting down his carry time and therefore creating a savings. A technical advisor is not needed in post production. We need a technical advisor for three weeks of prep and 14 days of shooting. We are paying the technical advisor $1,000 per week during prep and $500 per day during shooting.

The technical advisor working with Mr. Hackman on the saxophone will need a week before photography begins and two days during the filming. These would be days 19 and 20, when the saxophone appears on film.

85: Additional Expenses

Allow $500. (*See Computers on pages 123-124 for additional expenses.*)

85: Additional Expenses—Government Representative

Some foreign countries require you to hire a *government representative*. whose job it is to help you through the intricacies of their government's permit system, aid in obtaining clearances, and protect their local government from any derogatory comments about them in your movie. Sometimes this second function is performed by a censor, which the local government may require you to have on your payroll. In the United States we seldom need a government representative on the set. The exception is pictures which have military themes. In that case it would serve you well to contact the branch of the Armed Forces, have them read the script for veracity, and ask them for a Public Assistant Officer (P.A.O.) from their branch of the service to help you get the necessary clearances for filming around their facilities.

Such a person can be budgeted here or under the Location Account 3700.

85: Additional Expenses—Safety Officers

In the last few years, the safety laws administered by the California Occupational Safety and Health Administration or CAL-OSHA (and OSHA, the National body with the same function), have been revised to require more stringent safety procedures and active investigation of production accidents. By laws, production companies from the major studios to the smallest independent must adopt a formal IIPP or Illness and Injury Prevention Plan and must assign a **SAFETY OFFICER** to each work site. For practical purposes *work site* generally means *the set*, where the ADs usually act as *safety officers*. It also applies to other locations where personnel may be preparing or striking. All personnel must be properly trained in whatever equipment they handle from band-saws to bulldozers. As noted, safety officers disseminate information, hold meetings, and prepare additional paperwork relative to any production accident in which there is personal injury.

By law in California, any accident during work hours, whether it be during pre-production, production, or post-production, must be reported to CAL-OSHA within 24 hours of the occurrence. There must be a documented investigation by the production company to determine the cause of the accident, and there must be documented steps taken to prevent any recurrence. CAL-OSHA will examine the witnesses statements, the reports by the first AD, all medical reports, and the papers documenting any retraining programs instituted by the producer to prevent a recurrence. This applies to any serious accident, but especially to those which result in disfigurement, dismemberment, or loss of consciousness, however brief. The mere failure to adopt an IIPP, to report an accident, or to adhere to any other major safety requirement can result in a substantial fine by CAL-OSHA.

85: Additional Expenses—Office Expenses

Although on large projects each department might have its own offices, generally the entire production will be based in a single suite of offices. Most likely, you will rent a suite of offices. Each department will have its own area. There may be a common receptionist, and there will be a common machinery room where you will put your copier, fax, and so forth.

The most vulnerable areas in this account are the telephone, mobile phone, and security. Temporary office space is vulnerable to predators, and electronic machinery is a tempting target. Having your office wired with burglar alarms is far less costly than replacing computers, faxes, phone systems, etc. These expenses are found in Account 6200. If this film had been shot on distant location you would place these expenses in Account 4000.

85: Additional Expenses—Computers

Computers have become a necessity in all phases of production. Some of the more spectacular special effects are entirely computer-generated. Art directors have begun designing sets on computer and showing the director their work on a screen before beginning construction. Wardrobe designers can also design on computer.

The important thing to remember with computers is their vulnerability. A sudden power surge, such as during an electric storm, can destroy all your work. You need to protect yourself by buying a potent surge protector, and an uninterrupted power supply. These will guarantee that your system is not vulnerable to sudden electrical accidents. The other protection, which is absolutely necessary, is to make backup copies of you work. Do this at least once a day, and make two of these backups. [*Note: The newer Zip drives hold 100 MB of data and are currently selling for about $200.*] One backup copy should stay somewhere in the office where you can access it easily, and the other should go out of the building to a different location. That way if a catastrophe happens in the office you will have a backup to restore your data.

A computer is no place to save money, either. There are excellent inexpensive computers on the market which are more than adequate for your needs. Trying to save a few dollars by getting less memory or cheaper peripherals will often result in your spending much time trying to make the computer work properly, rather than being able to use it productively.

You should make sure your computer has an adequate virus-protection system. Having taken those few simple precautions, you will be able to use your computer to save you immense amounts of time and money. The unit production manager, production office coordinator, second assistant director and production accountant are renting their computers to the company. We will pay the unit production manager and production accountant a flat $1,500 each. The other three will be paid $1,000 each. This goes into Account 2085.

95: Miscellaneous

On *The Conversation,* additional compensation was given to the script supervisor as a *box rental* or allowance for her equipment (in this case stop watch, rulers, etc.) Box rentals are a common way of paying overscale without incurring additional fringes. The script supervisor also did another script timing. The first timing was accounted for in the Story and Screenplay Account 2050. We are allowing $1,000 here to cover the costs of the script supervisor's Polaroid film and script timing.

97: Production Board/Budget Prep

A good production board and budget cost money. If these were produced during the development period, that cost may charged back or recovered here. If not, estimate two times a unit production manager's weekly studio salary. The reasoning here is that the UPM usually does the board and budget in two weeks. In the development area we already budgeted $3,000, so we won't budget an additional amount here, however it is not unusual to pay around $5,000 for these services.

Account 2100

Extra Talent

PAGE NO. 11

PRODUCTION NUMBER	PRODUCTION TITLE	DATE

2100	EXTRA TALENT				SUBTOTALS		
ACCT NO.	DESCRIPTION	TIME	RATE	AMT.	A	B	C
01	Extra Casting Fee		12%	83,247			9,990
03	Payroll Fee		5%	83,247			4,162
05	Extra Casting Expenses ALLOW			1,000			1,000
10	Welfare Workers/Teach's ALLOW	2 WKS	1322		2644		
20	Extras & Stand-ins			83,247	83,247		
	(Detail Following Page 11A)						
35	Dancers/Swimmers		0				
43	Music Contractor		0				
45	Sideline Musicians ALLOW	30M/D	154	4,620	4,620		
	Scn. 188-194 Golden Gate Park						
	Scn. 1-9, 28, 33, 58, 62, 64, 68,						
	71, 87, 107, 182, 185, 222						
	Cartage	3 M/D	6 dy	180		180	
48	Interviews/Fittings ALLOW			500	500		
60	Extras Mile. Allow.						
	Buses (See Transp. Acct 4603)						
	Meals (See Catering Acct 3620)						
70	Rehearsal Expenses		0				
	Additional Hire						
85	Additional Expenses		0				
	Wardrobe changes, mileage, car rental, etc.		ALLOW	20,000		20,000	
95	Miscellaneous		ALLOW	500			500
99	Loss, Damage, Repair		ALLOW	750			750
				SUBTOTALS	91,011	20,180	16,402
				TOTAL ACCT 2100	127,593		

A = Fringeable/Taxable
B = Non-Fringeable/Taxable
C = Non-Taxable

ACCOUNT 2100—Extra Talent

PAGE NO. 11A

PRODUCTION NUMBER | PRODUCTION TITLE | DATE

2100 EXTRA TALENT – DETAIL

DAY NO.	BREAK-DOWN PAGE	SCENE NO.	SCENE NAME/ DESCRIPTION	A – GENERAL B – STAND-INS NO.	RATE	AMOUNT	C – SILENT BITS D – SPECIAL EXTRAS NO.	RATE	AMOUNT	O.T. ADJ.	MILEAGE NO.	RATE	AMOUNT	SUBTOTALS A	B
1		195-198	Ext. Financial District	A 8	105	840									
		226-229	Ext. Financial District (Phone Booth)	B 2	157.50	315									
		188-194	Ext. Golden Gate Park	N* 17	78.82	1,340									
2		34, 36 37	Ext. Street/Elect. Bus/	A 9	105	945									
		35	Int. Elect. Bus	B 1	157.50	158									
		38	Int. Market	N 36	78.82	2,838									
3		365	Ext. Street (Burning Car)	A 8	105	840									
		45	Int./Ext. Elect. Bus and Street	B 2	157.50	315									
				N 2	78.82	158									
4		96, 97	Ext. Financial District	A 8	105	840									
		271, 272	Ext. Financial Plaza	B 2	157.50	315									
		282, 283	Ext. Director's Bldg. (Bus 1 & 2)	N 67	78.82	5,281									
5		1-9	Ext. Union Square	A 7	105	735									
				B 3	157.50	473									
				N 118	78.82	9,301									
6		58, 62, 64, 66, 68, 71, 87, 107	Ext. Union Square	A 7	105	735									
													SUBTOTALS	25,429	
													TOTAL DETAIL ACCT 2100		

A = Fringeable/Taxable
B = Non-Fringeable/Taxable
C = Non-Taxable
* = Non-Union

PAGE NO. 11AB

PRODUCTION NUMBER | PRODUCTION TITLE | DATE

2100 EXTRA TALENT – DETAIL

DAY NO.	BREAK-DOWN PAGE	SCENE NO.	SCENE NAME/ DESCRIPTION	A – GENERAL B – STAND-INS NO.	RATE	AMOUNT	C – SILENT BITS D – SPECIAL EXTRAS NO.	RATE	AMOUNT	O.T. ADJ.	MILEAGE NO.	RATE	AMOUNT	SUBTOTALS A	B
12	(cont.)	104	Ext./Int. Amy's Apt.	A 9	105	945									
				N 1	78.82	79									
13		98	Int. Mr. C's Bldg.	B 2	157.50	315									
		199, 276, 277, 281	Int. Elevator	A 8	105	840									
			Int. Lobby – Mr. C's Bldg./Newsstand	N 42	78.82	3,310									
14		200-205	Int. Mr. C's Suite, Lobby & Corridor	A 7	105	735									
		273-275, 369-371	Int. Mr. C's Suite, Reception Area	B 3	157.50	473									
		372-376		N 68	78.82	5,360									
15		99-102	Int. Suite/Reception/ Corridor/Office	A 7	105	735									
				B 3	157.50	473									
				N 3	78.82	236									
16		206-221, 223-225	Int. Mr. C's Office	B 4	157.50	630									
17		93-95	Int. Lawyer's Office	B 2	157.50	315									
18		40, 41	Int. Harry's Apt.	B 2	157.50	315									
19		42-44	Int. Harry's Apt./ Living Rm./Kitchen	B 3	157.50	473									
20		48, 49	Int. Harry's Apt.	B 3	157.50	473									
													SUBTOTALS	15,707	
													TOTAL DETAIL ACCT 2100	see Pg. 11AE	

A = Fringeable/Taxable
B = Non-Fringeable/Taxable
C = Non-Taxable
* = Non-Union

PAGE NO. 11AC

PRODUCTION NUMBER | PRODUCTION TITLE | DATE

2100 EXTRA TALENT – DETAIL															
DAY NO.	BREAK-DOWN PAGE	SCENE NO.	SCENE NAME/ DESCRIPTION	A – GENERAL B – STAND-INS NO.	RATE	AMOUNT	C – SILENT BITS D – SPECIAL EXTRAS NO.	RATE	AMOUNT	O.T. ADJ.	MILEAGE NO.	RATE	AMOUNT	SUBTOTALS A	B
20	(cont.)	377-	Int. Harry's Apt./ Corridor												
21		92	Ext. Phone Booth	A 9	105	945									
		230-231	Int. Catholic Church Confessional	B 1	157.50	158									
		39	Int. Laundry	N 19	78.82	1,498									
		120 pt 123, 125	Int. Aud/Slides												
22		232-238	Ext./Int. Continental	A 9	105	945									
		254		B 1	157.50	158									
				N 6	78.82	473									
23		239-255	Int. Motel Room B-5 Harry	B 1	157.50	158									
24		255-268, 270	Int. Motel Room B-7	B 1	157.50	158									
		354	Int. Motel Room & Bathroom	A 9	105	945									
		269	Ext. Motel Window B-7	N 16	78.82	1,261									
25		356, 359-361, 363	Int. Motel Room/Bath B7	B 3	157.50	473									
26		284, 285	Ext./Int. Bus #1	A 8	105	840									
		289, 291		B 2	157.50	315									
		298-306		N 2	78.82	158									
													SUBTOTALS	8,485	
													TOTAL DETAIL ACCT 2100	see Pg. 11AE	

A = Fringeable/Taxable
B = Non-Fringeable/Taxable
C = Non-Taxable
* = Non-Union

PAGE NO. 11AD

PRODUCTION NUMBER | PRODUCTION TITLE | DATE

2100 EXTRA TALENT – DETAIL

DAY NO.	BREAK-DOWN PAGE	SCENE NO.	SCENE NAME/ DESCRIPTION	A – GENERAL B – STAND-INS NO.	RATE	AMOUNT	C – SILENT BITS D – SPECIAL EXTRAS NO.	RATE	AMOUNT	O.T. ADJ.	MILEAGE NO.	RATE	AMOUNT	SUBTOTALS A	B
27		286, 290, 294	Ext. Poles & Lines (Insert)	A 8	105.00	840									
		297	Ext. Street & Harry's Bus	B 2	157.50	315									
		287, 288, 292, 293, 295, 296	Int. Bus #2 & Street	N 2	78.82	158									
		307, 308	Ext. Bus & Street												
28		309-316	Ext. Stepped Street	B 2	157.50	315									
		317-319, 321-332	Ext. Park												
29		380-296, 367	Int. Harry's Room	B 1	157.50	158									
30		50	Ext. Harry's Warehouse	A 8	105.00	840									
		51-57, 59-61, 63, 65, 67	Int. Harry's Warehouse	B 2	157.50	315									
		69-70, 72-80, 82-86, 88-91		N 17	78.82	1,340									
31		69-70, 72-80, 82-86, 88-91	Int. Harry's Warehouse	A 8	105.00	840									
		82-86, 88-91		B 2	157.50	315									
				N 17	78.82	1,340									
32		160-173	Int. Warehouse	B 3	157.50	473									
33		160-173	Int. Warehouse	B 3	157.50	473									
34		160-173	Int. Warehouse	B 3	157.50	473									
													SUBTOTALS	8,195	
													TOTAL DETAIL ACCT 2100	see Pg. 11AE	

A = Fringeable/Taxable
B = Non-Fringeable/Taxable
C = Non-Taxable

ACCOUNT 2100—Extra Talent

PAGE NO. 11AE

PRODUCTION NUMBER — PRODUCTION TITLE — DATE

DAY NO.	BREAK-DOWN PAGE	SCENE NO.	SCENE NAME/ DESCRIPTION	A – GENERAL B – STAND-INS NO.	RATE	AMOUNT	C – SILENT BITS D – SPECIAL EXTRAS NO.	RATE	AMOUNT	O.T. ADJ.	MILEAGE NO.	RATE	AMOUNT	SUBTOTALS A	B
2100	EXTRA TALENT – DETAIL														
35		174-181, 183, 184	Int. Warehouse	B 1	157.50	158									
36		186, 187	Int. Warehouse	B 1	157.50	158									
37		337-353, 355, 357, 358, 362, 364	Int. Warehouse	B 1	157.50	158									
		333-336	Ext. Warehouse Alley												
38		144, 146-149, 151-153, 155, 157-159	Int. Car (Traveling)	B 5	157.50	788									
		145, 150, 154, 156	Ext. Street - Sedan & Mustang												
39		133-136	Int. Convention Bar	A 5	105	525									
				B 5	157.50	788									
				N 120	78.82	9,458									
		137-142	Int. Convention Booth Area												
		143	Ext. Parking Lot												
40		109-117, 119	Int. Convention Lobby/ Booth Area	A 7	105	735									
		120pt 121-124	Int. Convention Auditorium	B 3	157.50	473									
				N 118	78.82	9,301									
41		126-128	Int. Convention Booth Area	A 5	105	525									
				B5 N20	157.50 78.82	788 1,576									
													SUBTOTALS	25,431	
													TOTAL DETAIL ACCT 2100	83,247	

A = Fringeable/Taxable
B = Non-Fringeable/Taxable
C = Non-Taxable

2100—EXTRA TALENT

EXTRAS ARE ALSO CALLED *BACKGROUND PERFORMERS* and *atmosphere*. Without them a picture would be very dull. They add life to a scene, supplying the needed movement and color that makes a scene look natural.

The difference between an extra and an actor is quite simple. An actor has lines (or other meaningful sounds) in the script and is directed by the director. An extra has no lines in the script and is directed by the *assistant* director.

01: Extras Casting Fee

Central Casting in Los Angeles, the oldest and certainly best-known service for casting extras, has acquired a lot of competitors in recent years. For a while in the 1980s the demise of the Screen Extras Guild as an effective, industry-wide bargaining agent meant that many independent producers in features and television went to nonunion extras to save money. In New York, extras have long been covered by the Screen Actors Guild agreement. In the most recent negotiations that coverage was extended to the Los Angeles area as well. Currently the rates are $65/day for extras $90/day for stand-ins. A day is considered eight hours work, with overtime after the eight hours. For large scenes SAG permits nonunion extras to be hired at a reduced rate after a minimum number of union extras have been set. This was SEG's previous policy. The usual rate for a nonunion extra is $40 for eight hours.

Just as it is possible to cast your actors without employing a casting person, it is possible to cast extras without using a service. However, in the long rung, it is far simpler and cheaper to use extras casting company. Their fees will vary depending upon what you want the casting company to be responsible for, the difficulty of the project (e.g., period picture with wardrobe restrictions) and the deal you negotiate. Standard fee ranges from eight percent (8%) to 12 percent (12%) based upon the gross salaries earned by the extra talent players. Since all extras casting companies maintain accurate and up-to-date rosters of available people, when casting on distant location, it is essential to hire a local person who does casting professionally and/or is familiar with the people available in that area.

If the production company has an unusual request such as needing several "little people" for a scene who can wire walk (considered a *special ability*), the extra casting company will charge more since this is such a specialized search requiring extra work on their part. *The Conversation* had no special requirements.

03: Payroll Fee

This job is normally handled by the *Extras Casting Firm.* Such paperwork as computing the wages of the extra talent used, writing the checks, deducting the pension, health and welfare payments (if they are union members), deducting worker's compensation and maintaining the records and issuing the yearly W-4's is a full time job.

In order for an extra company to stay in business they will probably bill you every two days. This allows the extra casting company to maintain a reasonable cash flow.

The fee will total between three percent (3%) and five percent (5%) of the gross extra costs billed.

05: Extra Casting Expenses

You must allow for phone calls, meals, etc., on behalf of the extras casting people.

Also, your show may require your extras casting director to have additional costs such as placing an ad in a local paper to request people for a large crowd scene, or do a mailing to a certain group of charity organizations willing to have their members be extras. It is advisable to allow $1,000 for any such unusual requirements.

10: Welfare Workers/Teachers

Whenever there is a working minor on the set even if the child is an extra and not an actor, there must be a *Welfare Worker/Teacher* on set. Her duties are outlined in the Cast section before (Account 1310, page 25). During school holidays or when working with preschool age children, the welfare worker/teacher's responsibility is to ensure that all regulations governing working children are followed. On school days, the welfare worker/teacher will supervise the school work of the child who has been hired to work for at least three hours per day. Those three hours (and one hour of recreation which may be waived) are part of the child's total permitted work time.

For infants and other very young children whose inability to speak tends to place them in the category of extras and not actors, there are additional requirements which may include having a nurse present, transportation to and from the set, and very restricted work time detailed down to the minutes which can be spent on the set under the lights. If you are employing actors who are under the age of 18 and not emancipated minors (or deemed by the courts to be adults), you will need a **STUDIO TEACHER**. Although with the exception of some rules and regulations in the state of New York there is no organized department in the other 48 states whose prime responsibility is to govern and administer rules over minors used in the entertainment industry. All child actors are governed by California rules because the Screen Actors Guild has incorporated those regulations into its basic agreement. Even when child extras work outside California, it is a good idea to follow California State laws. All minors must also be accompanied by a parent or guardian who is not paid to be there but, as was noted under Travel and Living, must also be fed, transported and housed.

The studio teacher must have the proper California State teaching credentials and must be experienced in labor law supervision. She must also be certified by the Work Permit Office of the Los Angeles Unified School District or the local Labor Commissioner's office. The studio teacher is also assigned from the Work Permit Office. If you wish to request someone with whom you have worked before and fulfills the above mentioned requirements, you may make such a request.

There are strict rules and regulations governing the use of minors, from minimum increments of school time (20 minutes) to the earliest and latest times they can work, which varies according to age. Because one of the key restrictions is time, this may severely restrict the scheduling of child actors. The rules were established for the protection and well being of the minor and rules must be adhered to strictly.

A studio teacher need not be present when minors come in for wardrobe fittings, looping, for publicity or personal appearances so long as their time is limited to under one hour. They also must be accompanied by a parent and/or guardian. In the schedule of *The Conversation*, we have two minors on the schedule: TONY, Harry Caul's Niece on Day 17 and the LAUNDRY LADY'S LITTLE BOY on Day 21. Both days will require a studio teacher. Figure two days worked at the daily minimum for an 11 hour day. In addition, time must be allowed for street scenes. Over all allow two weeks.

Union (**IATSE**) welfare workers may be hired through Central Casting or other agencies. There are several companies that specialize in non-IATSE, certified teachers. Studo teachers can be budgeted here or under the Production Account.

20: Extras & Stand-ins

The Screen Actors Guild has established various studio zones throughout the United States. When local-resident SAG actor-members work outside these boundaries, they are deemed to be on distant location. These zones and/or boundaries also deem the areas within which SAG extras must be used. Established contracted fees and working conditions vary according to zone. Outside Los Angeles and New York verify if SAG has jurisdiction.

Since extras are the newest addition to the SAG agreement in Los Angeles, SAG has been (and will remain for some time to come) negotiable on how many SAG extras must be employed on a project. While there are no set rules, on a picture budgeted between $1 million and $2 million, SAG may only ask that you pay 40 extras at the union rate. Because there is no set rule, you should budget according to established SAG minimums unless you strike a better deal.

On the production board for *The Conversation* (this is in the fold-out section of *Film Scheduling*, Lone Eagle Publishing Co.) we indicated the number of extras needed each day and circled that number on the individual strips. The strips represent scene(s) in the screenplay. Look at Day One—a Sunday—Scenes 195/196: *"Sunday. The district is quiet and deserted. Large new buildings empty. The plazas and courtyards without people. We see a single man (Harry Caul) cross the street on his way to the Financial Building. . ."*

The extra count is "one"—a uniformed security guard (asked for by the director). The writer/director wants the city to look deserted. The production company chose Sunday as it was the only time during the week that this effect could be achieved.

Scenes 197 (Plaza Area) and 198 (Elevator Area) are also deserted. Scenes 226-229 find Harry again alone in the bleak desolate financial district. Once the film company has completed photography in the financial district, the company moves to Golden Gate Park. Activity in a city park is usually high on a Sunday unless the weather is bad. Kids on bicycles, joggers, lovers on a slow walk and, of course, the band playing in the band shell. Now, the band members are not extras. They fall under sideline musicians. Twenty-five extras will be enough for the sequence, considering the size of the park and how wide the establishing shot will probably be. Judging from the script, most of the people sitting on the benches are very old.

The Security Guard (Scenes 195, 196), photographed in the morning, can be used in the park scenes in the background. This will call for him to change wardrobe. The total count for Day One is 25.

On Day Two we begin with an establishing shot of an electric bus in motion (Scene 34). A question mark is next to *HARRY CAUL's* name. Does the director want to see him sitting (in the scene) on the bus? The bus itself has passengers. It is late afternoon and some people are returning home from work. How do we know this? In

Scene 33, before this, the STREET MUSICIANS have stopped playing and are putting their instruments away. Lunch hour is long over. MARK says in Scene 26, "We'd better get back, it's almost two." At the end of Scene 33, there is a FADE OUT, giving us a time transition. HARRY probably went to the warehouse with the tapes and we pick up with him as "one of many tired people on their way home from work" (Scene 35). Figure 25 extras for the interior of the bus (Scene 35), the same 25 for the bus exterior (Scene 34). "*The non-pleased driver (electric bus), hops up, moves outside the big steps, and expertly begins to pull the cables to reset the connection.*" The driver knows the piece of equipment. It is not uncommon to hire a professional and get a waiver if it is necessary.

HARRY is outside the bus in Scenes 36, 37 and is walking through his neighborhood. Here we can tell a great deal by the types of people who inhabit HARRY's working class neighborhood. There is construction going on. An old building is being replaced. Another 20 people will give you the feeling of a late afternoon in the San Francisco urban suburb. HARRY goes to his local market (Scene 38) to select his dinner. There will be other customers doing the same thing and there's the man behind the counter. With wardrobe changes, you can use some of the 45 people (25 from the electric bus and 20 from the street) in the market. The COUNTER MAN will need an apron or coat from wardrobe. Your extra count for Day Two is 45.

As you go through each scheduled day, you must analyze where you can repeat your extras. This must be done with caution because you do not want to see the same faces unless you are creating an atmosphere of familiarity.

For the sake of the budget, we are going to figure using non-union extras and stand-ins. On the budget form, use 12 hours for the amount of time budgeted each day. After you have analyzed each day, total your number of extra work days and stand-in work days and place the total on page 11.

Although it is not unusual to all lump all nonspeaking actors in the extras category. There are distinct categories of extras which are defined on the following pages.

STAND-INS

While covered by the same contracts and permitted to work in front of the camera, a *stand-in* is not really an *extra*. Rather stand-ins usually have similar physical characteristics as the principal actors and work on the set throughout the day. They watch rehearsals or run-throughs of the master scenes and note the position of the actors at various moments, some of which will also be marked on the floor with tape by the second assistant camera person. When the set is turned over to the director of photography for the scene to be lit, the principal actor goes back to his trailer and the stand-in *stands-in* the actor's place while the crew completes the more tedious work of setting the lights and adjusting the camera angles. The key stand-ins work every day of production and are as much a part of the crew as the grips and electricians. Many directors of photography, first ADs, and stars have favorite stand-ins with whom they work. Any or all or them may have a say on which stand-ins are hired for a project.

SILENT BIT

A *silent bit* is an extra who has no lines but performs a scripted *bit* of business, such as handing an item to an actor or being told to do something by an actor and silently complying. The minimum adjustment, which like a stunt adjustment is added to the basic compensation, is $10. This can increase if the scene merits.

SPECIAL ABILITY

Special ability extras are much like photo doubles who double for actors in non-stunt scenes. Any extra requiring a special ability for a particular scene or sequence will be paid an adjustment. Adjustments start at $10 and work up. Driving a car need not be a special ability, as most people already can drive. Driving a bus or a truck, however, would definitely be special ability, as would ice skating, being a croupier, or working a steam press. Most extra casting services have people with common special abilities on their rosters and have a usual rate of pay. The highest compensation will be for body doubles or other nude or semi-nude performers whose rates may equal or exceed SAG Day Player minimums. All these rates are negotiable in advance. In cases such as needing someone to operate heavy equipment as part of their requirement, it is always permitted to hire non-SAG members and **TAFT-HARTLEY** them.

In *The Conversation* we need a mime for the opening scenes. As he has no lines, he would be considered a special ability extra.

35: Dancers/Swimmers

When a script calls for a *dancers* in chorus line in a nightclub sequence, the dancers must be prepared beforehand by rehearsing with a choreographer. The dance must be planned for the camera. This is far more complicated if your movie is about the ballet. In any case the dancers must be paid more than regular extras.

Swimmers who are not stunt performers still merit more salary than other extras when the script requires them to be immersed in a pool or the ocean. There are no swimmers or dancers in *The Conversation* so we budget nothing for them.

43: Music Contractor

The *music contractor* is responsible for coordinating all financial and business activities and must be present at all recording sessions. There are two different types of contractors: non-playing and playing.

The minimum rate for a contractor under an American Federation of Musicians (AFM) contract is $130.64 per day. This rate is doubled if the contractor plays an instrument.

Where there are no sideline musicians and/or on non-AFM shows, the contractor may be placed in the Music Account and is often included in the package deal with the composer.

45: Sideline Musicians

Sideline musicians may be budgeted here or under the Cast Account. A non-playing contractor receives a sideline musician's scale rate which is $153.96. This reduces to $130.64 if more than ten musicians are present. A contractor must be hired whenever ten or more musicians are used in any session.

Musicians who work at the recording sessions for the underscore are budgeted under the Music Account. SAG cover all singers, whether they are seen in the picture or heard on the underscore. If you know that either or both types will be used, budget them here.

As with many union and guild contracts, the scale wage is governed by first the type of entertainment project you have (e.g., theatrical, videotape, pay-cable television, etc.) In the case of *The Conversation*, we are dealing with theatrical and the rules and regulations governing the theatrical and television film.

Cartage

Cartage is the cost of transporting a musician's instruments and any other equipment needed to perform that the musician cannot easily carry by himself (e.g., a piano.) The production must pay to transport the instruments from their storage place to the set and back again.

48: Interviews/Fittings

At times for a special look or a special ability, the director may want to *interview* several candidates. *Fitting* an extra for wardrobe may also be done before the actual set work. The rate varies depending upon whether the extra is union or nonunion. You will need to pay a small mileage fee for driving to your office prior to filming for an interview or fitting.

In *The Conversation* all our extras are dressed in contemporary clothing so no fittings are necessary. The Mime will be able to bring his own theatrical clothing, for which he will receive a small reimbursement. We will allow $500 here.

70: Rehearsal Expense

Rehearsal time is considered work time. Both extras and musicians will be paid accordingly.

85: Additional Expense—Crowd Controllers
If there are large crowds scenes such as in Union Square, additional people will be needed for *crowd control.* Some extras casting services ask for and/or provide coordinators as part of their deals. On calls requiring large crowds, most services will send a representative at the main extra call time to help check people in and verify those people showing up are the ones who were called. Paid controllers or coordinators will usually be on an extra voucher themselves, but at a slightly higher daily rate.

Wardrobe Allowance
When extras are required to arrive on the set with, for instance, period wardrobe for a 1940s full-dress ballroom scene, you will pay them an additional fee for the use of their clothing.

The fee for special wardrobe has been set at $9 for the first change and $6.25 for each change thereafter.

Car Rental
When *nondescript* — ND—cars are needed for specific background action on the street, the most efficient method of obtaining them is to hire extras who have vehicles.

The rate for car rental for $15 per day/nonunion and $27 per day union. Even special vehicles may be obtained this way by the ADs or transportation coordinator and charged here rather than in picture vehicles. The fee is negotiable and can range from $50 to more than $200 a day.

95: Miscellaneous
If the charge doesn't fit anywhere else within this area, then use this account number. An allowance $500.

99: Loss, Damage, Repair
Since your deductible on your insurance will probably be high ($10,000 deductible per incident per claim or higher), it is good to provide some money to curtail costs. Seven-hundred and fifty dol-

lars is recommended. Remember we are talking extras and a contemporary film. This amount will be higher if it's a period or futuristic story.

Account 2200

Art Department

PAGE NO. 12

PRODUCTION NUMBER | PRODUCTION TITLE | DATE

2200 ART DEPARTMENT

ACCT. NO.	DESCRIPTION	LOCAL/ On Loc.	PREP	SHOOT	WRAP	TOTAL	RATE	SUBTOTALS A	B	C
01	Production	Local	10	8.2		18.2	4,000	72,800		
	Designer	On Loc.								
02	Art Director	Local	8	8.2	16.2		2,096	33,955		
		On Loc.								
03	Assistant	Local								
	Art director	On Loc.								
04	Set Designer	Local	3.8	8.2		12	1531	18,374		
	10 hr. dy. 27.84 hrs	On Loc.								
		Local								
		On Loc.								
05	Draftsman	Local								
		On Loc.								
		Local								
		On Loc.								
09	Sketch Artist	Local	8	2		10	1665	16,650		
		On Loc.								
10	Set Model Builders	Local	10 dys			10 dys	306	3,062		
	10 hr. dy. 27.84 hrs	On Loc.								
15	Set Estimator	Local								
		On Loc.								
	Additional Hire	Local								
		On Loc.								
		Local								
		On Loc.								
		Local								
		On Loc.								
30	Rentals									
	P.D. Car Allowance: 18.2 wks. x 150/wk.									2,730
	Box Rentals/Car: 16.2 wks. x 1,000/wk									16,200
40	Purchases									
	Office supplies, etc.						ALLOW			1,000
	Materials for set models						ALLOW			300
70	Research					ALLOW				5,000
85	Additional Expense									
	Blueprints						ALLOW			7,500
95	Miscellaneous					ALLOW				500
99	Loss, Damage, Repair									
							SUBTOTALS	144,841		33,230
							TOTAL ACCT 1200	178,071		

A = Fringeable/Taxable
B = Non-Fringeable/Taxable
C = Non-Taxable

2200—ART DEPARTMENT

THE PRODUCTION DESIGNER AND THE REST of the Art Department are charged with creating the material look of the script. That look should be detailed and realistic enough to convince an audience that any set on a sound stage or a location is what it is depicted to be. However, it should not so authentic that is costs as much or more as the real thing to create. While an anachronism, such as Revolutionary War character wearing a wristwatch, will obviously jerk the audience out of its involvement with the picture, anything from a cheap-looking suit on a supposedly wealthy character to a bad color scheme to can be subtly unsettling as well.

01: Production Designer

Since the *look* of a picture is so critical, one person—the production designer—is normally in charge of coordinating all its elements. This includes not just the props and set decoration, but the costumes, picture cars, locations; every place or thing that it to be photographed.

To accomplish this within your budget, you must give your production design team enough time to do their jobs properly. If your picture takes place at any time period other than the present, the art department will need more time to design and build your sets, or to find locations which are sufficiently old or modern to suit.

We will give the production designer of *The Conversation* ten weeks to prepare, find and rework the sets and locations we will use for the shoot. His employment will last through the filming, ending on the last day of the shoot. A designer earns between $4,000 or $5,000 per week for work in the Los Angeles area on a high-budget project. Some production do command more. Lower budgeted films pay around $1,500-$2,500 per week.

02: Art Director
According to union and Academy regulations there is no official job category for *production designer*. This title is given at the discretion of the producer. In *The Conversation*, the art director works with the production designer. The art director will have a great deal of independent responsibility, but most of his work will be done under the authority of the production designer. The art director will have eight weeks of prep and no wrap time.

Bear in mind that with the art department, as with almost all departments, the process of prep-shoot-wrap is ongoing. When you shoot a movie you don't build all the sets at the same time during prep, then shoot them all, then wait until the wrap period before striking the sets. You design the sets before filming. However, the actual prep time may take place during the few days before you actually shoot that scene, even if filming is happening on the sets for the scenes just prior in the schedule. For instance, we are not going to film HARRY'S MOTEL ROOM until Day 23. We will be filming in the Continental Motel lobby on Day 22. It will not take us a day to redress the room for the filming. So rather than dress the room a week or so ahead of time, costing the company money in room rental, we wait until Day 19 or 20 before we start bringing in furniture, hanging pictures, etc. Why so early? Because we may need the room as a cover set in case the exterior of the motel has a rainstorm and we cannot film exterior.

We will film in the room on Days 23, 24, and 25. We will not see that film until Day 26 some time, so *we will not strike the set until Day 27, after we have seen the dailies*. Why? In case the director and producer decide that something must be reshot, we have kept the set in order and do not have to redress it. We will still have the actors from that scene available and can easily return to the motel and do a quick reshoot. If there are special circumstances where for some reason you cannot hold onto the set or location (actor's cost; availability of set, etc.) then with the OK from the producer, director and studio you can strike the set based upon the negative report from the lab the next morning.

On a local shoot for high-budget pictures the rates range between $2,500 to $3,500 per week. On lower budget films the production designer and art director the same person.

04: Set Designer

The production designer and/or art director decide what the set will look like, but someone has to do the mechanical drawings from which the blueprints will come. This person is the *set designer.* The mechanical drawings show the scale, the exact dimensions, and all the other relevant information which gives the construction team the practical knowledge they need to physically build the sets. The set designer also draws the actual plans for the set. In some instances, the designer or the art director may also execute these drawings or make models or even draft blueprints, which eliminates the need for a set designer.

For a five-day week the set designer makes $1,500 to $2,000 per week, based on an hourly rate.

09: Sketch Artist

As with the set designer, you may not always need a *sketch artist.*In *The Conversation* we have a sketch artist for ten weeks, to help the designers to better visualize their ideas, and to communicate that vision to the director. Again, the rate here varies from $1,650 to $2,000 per week for five days.

10: Set Model Builders

Some designers create models themselves. Other times *set model builders* are hired to do this. Models can be quite helpful to directors, directors of photography, and others in planning the shots. These models are similar to a doll's house without the roof. There might be tiny furniture and little cardboard cutout characters to move around. This is a great help when a picture will take place in sets which have not yet been built. Spatial relations become obvious to the director, and much valuable shooting time can be saved because the director has plotted out the camera angles beforehand. The union minimum for a set model builder is $1,142.54 for a five-day week. An assistant set model builder will earn $828.03 for the same period.

15: Set Estimator

On large or complex projects, the production designer and/or construction coordinator may require the assistance of a *set estimator* to help produce a detailed and accurate budget.

The set estimator's rate is approximately $1,000 per week for five days.

30: Rentals—Car Allowance

This subaccount appears in many departments. Since the production designer will have a lot of driving around from one location to another, we provide a car allowance of $150 per week. That should cover out-of-pocket expenses for gas, oil, etc.

30: Rentals—Box Rentals

This subaccount also appears in many departments. We have already paid for the car allowance, so this is for the *box rental*, i.e., the specific tools from a drafting table to T-squares that members of this department will provide for themselves. Many crew members have a very specific set of tools they use in their craft. The Art Department crew is no different. It is less expensive to let the designers use their own tools than to buy all new tools.

70: Research

It takes a great deal research to find out how all the surveillance devices looked. This where the cost for that research goes. *[Note: Current costs for that equipment should be less as today's equipment is smaller, lighter and more powerful.*]

85: Additional Expense—Blueprints

Cost of printing of multiple sets of blueprints goes here.

95: Miscellaneous—Concept Design Fees

Some pictures will need for a specific piece of equipment to be designed for that show only. The Batmobile for *Batman* or the space ship in *Independence Day*. The design of the object would go here in the budget, but the actual construction would be under the Construction Account. The bench tables used inside the surveillance van where created by the production designer in *The Conversation*.

Account 2300

Set Construction

PAGE NO.13

PRODUCTION NUMBER | PRODUCTION TITLE | DATE

2300 SET CONSTRUCTION

ACCT. NO.	DESCRIPTION	No.	LOCAL/ On Loc.	PREP	SHOOT	WRAP	TOTAL	RATE	SUBTOTALS A	B	C
01	Construction		Local	3	8.2		11.2	2,000	22,400		
	Coordinator		On Loc.								
05	Construction		Local								
	Foreman		On Loc.								
	Labor	No.									
11	Painters		Local				51M/D	23.14 hr.	16,522		
	12 hr dy. 23.14 hrs.		On Loc.					(14 pay hr)			
12	Scenic		Local								
	Artist		On Loc.								
13	Carpenters		Local				84M/D	23.14 hr.	27,213		
	12 hr. dy.		On Loc.					(14 pay hr)			
14	Propmakers		Local								
			On Loc.								
15	Laborers		Local				26M/D	18.05 hr.	6,570		
	12 hr. dy.		On Loc.					(14 pay hr)			
16	Plumbers		Local								
			On Loc.								
17	Electrical		Local								
	Fixtures Man		On Loc.								
18	Plasterers		Local				14M/D	22.70 hr.	4,449		
	12 hr. dy.		On Loc.					(14 pay hr)			
			Local								
			On Loc.								
	Additional Hire		Local								
			On Loc.								
20	Set Contruction Materials (See 13A)				ALLOW						50,217
30	Set Equipment/Rentals (See 13A)										4,000
35	Backings										3,000
40	Set Equipment/Purchases										
55	Set Striking Maintenance (See 13A)								11,574		
	Rigging (See 13A)								32,500		27,500
	Greens (See Set Dressing Accts 2410 & 2440)										
	Construction Painter Box Rental, 350/wk. x 10 wks.										3,500
75	Pickup and Delivery										
	Rigging Gaffer Box Rental, 250/wk. x 4 wks										1,000
85	Additional Expense Coordinator Box Rental 11.2 wks. x 1,000										11,200
95	Miscellaneous										
99	Loss, Damage, Repair										
								SUBTOTALS	121,228		100,417
								TOTAL ACCT 2300	221,645		

A = Fringeable/Taxable
B = Non-Fringeable/Taxable
C = Non-Taxable

ACCOUNT 2300—Set Construction

PAGE NO. 13A

PRODUCTION NUMBER | PRODUCTION TITLE | DATE

2300 SET CONSTRUCTION DETAIL							SUBTOTALS		
SET NO.	SCENE NAME/NO. DESCRIPTION	LABOR	MATER-IALS	BACK-INGS	RIGG-ING	STRIK-ING	A	B	C
20	Harry's Apt.								35,217
	Local Locations		ALLOW						15,000
30	Scaffolding		ALLOW						4,000
55	Grip	16,250	8,750				16,250		8,750
	Electric	16,250	18,750				16,250		18,750
	Set Striking								
	Maintenance 11% of Construction Cost (105,217)						11,574		
						SUBTOTALS	44,074		81,717
						TOTAL ACCT 2300	-		

A = Fringeable/Taxable
B = Non-Fringeable/Taxable
C = Non-Taxable

2300–SET CONSTRUCTION

A SET IS A TEMPORARY ARTIFICE WHICH MUST look good to a camera for a brief period of time, then must be dismantled and removed quickly and easily. Many walls should be *wild* or easily removed to permit free camera placement and movement. A set is built to be sturdy, moveable, flexible, and pleasing to the eye. It must be efficient. If you will not see into a building, but just see the outside façade, painting or decorating the interior is a waste of money. But the set must be sturdy enough to accommodate shooting needs also. Walls have to be strong enough to hold up the movie lights clamped to the wall tops. Ceilings have to hold chandeliers. And you'll need scaffolding or a tall ladder to get the electrical fixture person out to the center of the ceiling to hang the chandelier without risking injury.

If you are shooting a unique location, whether it's the Oval Office or a space station, a sound stage may be the only place where your set actually exists. Shooting on a sound stage at a studio lot may present many other advantages: greater control over the surroundings, a lack of unwanted sounds, convenient permanent dressing rooms, a commissary for meals, as well as the ease of working on a constructed set.

Even when shooting on a practical location you may need to *build out* or add additional elements to an existing structure which the script or director have indicated should be there.

Depending on the project's requirements, the production designer may advise that it is less expensive to contract out the set construction to one or more independent companies. For a package fee these companies will build, transport to your location, erect, and strike the sets. If your film is union, you must keep union requirements in mind. You can not build or strike a set with nonunion personnel on a union stage. You can also rent all or part of a prefabricated set. In the case of the Oval Office, there are several in scene docks or set storage areas at various studios in Los Angeles. You may even rent part of such a set, such as the walls and doors, from one studio and another part, such as the rug and chandelier, from another. Again remember that you must budget for not just the rental but for any transportation, assembly, finishing construction, and striking that is needed.

A final possibility to be considered is to find a *standing set* or one which is maintained in a semi-ready to shoot condition at a studio. In Los Angeles, for example, there are several studio facilities with standing jail house, courtroom, and airplane interior sets.

01: Construction Coordinator

Many art directors have established relationships with *construction coordinators* and consider that person part of an established team. Even when an outside firm is contracted to build sets for a project, it may be appropriate to hire an experienced construction coordinator to keep track of the finances and logistics of construction.

For *The Conversation*, we will give our construction coordinator three weeks of prep. He won't need to have any construction until Day 11, (Int. Amy's Apartment), so there will be over four weeks to prepare that practical location as well as the other locations. It would be ready one week prior to filming, in case Francis Coppola wants a few changes made. It also could serve as a cover set in case it rains on Union Square the week prior. We are therefore renting this location for a longer time than normal.

The construction coordinator will stay on payroll until the end of the picture. He will supervise set striking and removal. (*See Account 2355.*)

05: Construction Supervisor

When several construction sites are used for a project, it is efficient to hire a *construction supervisor* to oversee the construction. The supervisor is responsible to the construction coordinator for those sites, and the coordinator is responsible for all sites. Daily progress reports must be maintained and budget updates can be tracked by each foreperson. The minimum rate is $1,335.84 per week for five days.

Construction Labor

We have determined that we will need *construction labor* amounting to $16,522, to cover our construction costs. On much larger projects, especially period pieces, this cost would be far more.

11: Painters

We have included the costs of paint, carpentry, plumbing, electrical fixtures, plasterers, and construction labor in the overall labor cost.

Painters usually receive $300 to $350 per week for their box rental.

Additional Hire—First Aid

A *first-aid person* is required only on Los Angeles-based productions and is covered on union films by Local 767.

A first aid person on a set or a construction site is like buying cheap affordable insurance. When you don't have a medic on site things will happen. Sometimes when a medic is on site things happen anyway. In *The Conversation* our medic is included in the overall construction labor cost.

Security Guard

During construction, and indeed after construction has finished, you will want to guard your set to prevent pilferage etc. This pertains especially when you have built inside a warehouse in a less than secure neighborhood (*See Account 3609.*)

20: Construction Materials

As our set construction is limited we only need a small amount for materials. We will be reworking existing locations rather than building sets from scratch. When we film the scenes which occur in a warehouse we will use a real warehouse. Some construction is always necessary, a wall here, a backdrop there, but basically we will be using existing locations as themselves.

35: Backings

Backings are very cleverly devised to emulate exterior scenes which are visible through the windows, doors, or other openings on a stage set. They are either painted drops which are lit from the front or huge transparencies which are lit from the rear. Ocean backings usually have bits of tinsel attached from which you can bounce light to appear like sunlight sparkling on the water. Some building backings have translucent window panes which can be lit from behind during night scenes to appear as if there are lights on in the house. The audience is not going to be staring at your backings outside the set windows, so the backings should be realistic but not intrusive.

Fifteen-thousand dollars is a fair figure for having backings made. In *The Conversation,* since we have only one set and the backings are not complicated, we will rent from the backing company's stock. We will allow $3,000.

55: Set Striking Maintenance—Striking

Remember, what goes up must come down, and that includes sets. Whether you build a set in a studio or in a warehouse or on the street on a vacant lot, you will have to dispense with it somehow when you have finished shooting. Be sure to construct it for ease of use and dismantling, as every day spent tearing down a set will cost you stage rental and construction crew costs.

If you have made set striking and hauling part of your deal with a set construction firm, it will be to their advantage to keep striking costs to a minimum, as they are responsible the extra days' payroll—not you.

If you are building a large set do not underestimate the amount of trash you will generate during construction, everything from paper wrappings for set dressing to discarded plaster pieces which came from the mold unfinished.

Trash Removal/Recycling

Rented stages are normally contracted to be returned in a *clean and swept out* condition. Trash removal may involve nothing more than filling a few dumpsters already on a studio lot and paying the set fee for a pickup or renting a larger drop bin. In either case $250 to $500 would be a reasonable allowance. For larger sets where the strike is not already contracted, more should be allowed. I have allowed for it within set construction.

New Federal Environment Protection Agency laws have made it mandatory for movie companies to safely dispose of construction materials. Anything can be hazardous waste. Legally, anything you use for construction becomes your responsibility until you legally dispose of it. Unused paint, wallpaper, plastic, all must now by law be recycled as much as possible. Documentation must be kept by the production company to show that the law has been obeyed, because the E.P.A. may eventually ask for proof that you have obeyed the law. Recycling is a useful if not required adjunct of waste disposal. Sets and parts of sets can be recycled often by being sold or donated to other companies or scene docks. Paper, plastic, and other materials can be reused, if not by you, then surely by one of the many firms which will *pay you* for the privilege of carting your recyclables away. This is true not only of sets but also of office supplies, props, anything and everything that could conceivably be reused.

Account 2400

Set Dressing

PAGE NO.14

PRODUCTION NUMBER	PRODUCTION TITLE	DATE

2400 SET DRESSING

ACCT. NO.	DESCRIPTION	LOCAL/ On Loc.	DAYS/WEEKS PREP	SHOOT	WRAP	TOTAL	RATE	SUBTOTALS A	B	C
01	Set Decorator	Local	6	8.2	2	16.2	1910	30,942		
	27.30	On Loc.								
05	Swing Gang /Leadman	Local	6	8.2	2	16.2	1619	26,228		
	12 hr. dy/23.13 p. hr.	On Loc.								
06	Swing Gang/2nd Leadman	Local	6	8.2	1	15.2	1512	22,982		
	12 hr. dy/21.60 p. hr.	On Loc.								
07	Swing Gang/12 hr. dys.	Local	6	8.2	1	15.2	1512	45,965		
	Local 21.60 p. hr. x 2	On Loc.								
10	Greensman	Local		1		1	1553	1,553		
		On Loc.								
12	Draperer ALLOW	Local	1	1		2.	1466	2,932		
		On Loc.								
15	Standby Painter	Local	.40	8.2	.20	8.8	1703	14,987		
	12 hr. dy/24.33 p. hr.	On Loc.								
	Additional Hire	Local	15 MDs	20 MDs		35 MDs	302 d.	10,584		
	21.60 p. hr. ALLOW	On Loc.								
	On-set Dresser	Local		8.2		8.2	1512	12,398		
	12 hr. dy/21.60 p. hr.	On Loc.								
20	Set Dressing Manufactured – Labor									
25	Drapery and Upholstery – Labor (1466 p.per.per.wk.) install ALLOW							4,000		
26	Carpets (1466 p.person p.wk.) Strike ALLOW							4,000		
30	Rentals									
	Set Dressing (See Detail Page 14A) ALLOW									57,000
	Paint Box (8.8 wks. x 250)									2,200
	Greens									2,500
	Leadman Car Rental (16.2 wks. x 150)								2,430	
40	Purchases									
	Set Dressing (See Detail Page 14A) Drapery/Carpets/Fixtures									27,800
	Expendables (Manufacturing 50,000/Purchases 60,000)									110,000
	Paint ALLOW									5,000
	Greens ALLOW									2,500
	Carpets: Install/Strike ALLOW 4,000							4,000		
75	Delivery and Pickup Charges									
80	Fixture Man: 1466 p. person p.w. x 3 wks.							4,398		
85	Additional Expense Clean/Dye									200
95	Miscellaneous ALLOW									1,500
99	Loss, Damage, Repair ALLOW									1,000
							SUBTOTALS	184,969	2,430	209,700
							TOTAL ACCT 2400	397,099		

A = Fringeable/Taxable
B = Non-Fringeable/Taxable
C = Non-Taxable

ACCOUNT 2400—Set Dressing

PAGE NO.14A

PRODUCTION NUMBER | PRODUCTION TITLE | DATE

ACCTS 2430 & 2440 SET DRESSING – DETAIL								
SET	SCENE NAME/NO.	VEHICLES		RENTAL			PURCHASES	
NO.	DESCRIPTION	QTY	DESCRIPTION	TIME	RATE	AMOUNT	AMOUNT	✔
2430	RENTALS:							
	Drapery					2,000		
	Over All Purchases					55,000		
2440	PURCHASES:							
	Drapery						8,000	
	Carpet						7,800	
	Fixtures						12,000	
	EXPENDABLES:							
	Manufacturing						50,000	
	Purchases						60,000	
					SUBTOTALS	57,000	137,800	
			TOTAL DETAIL ACCTS 2430 & 2440			194,800		

A = Fringeable/Taxable
B = Non-Fringeable/Taxable
C = Non-Taxable
4= Recoupable

2400—SET DRESSING

THIS DEPARTMENT IS RESPONSIBLE FOR PROVIDING all the set dressing or decoration, items which would have been in the set anyway and which are not specifically handled by the cast as part of the story are all set dressing. A chair is *set dressing*. If an actor picks one up and throws it at another character, it's a *prop*.

01: Set Decorator

The production designer normally chooses the *set decorator* and works with on the dressing requirements and budget for both stage sets and practical locations. The decorator then goes to property, and set dressing rental houses and stores in the town to find the dressing necessary to give life to the sets. Sometimes you can make a comprehensive all-in rental deal with a particular source.

We are giving the set decorator six weeks to prepare the first few sets of *The Conversation*. Remember, only the first few sets have to be prepared. The ones later on in the shooting schedule will be dressed as you get closer to filming them.

You still have to give a week or so of wrap after the film is over for the set dressing crew to return the furniture to the rental houses. When dressing has been purchased it may be offered for less than the purchase price to the cast and crew, usually discounted to 50 percent (50%) of the purchase price. This recoups part of the cost of the movie and disposes of objects which would have needed to be stored.

05: Lead Person

The *leadperson* is the foreperson of the set dressing crew, who are known collectively as the *swing gang*. (See following page.) Many times the leadperson is a set decorator in training, and is given more responsibility in using his best judgment in choosing the pieces for a particular set.

The leadperson usually receives a car rental of about $150 to $200 per week in addition to a weekly salary.

06: Swing Gang

The *swing gang* is a group of people who transport and place the furnishings on the set for you. Normally, the decorator, lead, and swing gang work off-production, that is they take their own calls and work their own hours as needed to the have the sets ready per the shooting schedule.

07: Local Labor

When you are on a distant location you will need a person who lives in the area to help you find those little hidden places where you can find the right set dressing for your show. The Yellow Pages is a big help, but a person with the knowledge you need is far more useful and efficient.

Since *The Conversation* is filmed in San Francisco where there is a large pool of talented, experienced film crew persons, we will hire the entire crew, including the decorator, in San Francisco.

10: Greens People

When your set needs plants, flowers, etc., the *greens people* are whom you call. Most major studios keep on hand a large collection of trees, shrubs, and plants of various sizes and shapes which are native to many parts of the world. These are usually dead. When you need them, the greens crew goes out and sprays them a nice, live green color, places them in the set (to suit the camera, of course), and later removes them back to their nursery. For independent producers in Los Angeles, there are several companies that specialize in production rentals of live and prop plants.

Greens are also used on both exterior and interior practicals, often as foreground cutters or pieces that block off part of the camera's view and conceal an unwanted fixture such as a sign or fill light.

[Note: on non-IATSE productions, and even on some low-budget IA shows, there is full interchangeability in the Art Depart-

ment, so that any member can apply paint or handle props, dressing, greens, drapes, etc., and specialists are not required. I am allowing one week since little is called for in The Conversation.*]*

12: Draperer

A *draperer* handles drapery, curtains, or any hanging fabric In *The Conversation*, you have curtains on the windows of HARRY CAUL's apartment are hung.

15: Standby Painter

Standby painters stay on the set—location or studio—touching up any damaged or chipped paint, changing the color of something per the DP's requests, or aging an item by stippling it with smudges and scuff marks. Box rental will be paid for materials amounting to $150 to $200 per week (Account 2430).

We will have a set painter on the set for *The Conversation*. Most set painters actually are sign painters and can do wonderful things on short notice which will enhance your film. Suppose we have rented the panel truck for the surveillance team in Union Square, and it arrives on the set with the wrong lettering on it. We can ask the standby painter to change it in a short time and we are ready to shoot.

We will give our standby painter two days to prepare for the shoot and one day to wrap out.

On-Set Dresser

The *onset dresser* is a member of the swing gang who remains on the set while filming is taking place, to move set dressing pieces to suit the camera. This is necessary when rest of the swing gang is out gathering the dressing for tomorrow's set.

20: Set Dressing Manufacturer—Labor

This applies to any set dressing which must be manufactured for the film is budgeted here. There were no special pieces built for *The Conversation*.

25: Drapery and Upholstery—Labor
Almost every film has some drapery or upholstery which is given to an outside company to do. Many studios have departments which do this work in-house.

26: Carpets
An most shows, laying and removing carpeting is done by the swing gang. Remember that tools are necessary in affixing floor coverings to the floor, and more than likely there will be expendable supplies such as carpet tacks, duct tape.

30: Rentals
Your script and breakdown sheets will indicate a huge amount of set dressing *rentals* to help create the look of the film.

40: Purchases
Be sure you are covered in this and the rentals area. It is always embarrassing to try to photograph sets with no furniture in them. In *The Conversation* there is not much money in these accounts because the film does not call for much set dressing. Quite a few scenes take place in a nearly empty warehouse with practically no furniture in it at all. Other scenes are set in locations which are basically dressed already, such as hotel lobby, corridor, etc.

80: Fixtures
Fixtures are ceiling and wall lights. The set dressing crew hangs them and leaves their power cords accessible, so that if they will be lit while photographed and require electricity, the rigging or production crew (electric) can hook them up to a controlled power supply.

85: Additional Expense
Here we would list costs for such items as cleaning and dying.

99: Loss, Damage, Repair
Try not to leave this account in any department empty. The chances of finishing a project with limited dressing requirements without

some small mishap are so small as to be irrelevant. Most of this damage will be well below the deductibles of your insurance. One-thousand dollars should be enough at the low end; allow as much as $5,000 for larger projects. Let's use $1,000 here.

Account 2500

Prop Department

PAGE NO.15

PRODUCTION NUMBER | PRODUCTION TITLE | DATE

2500	PROP DEPARTMENT									
ACCT.		LOCAL/	DAYS/WEEKS					SUBTOTALS		
NO.	DESCRIPTION	On Loc.	PREP	SHOOT	WRAP	TOTAL	RATE	A	B	C
01	Propmaster	Local	8	8.2	2	18.2	1833	33,366		
	12 hr. dy/2619/hr.	On Loc.								
		Local								
		On Loc.								
02	Asst. Propmaster	Local	7	8.2	2	17.2	1619	27,849		
	12 hr. dy/23.13 hr.	On Loc.								
		Local								
		On Loc.								
03	Add'l. Asst	Local								
	Propmaster	On Loc.								
		Local								
		On Loc.								
		Local								
		On Loc.								
	Additional Hire	Local								
		On Loc.								
		Local								
		On Loc.								
		Local								
		On Loc.								
		Local								
		On Loc.								
		Local								
		On Loc.								
		Local								
		On Loc.								
30	Prop Rentals (See Detail Page 15A)									62,730
	Video Playback System									
	Prop Box (8.2 wks. x 300/wk)								2,460	
40	Prop Purchases (See Detail Page 15A)									40,000
50	Props Manufactured – Labor (65%)							35,750		19,250
	Sideline Food									12,500
55	Props Manufactured – Materials									
65	Permits (Guns and Ammo.)									
75	Pickup and Delivery									
85	Additional Expense									
95	Miscellaneous	ALLOW								1,000
99	Loss, Damage, Repair	ALLOW								1,500
							SUBTOTALS	96,965	2,460	136,980
							TOTAL ACCT 2500	236,405		

A = Fringeable/Taxable
B = Non-Fringeable/Taxable
C = Non-Taxable

PAGE NO.15A

PRODUCTION NUMBER	PRODUCTION TITLE	DATE

ACCTS 2530 & 2540 PROPS – DETAIL

SET NO.	SCENE NAME/NO. DESCRIPTION	VEHICLES QTY	VEHICLES DESCRIPTION	RENTAL TIME	RENTAL RATE	RENTAL AMOUNT	PURCHASES AMOUNT	✔
2530	Prop Master Vehicle		Vehicle Allowance	18.2 wks	150	2,730		
	Overall Rentals				ALLOW	60,000		
2540	Overall Purchases				ALLOW		40,000	
					SUBTOTALS	62,730	40,000	
					TOTAL DETAIL ACCTS 2530 & 2540	102,730		

A = Fringeable/Taxable
B = Non-Fringeable/Taxable
C = Non-Taxable
4= Recoupable

2500—PROP DEPARTMENT

THE RULE OF THUMB FOR DIFFERENTIATING PROPS from set dressing is whether they are handled by the actors and extras and/or noted in the script. A hairbrush on a dressing table might normally be placed there by the decorator. If the script calls for an actor to pick up and use it, it becomes the responsibility of the property department. The lines between dressing, property, and sometimes wardrobe can become blurred. A police officer's gun, whether wielded by an actor or extra is a prop. But what about its holster, is it wardrobe or props? One of the organizational issues that should be resolved as departments break down and prepare the script is who will be responsible for items like these.

Props can add immeasurably to the scene. The propmaster, with small touches, can help with characterization.

01: Propmaster

A good propmaster has a very large collection of everything, the knowledge of where to obtain those items she doesn't have, and the good judgment to use it when the script calls for it. And it has to be not just any flag or microphone or pocket knife, but just the right item for the character. A good propmaster will have exactly what you need when you need it. Of course the director must explain what is expected for each scene. The propmaster will usually then bring a variety of items which approximate what the director has requested, and the director can make the proper choices.

The propmaster on *The Conversation* has much more to prepare than the set decorator, so the prep time will be eight weeks. The amount of prep is directly related to the amount and kinds of props to be obtained. In this case there will be many electronic instruments for *The Conversation*, and other intricate objects. Eight weeks will be barely enough time to find out what Francis Coppola wants HARRY CAUL to be using, and to have it built. (Not many Propmasters have bugging devices ready at hand in their prop boxes.)

We also will give the propmaster two weeks to return the rented and borrowed items. Again, cheap insurance. She will get signed receipts from the prop houses so that a month later they can't try to bill the company for items which have been returned.

02: Assistant Propmaster

On all but the simplest projects, no propmaster will have the time to do everything necessary to make the show work, so an assistant is essential, especially on a show using as many props as *The Conversation*. Furthermore, no matter how well prepared the Prop Department might be, there will always be the errant prop which has to be gotten ten minutes before the scene is shot. So the assistant propmaster will be sent to pick it up while the propmaster stays on set. One of these two people has to be on set all the time.

The Conversation needs an assistant almost full time, so we will start him one week after the propmaster, who will spend the first week breaking down the script and making her lists.

Additional Hire—Buyer

Sometimes a show is so heavy in props that someone has to be hired just to buy the necessary props. This would be necessary in, say, a science fiction picture where props were the most important elements of the show. *The Conversation* is not quite that heavy, so the propmaster will be able to handle it.

Additional Hire—Local Hire

People who normally live in the locale where you are filming can help obtain local props and also aid the propmaster on set when necessary.

Since *The Conversation* is considered a local film, local hire does not apply here, but the local union minimum would be $1,570.32 per week for five days.

30: Rentals

Many production centers have prop houses which specialize in renting props to movie companies. This is normally less expensive than buying everything and wondering what to do with it after the show is over. Remember that because of the risk of damage while filming, some key props, like key costumes, may need to be acquired in duplicate, triplicate or more; and this may be only possible by buying rather than renting.

We are going to allow $60,000 for *The Conversation* plus rental of the prop masters vehicle.

Video Playback System

If your script calls for the film's family to sit around the den watching a TV show, you need to have something to put on the screen. You will require a videotape and playback system to make the TV set work. Sometimes you can use a TV show which already exists. Then all you need is to obtain the videotape, and, the rights to show it in your show. If it is to be made specifically for your show, you also have to photograph the scene to be shown on TV *before* you photograph the scene in which the TV set is playing it. And remember that when actors appear in a movie within a movie they must still be paid per SAG rules as a single show, and a SAG contract will be necessary.

One very important item to remember is that the picture used on the TV screen must be in sync with the shutter of the camera. Otherwise it will produce that unpleasant roll bar effect which is evident in early films showing TV screens. Nowadays we have sync devices which eliminate it, but these must be arranged for beforehand. Merely photographing a TV screen with a camera will not produce a good picture.

In some budget forms, this equipment and persons who operate it are line items under the Sound Department.

Prop Box

Your propmaster will have his own box, boxes, or truck which have a fantastic stock of props you will need on the shoot. Renting this box or truck can only save you money and time.

40: Purchases
We have allotted enough money here to cover the costs of buying the electronic bugging devices as well as many other purchases, but the important ones are the actual props used by HARRY CAUL in his work.

Picture Food
Several scenes call for the characters to eat food on camera. Food on camera has to be edible. Actors should enjoy the food they are eating, if the script calls for them to like it. If the script calls for the actors to dislike the food, don't try to help. Give them enjoyable food and let them act as if they don't like it. And there should be enough, because you will need to replenish plates for retakes. Most television programs and some features try to avoid brand names in packaged food or other products. Most prop rental houses carry generic food, cigarettes, and other items with fictitious, cleared brand names for this purpose.

Obviously in the case of alcoholic beverages, the real thing is not used. Propmasters have a variety of recipes for concocting palatable look-alikes for any drink. For actors allergic to tobacco or minors who must smoke on camera, there are even cigarettes made from herbs.

50: Props Manufactured—Action Props
Since *The Conversation* calls for specialized electronic gear and the propmaster will not be able to buy everything needed off the shelf, some items will have to be built. Since this is a movie, the items don't actually have to work except for what the camera sees. In other words, if it is a tape recorder it does not have to record or play, but the reels have to revolve, and the dials and instruments have to light up as if it were working. Usually the Special Effects Department will step in here to make a prop practical.

85: Additional Expense—Armorer
While *armorer* may conjure up images of Medieval knights, it refers here to a prop person licensed to handle blanks, which like any

explosive device, requires a *powder license*. Many propmasters havea powder license and are familiar with the safe handling of weapons. On complex shows, such as those in which automatic or exotic weapons (such as the flintlocks in *The Last of the Mohicans)* are required, a specialist is the safest and most expedient course. Blanks are not harmless and can kill if used inappropriately.

You must always check with the local authorities as to which permits might be required to use firearms on a set. Don't even think of firing guns on a set without warning the local police beforehand. You could end up being arrested, even if it is only a movie.

Firearms

Be sure that you have provided not only for the firearms but also for the rounds of ammunition you will be shooting.

95: Miscellaneous

Most propmasters will already have their own Polaroid cameras, but you will probably have to buy the film for them. This is essential for matching props on the set from one day to the next. Make sure you have an allowance here.

99: Loss, Damage, Repair

Sometimes items break. Since by definition actors will handle props, someone will drop something sometime, or things will get lost or stolen. You should provide in this account for the deductible on your insurance to minimize your exposure. That is usually around $2,500. This makes it useless for you to put in claims smaller than that amount. Be sure to budget your deductible amount here, in case the inevitable happens. On *The Conversation* we are allowing $1,500.

Account 2600

Picture Vehicles

PAGE NO. 16

PRODUCTION NUMBER	PRODUCTION TITLE	DATE

2600 PICTURE VEHICLES		SUBTOTALS		
ACCT NO.	DESCRIPTION	A	B	C
01	Vehicle Drivers (Non-Teamsters/Vehicle's owner or representative)			
02				
	Transportation Allowance (See Location Acct 4005)			
30	Rental (See Detail Page 16A)			13,500
	Cars/Trucks			
	Motorcycles			
	Planes/Helicopters			
	Trains			
	Boats			
40	Purchases (See Detail Page 16A)			5,000
	Cars/Trucks			
	Motorcycles			
	Planes/Helicopters			
	Trains			
	Boats			
	Car Carrier (See Transportation Acct No 4600)			
45	Special Vehicle Use Permit (Check local regulations)			
48	Vehicle Alterations, Modifications, and Repairs			
	Gas and Oil (See Transportation Acct 4650)			
60	Permits, Parking, Tolls, Fees, etc. (See Transp. Acct 4669)			
65	Rigging Maintenance			
70	Storage			
72	Security			
75	Shop			
	Insurance (See Insurance Acct 6100)			
85	Additional Expenses			
95	Miscellaneous			
99	Loss, Damage, Repair			
	SUBTOTALS			18,500
	TOTAL ACCT 2600	18,500		

A = Fringeable/Taxable
B = Non-Fringeable/Taxable
C = Non-Taxable

PAGE NO. 16A

PRODUCTION NUMBER | PRODUCTION TITLE | DATE

ACCTS 2630 & 2640 PICTURE VEHICLES – DETAIL

SET NO.	SCENE NAME/NO. DESCRIPTION	VEHICLES QTY	VEHICLES DESCRIPTION	RENTAL TIME	RENTAL RATE	RENTAL AMOUNT	PURCHASES AMOUNT	4
DY 2	Sc. 34, 35, 36, 37 Ext. St./Bus	1	Electric Bus	1 Dy	900/dy	900		
DY 3	Sc. 43 Int./Ext. Bus & St.	1	Electric Bus	1 Dy	900/dy	900		
DY 4	Sc. 282, 283 Ext. Dir. Bldg./Bus	2	Electric Bus 1 & 2	1 Dy	1,500/dy	3,000		
DY 26	Sc. 284, 285, 289, 291 Ext./Int. Bus	2	Electric Bus 1 & 2	1 Dy	1,500/dy	3,000		
DY 27	Sc. 297-306, 286, 290, 214 Ext./Int. Bus	2	Electric Bus 1 & 2	1 Dy	1,500/dy	3,000		
	Sc. 287, 288, 292, 293, 295, 296 Int. Bus 2							
	Sc. 307, 308 Ext. Bus & Street							
DY 3	Sc. 365 Ext. Street	1	Mercedez Benz				5,000	
DY 5	Sc. 1-9 Ext. Union Square	1	Mirror Van	2 wks	600/wk (incl. prep)	1,200		
DY 6	Sc. 1-9 Ext. Union Square	1	Mirror Van					
DY 8	Sc. 13, 30 Ext. Van/Union Sq.	1	Mirror Van					
DY 9	Sc. 13, 30 Ext. Van/Union Sq.	1	Mirror Van					
DY 10	Sc. 12, 14-16, 27, 29 Int. Mirror Van	1	Mirror Van					
DY 38	Sc. 144, 146-149, 151-153, 155, 157-159	2	Paul's Sedan	1 Dy	100/dy	200		
	159							
	Int. Car	2	Willie's Mustang	1 Dy	150/dy	300		
	Sc. 145, 150, 154, 156	1	Paul's Sedan	1 Dy	500/wk Prep	500		
	Ext. Street Sedan & Mustange	1	Willie's Mustang	1 Dy	500/wk Prep	500		
					SUBTOTALS	13,500	5,000	
			TOTAL DETAIL ACCTS 2630 & 2640			18,500		

A = Fringeable/Taxable
B = Non-Fringeable/Taxable
C = Non-Taxable
4= Recoupable

2600—PICTURE VEHICLES

PICTURE VEHICLES APPEAR IN THE PICTURE. Production vehicles carry your equipment around. Some budgets include this entire account and its subsidiary categories as a subaccount under Transportation. We have separated it out here so that it doesn't get mixed in with all the other vehicles listed in the Transportation Account. This category includes all vehicles from ordinary sedans and station wagons to police cars,fire trucks, helicopters and airplanes.

01: Vehicle Drivers—(Non-Teamsters/Vehicle's Owner or Representative)

There are special cars which need not be driven by a teamster if the owner prefers to do it himself, or designate a special driver to do so. A number of collectors of antique or unique vehicles live in various parts of the country. These owners will rent you their vehicles for use in your film, and they usually will drive the vehicles to and from location for you as well. Sometimes they will also act as extras so that they can drive their own vehicles in your picture. Frequently they have all the necessary period wardrobe.

Coordinator

If there are large numbers of picture vehicles you may need a *coordinator* to handle just those.

02: Transportation Allowance

Getting the vehicles to and from the set can be costly, especially if they have to be transported on flatbed trailers. Budget this in Account 4005.

30: Rental

In *The Conversation* we have four very specific vehicles which must be prepared for the show. First, the *panel van* with the mirrored windows must be rented or purchased in advance of the filming, rigged with the mirrored windows, painted with the appropriate advertising signs, and fitted inside to handle the electronic gear for the surveillance. And this should be done far enough ahead of the filming to allow the director time to see the work and to make any changes he deems necessary.

Second, the *Mercedes* in which Mr. C's body is cremated must be specially prepared for the film. This is especially difficult because the current laws require automobiles to be manufactured with nonflammable materials. It is almost impossible to burn an automobile without considerable special effects preparation in advance of the scene. And when the scene is filmed it will be necessary to have the prerequisite fire department personnel with their equipment to make sure that the fire stays within the confines of the scripted scene. The Mercedes must be purchased since we are going to burn it.

Next come our chase cars: Paul's *Sedan* and Willie's *Mustang*. Both can be rented. You should also rent doubles for each as well. You will put camera mounts on the doubles. The time you save by doing so will be well worth it.

Planes/Helicopters

These *airplanes* and *helicopters* are not those which serve as flying camera platforms for aerial shots—these are the ones you actually see on film. Their costs are line items under Special Equipment—Account 3000.

The pilot of picture planes or helicopters, whether or not he speaks on camera, is covered by the SAG Basic Agreement. Weekly scale for a pilot appearing on camera is the same rate as a weekly stunt player *plus* a minimum adjustment every time he flies or taxis. Daily scale is 35% higher than for a day player. The pilots should be budgeted under Cast where they will automatically have their fringe benefits added in. The equipment is detailed here.

Most companies renting airplanes and helicopters to the motion picture industry can prepare them either to be photographed or to used in aerial photography. You may often require one plane or helicopter to photograph another in flight. These companies can make you a package price including SAG pilots and special camera operators trained in aerial photography. If you are including such an all-in quote in your budget you may wish to place the entire package price in a single account instead of breaking it out into several other areas.

Whenever you use a helicopter, you must notify the local FAA. You will need permission to land wherever you land. You will need to communicate with the helicopter pilot. It's best to request that the pilot bring you a set of walkie-talkies set to his frequency. Usually his system (ground to air) is the best.

Trains

Modern *trains* can be arranged through the local freight lines or Amtrak. Period trains are maintained at movie ranches in various parts of the country. A well-maintained narrow-gauge railroad might be necessary for a Western movie.

Trains are complicated and cumbersome mechanisms that require specialized operators and ample time to reset for Take Two. Allow plenty of time for these shots, and make sure you have taken adequate safety precautions.

Special Vehicles

Golf carts, Formula One racers, bulldozers that may appear in picture are all considered *special vehicles*.

In *The Conversation* we will need electric buses. One bus rents for $900 per day, and two rent for $1,500 per day. The rental price includes the labor (driver). If the sequence is complicated or dangerous, a supervisor must be present at $50 per hour.

Vintage cars are also itemized here. There are a number of companies across the country which specialize in handling vintage cars for the movies. Antique cars are not as reliable as contemporary vehicles. If you keep them running between takes they will probably overheat. And hand-cranking to restart them is no fun! Even if you have a standby mechanic for your production vehicles, you may want to include a specialized standby person on the days when you have problem vehicles. Put those costs either in this account or under Transportation.

Pickup/Delivery Charges
The costs of picking up and/or delivering picture vehicles goes here.

Car Carriers
If your show calls for many vehicles—particularly ordinary cars that would otherwise each be assigned a Teamster driver—it will usually be less expensive to transport them on a *car carrier*.

48: Vehicle Alterations, Modifications, and Repairs
You may have to specially prepare a picture vehicle for the run of the show. This may be no more involved than painting several cars alike to have duplicates or more complicated in creating several identical custom cars. You may anticipate a problem with a lot of running shots (i.e., shots of occupants inside the car as it moves) and decide to pre-rig the car so that car mounts or platforms for the camera may be easily attached and removed. Even if you're not doing *Thelma and Louise II*, pre-rigging can save valuable production time. [*Note: Having duplicates of important picture cars, especially those involved in stunt sequences, is not an extravagance—it is a necessity in most cases.*]

Stunt Cars
Nondescript (ND) *stunt cars*, built to be crashed, may be purchased from many companies that specialize is picture vehicles. These specially equipped cars come fitted with roll-bars and other safety devices. If you must wreck a key picture car, make sure you have a duplicate outfitted and ready to go in case you need to reshoot. Itemize those expenses here.

Gas and Oil—Gas Trucks
For both production and picture vehicles it can be less expensive as well as more efficient to refuel on the spot, instead of having to drive to the local gas station. A *gas truck* or fueler—a crew cab with

one or more 50-gallon drums that pump gasoline or diesel—can be arranged. Budget those costs here or under Transportation.

70: Storage

Rare rentals or specially built cars should always be assigned a security guard or stored safely elsewhere. Other conditions, such as keeping a rental car painted with easily removed water-base paint out of the rain, may require a garage or other form of safe *storage.*

Account 2700

Special Effects Department

PAGE NO.17

PRODUCTION NUMBER | PRODUCTION TITLE | DATE

ACCT. NO.	DESCRIPTION	LOCAL/ On Loc.	PREP	SHOOT	WRAP	TOTAL	RATE	A	B	C
2700	**SPECIAL EFFECTS DEPARTMENT**									
			DAYS/WEEKS					SUBTOTALS		
01	Sp. Eff. Foreman	Local	3	8.2	.4	11.6	1860	21,576		
	12 hr dy/26.57 p. hr	On Loc.								
		Local								
		On Loc.								
02	Asst. Sp. Eff. Men	Local	2.6	8.2	.2	10.4	1718	17,867		
	12 hr dy/24.54 p. hr	On Loc.								
		Local								
		On Loc.								
	Additional Hire	Local			ALLOW	1.	1718	1718		
		On Loc.								
		Local								
		On Loc.								
05	Rigging	Local								
		On Loc.								
		Local								
		On Loc.								
06	Striking	Local								
		On Loc.								
30	Equipment Rentals				ALLOW					15,000
	Wind									
	Rain									
	Snow									
	Fog									
	Fire Hose Wet Downs									
	Box Rental (Water Wagon – See Transportation Acct 4630)									
	9.2 wks x $1,000 p. wk.									9,200
40	Equipment Purchases				ALLOW					25,000
	Explosives, Breakaways, etc.									
50	Manufacturing – Labor (65%) (Total $12,500)				ALLOW			8,125		
55	Manufacturing – Materials (35%)									4,375
65	Permits (Explosives, Fire, etc.)				ALLOW					500
79	Other Charges, Permits, Fees, etc.									
85	Additional Expense Surveillance Equipment – Labor									
	Materials to make practical				ALLOW					1,500
95	Miscellaneous									
99	Loss, Damage, Repair									
							SUBTOTALS	49,286		55,575
							TOTAL ACCT 2700	104,861		

A = Fringeable/Taxable
B = Non-Fringeable/Taxable
C = Non-Taxable

PAGE NO.17A

PRODUCTION NUMBER | PRODUCTION TITLE | DATE

ACCTS 2730 & 2740 SPECIAL EFFECTS – DETAIL

SET NO.	SCENE NAME/NO. DESCRIPTION	VEHICLES QTY	VEHICLES DESCRIPTION	RENTAL TIME	RENTAL RATE	RENTAL AMOUNT	PURCHASES AMOUNT	✔
1	Dy 2: Ext. St./Bus/ Neighborhood		Sparks from Bus					
	Sc. 34, 36, 37							
2	Dy 3: Ext. Street		Merdedes - Car Barn					
3	Dy 4: Ext. Directors Bldg. (Bus 1 & 2)		Fog					
	Sc. 283							
4	Dy 5, 6, 8, 10: Int/Ext. Union Square		Mirrored Van w/ Electronic Device					
	Sc. 1-9, 58, 62, 64, 66, 68, 71, 87, 107, 10, 11							
	25, 26, 17, 31, 18, 23, 24, 103, 32, 13, 30, 12,							
	14, 15, 16, 27, 29							
5	Dy 24: Int. Bathroom B-7 Sc. 261-268		Water in toilet becomes bloody					
6	Dy 25: Int. B-7 Motel Room & Bath		Stab wounds on body, blood					
7	Dy 26: Ext./Int. Bus #1 & 2 Sc. 284, 285,		Fog					
	289, 291, 298, 300, 301, 302, 299, 303-306							
8	Dy 27: Ext. Poles & Lines Sc.		Short in Wires Fog					
	Sc. 286, 290, 294							
9	Dy 28: Ext. Stepped Street Sc. 309-316		Fog					
10	Dy 29: Ext. Park Sc. 317-319, 321-332		Fog					
11	Dy 30, 31: Int. Warehouse		Tape Recorders Misc. Equipment					
	Sc. 50-57, 59-61, 63, 65, 67, 69, 70, 72-80,		Electronics					
	82-86, 88-91		"					
	Dy 32-34 Int. Warehouse		"					
	Sc. 160-173		"					
	Dy 35, 36: Int. Warehouse		"					
	Sc. 174-181, 183, 184, 186, 187		"					
					SUBTOTALS	see 17AA		
	TOTAL DETAIL ACCTS 2730 & 2740							

A = Fringeable/Taxable
B = Non-Fringeable/Taxable
C = Non-Taxable
4= Recoupable

PAGE NO.17AA

PRODUCTION NUMBER | PRODUCTION TITLE | DATE

ACCTS 2730 & 2740 SPECIAL EFFECTS – DETAIL								
SET NO.	SCENE NAME/NO. DESCRIPTION	VEHICLES		RENTAL			PURCHASES AMOUNT	✔
		QTY	DESCRIPTION	TIME	RATE	AMOUNT		
11 (cont)	Dy 37: Int. Warehouse		Tape Recorders Misc. Equipment					
	Sc. 337-353, 355, 357, 358, 362, 364, 333-336		Electronics					
12	Dy 38: Int. Car (travelling)		Action between Mustang & Sedan					
	Sc. 144, 146-149, 151-153, 155, 157-159							
	Dy 38: Ext. Street Sedan & Mustang		Action between Mustang & Sedan					
	Sc. 145, 150, 154, 156							
			Allow					
					SUBTOTALS	15,000	25,000	
	TOTAL DETAIL ACCTS 2730 & 2740					ALLOW 40,000		

A = Fringeable/Taxable
B = Non-Fringeable/Taxable
C = Non-Taxable
✔= Recoupable

2700–SPECIAL EFFECTS DEPARTMENT

01: Special Effects Supervisor

THE SPECIAL EFFECTS SUPERVISOR BEGINS BY BREAKING DOWN the script and isolating all the *mechanical effects*—those which will be produced while filming and not by optical manipulation of the image in post-production. Effects from sparks to ships sinking may be achieved either mechanically or optically. The relative cost and safety will be key factors in deciding which way to proceed. Ultimately many of the effects seen in the finished picture may end up as a combination of mechanical and optical methods. Many mechanical effects from bullet hits to explosions require a crew of licensed and/or certified specialists led by a supervisor who is experienced in the particular demands of your script. Just as a stunt coordinator who may be adept at both car chases and high falls may bring in a special consultant for underwater work, a good special effects supervisor will know when and how much additional help is needed. If this is more than you have budgeted, safety demands that either the effect be eliminated or simplified, or the budget be increased.

Before deciding that you have a very simple show and do not need an effects person, keep in mind that on union productions there are many less spectacular, nonexplosive effects from elevator doors opening on a stage set to using fans to simulate a breeze that are supposed to handled by a special effects person.

For *The Conversation* there is not much in the way of special effects—MR. C's car explodes on Day Two and there are some sparks from the electric bus on Day One. We will hire a Supervisor for the run of the show, however, in case the director changes his mind and wants some additional effects. The supervisor will have three week's prep time.

02: Assistant Special Effects
The *special effects assistant* will have 2.6 weeks of prep to get the car ready and aid the department head in preparing the show.

Additional Hire
Whenever you burn something or blow it up, you must always have people standing by with the proper fire prevention equipment (e.g., fire extinguishers, water truck, goggles, ear protectors.) Allow one week's salary here to cover yourself.

05: Rigging
In order to prepare the Mercedes to be burned, it will require a few days' time. The car's gas tank and fuel lines have to be removed. Any fluids that could explode under the intense heat are also removed. All flammable materials have to be pretreated prior to filming.

06: Striking
Don't forget that you can't leave the burned car in the streets. It has to be removed and legally disposed.

30: Equipment Rentals—Wind/Ritters
A *Ritter* is actually an airplane propeller enclosed in a safety cage. It requires its own operator. The wind it creates can be not only dramatic but also quite dangerous.

30: Equipment Rentals—Rainbirds
Rainbirds are flexible arrangements of pipes and sprinkler heads which may be set at variable heights and connected to a hydrant, stand pipe, or water truck to produce artificial rain. Even if you are actually filming in the rain, devices of this sort are needed to fill in behind close-ups and provide continuity if the rain should stop.

30: Equipment Rentals—Special Materials
Special materials here include snow throwers, remote control devices, and anything else which performs movie magic on camera.

There were no special materials on *The Conversation* except for the electronic surveillance equipment.

30: Equipment Rentals—Box Rental/Truck & Trailer Rental

Many special effects people have a wide range of equipment that they store in their own trucks or trailers. It is normal to rent the entire rig and even purchase certain expendables as part of a package. In fact, certain companies and individual will bid a package price to provide the personnel and material to produce every mechanical effect in your script.

40: Purchases

The expendables and manufacturing are probably quite reasonable at $25,000. It takes quite a bit of effort and materials to do a burning sequence. If the director decides to see MR. C'S BODY in the car, this will have to be purchased and prepared for the scene.

85: Additional Expense—Firearms/Weapons

Even if your propmaster has a powder license, complex sequences or the use of weapons with squibs or dustguns (which fire small pellets of Fuller's Earth that produce a puff of smoke when striking walls, car doors, or other solid surfaces to simulate bullet hits), should be supervised by an effects person.

85: Additional Expense—Electronics Effects (Surveillance Equipment)

When you order electronic effects you must budget not only for the effects themselves but also for all the accompanying expenses such as: transporting the effect to the set, hiring operators to make it work.

[*Note: If you are featuring computers in the scene be sure to preprogram the equipment so that it performs on cue when the director asks for it.*]

Account 2800

Camera Department

PAGE NO.18

PRODUCTION NUMBER | PRODUCTION TITLE | DATE

2800	CAMERA DEPARTMENT									
ACCT. NO.	DESCRIPTION	LOCAL/ On Loc.	DAYS/WEEKS PREP	SHOOT	WRAP	TOTAL	RATE	SUBTOTALS A	B	C
01	Director of Photog	Local	3	8.2		11.2	4320	48,388		
	12 hr. dy/61.72 hr	On Loc.								
		Local								
		On Loc.								
		Local								
		On Loc.								
02	Camera Operator	Local		8.2		8.2	2725	22,345		
	12 hr dy/38.92 hr	On Loc.								
03	Additional	Local		2		2	2725	5,450		
	Camera Operator	On Loc.								
		Local								
		On Loc.								
05	1st Ast. Cameraman	Local	1	8.2	.4	9.6	2187	20,997		
	13 hr dy/27.34 hr	On Loc.								
	Add'l 1st Ast	Local		2		2	2187	4,374		
	Cameraman (same)	On Loc.								
10	2nd Ast. Camerama	Local	.4	8.2	.2	8.8	2010	17,692		
	13 hr dy/25.13 hr	On Loc.								
12	Add'l 2nd Ast.	Local		2		2	2010	4,021		
	Cameraman (same)	On Loc.								
	Still Photographer	Local								
	(See Publicity, Act. 6000)	On Loc.								
15	Special	Local								
	Camera Operator	On Loc.								
	Video Asst. Op.	Local	.4	8.2	.2	8.8	1991	17,519		
	12 hr dy/28.44 hr	On Loc.								
30	Rentals									
	First Camera System 8.2 wks. x 10,000/wk									82,000
	Second Camera System 2 wks. x 5,000/wk.									10,000
	Through-The-Lens Video System Videotape 8.2 wks x 1,000 wk.									8,200
	Other									
	Filter 8.2 wks. x 200/wk									1,640
	1st A.C. Box Rental 8.2 wks. x 50/wk.									410
40	Purchases ALLOW									5,000
85	Additional Expense									
95	Miscellaneous									
99	Loss, Damage, Repair									
							SUBTOTALS	140,786		107,250
							TOTAL ACCT 2800	248,036		

A = Fringeable/Taxable
B = Non-Fringeable/Taxable
C = Non-Taxable

2800—CAMERA DEPARTMENT

THERE ARE TWO KEY ASPECTS TO THE WORK of the director of photography: supervision of camera placement and movement, and lighting the scene. Just as the many departments from construction to wardrobe which work with the production designer are guided by the designer's supervisory influence, so are camera, grip, and electric related to the director of photography. In both instances, the key person will have much to say about all those who head up and work in the subsidiary departments.

01: Director of Photography

The *director of photography* (also called *cinematographer*), will be the director's primary technical assistant during production. Most feature directors expect to work with a director of photography of their choosing. Producers will consult with the director as to his choice, but the decision usually rests with the director.

Choosing a director of photography, or DP, is not a simple matter. DP's sometimes specialize in a particular kind of cinematography. Having a good eye is essential as well as being able to establish a certain kind of verbal shorthand with the director.

A cinematographer must know how to *position* the camera, and, when necessary, *move* it. He must know how to *light* a set, to get the maximum possible use of the elements available. Use of *color* is an essential part of a cinematographer's repertoire as color gives things psychological overtones.

A very important part of the cinematographer's tools is the camera crew. The DP must have a good selection of excellent craftspeople/artists to help in these tasks. The basic crew of DP, operator, gaffer, key grip, and camera assistants must work together smoothly and artistically to effectively realize the vision of the director.

When selecting a DP, the director usually suggests DP's with whom he has worked before. If the director suggests someone new, look at their sample reel. It will show what the person's work looks like. Then, if you like the work, call at least two former employers to find out what the DP is like on the set. Pay particular attention to how quickly does he sets the camera, lights the set and how efficiently he works with the crew.

For *The Conversation* we will give the DP three weeks of prep, to scout locations and determine the camera needs of the picture.

Rates for DP's vary. Scale is $465.42 per day. The realistic range is $5,000 to $15,000 per week, although some DP's demand—and get—hundreds of thousands of dollars per picture. For lower budgets, the rates may be reduced by 30 to 40 percent (30% to 40%.)

02: Camera Operator

The *camera operator*'s job is more critical than just operating the camera. Since the operator is the only one looking through the lens when the shot is in progress, the ability to interpret what the DP and director want is crucial. With the recent advent of *video assist*, more and more people can view the shot on a nearby video monitor. (See Account 2815 for *video assist operator*.) The operator alone guides the camera through its side-to-side pans, up-and-down tilts, and other movements, determining exactly what the audience will be seeing on the screen. In England and other countries, the camera operator is more responsible for helping the director set shots, and the DP (DOP in England) is often termed a *lighting cameraperson.*

On most shows, the operator needs little or no prep or wrap time.

03: Additional Camera Operators

Whenever you need more than one camera to photograph a scene you will also need *additional camera operators* to load it and run it. Each camera must have its own assistant and operator for that purpose.

For *The Conversation* we are allowing two weeks for an extra camera operator. This will cover the car burn and Union Square sequences.

05: First Assistant Cameraperson

As film sets are normally lit to take the maximum advantage of the speed or light sensitivity of the film stock being used, the F-stop or opening of the lens which regulates the amount of light is passes through will also be near maximum. This means that the depth of field of the range which appears to be in focus for a given lens will be narrow, and that as the key actors move around in the set, the focus setting of the lens will be changed during filming. This critical task falls to the *first assistant cameraperson*, or first AC, who is called a *focus puller* in England. The first AC is responsible with the physical care of the camera itself. She transports it to and from the set, changes the lens as required, attaches and loads the film magazines, and makes any other alterations to the camera's configuration. The technology has progressed to where the camera is run by computer chips, and the technician must know a motherboard from a CPU as well as an F-stop. On IATSE shows, first assistants are usually paid the higher scale of a technician.

The first assistant is the one with the measuring tape who checks the distance between the lens and the camera's subject and records the focus marks on the lens. The first assistant usually will rent you her *ditty bag*, which has a combination of necessary items like lens cleaners, filter frames, scissors, different size slates or clappers which identify and provide sync references for scenes, chalk to mark them, a Swiss Army Knife, mini-flashlight, and so on. It is cheaper and easier to pay the rent than to buy it yourself.

The first assistant will get one week of prep to check out the cameras, bench-test the lenses, load the camera/sound van, and make sure that everything is ready for filming. She will also get two days of wrap to return the cameras to the rental house at the end of filming and check everything back in.

10: Second Assistant Cameraperson
The *second assistant cameraperson* helps maintain the equipment and film inventory and does the paperwork associated with it. She also puts down marks for the actors and stand-ins, writes the scenes, takes, and footage information on the slate or clapboard and camera reports, and *marks* the scenes by closing the clapboard at the beginning or end of each shot.

On most projects, the second assistant cameraperson will have a couple of days of prep to help the first assistant prepare the cameras, and one day of wrap to return them.

Still Photographer
On most projects there will be a *still photographer* assigned to the project. You will need production stills, publicity stills, continuity stills, all sorts of still photographs. Still photographers are generally very careful not to be in the way of the camera or director, and only take their pictures when the first assistant director tells them. *(See additional comments under Publicity, Account 6000.)*

15: Special Camera Operator—Steadicam or Panaglide Operator
The trademarked names *Steadicam* and *Panaglide* both refer to a hand-held system which help the cameras remain steady or glide smoothly. As both systems require a harness, video taps (see Videotap on page 200), and other cumbersome attachments, there are a large number of camera operators who specialize in and have had special training in the use and maintenance of this equipment. Many Steadicam systems are owned by their operators who make daily, weekly, or run-of-the-picture package deals for both equipment rental and their services. Panaflex cameras are too heavy to be mounted on a normal Steadicam, so Panavision rents out the more heavy-duty Panaglide. Most videotaps are now wireless and focus pulling is by remote control. Because the operator does not physically look through the lens but is guided by a small, black-and-white video monitor, the focus pulling is also critical. Many camera assistants are also specialized in using these devices.

Whether your production calls for a single day or numerous sequences using these systems, experienced technicians are essential to a good result.

Additional Hire—Standby DP

Until recently, if a cinematographer from California worked in New York or Chicago, the production company was required to hire a local standby DP at scale rates. This DP basically stood around the set and observed. Now the three unions have merged into one Local 600. They still have three separate contracts and New York (Local 644) still has a higher wage rate. However, this should all be unified when one contract is available in the near future.

30: Rentals—Camera Package

Some directors of photography prefer only a Panavision package, others prefer Arriflex. While there are other systems available—particularly in Los Angeles—such as Moviecam or Ultracam, the compact, silent Panaflexes or Arri BLs are used on the vast majority of productions. Package prices vary mainly because of the peripherals. For example, it is typical for a high-speed, extremely sharp zoom lens to rent for almost as much as the camera itself. Additional lenses, magazines, batteries, etc., are all rented on an individual basis. Most productions will add or subtract from the basic package on an as needed basis. If you need a set of higher-speed prime lenses for a week's worth of night exteriors, rent them for that period only but make sure that you reserve them as far in advance as possible. If you are using a computerized editing system (*Liteworks, AVID,* etc.) then you will need a digital clip board.

For a major picture like *The Conversation*, $10,000 per week is not unreasonable.

Extra cameras

Many features will carry an Arri II or III as an extra camera. Panavision has modified for hard-front Arris which accept its lenses. These cameras are not blimped, so that the noise of their motors in unacceptably loud for dialogue scenes, but they are lighter, more easily transportable, and quite effective as second cameras in stunt or action sequences and shooting wider, non-dialogue establishing shots. Even if the director wants two sound cameras available at all times, it will seldom be necessary to have more than one set of lenses, tripods, etc., for both cameras

If you are filming a very intricate and involved special effect or stunt or both, you may wish to rent four or more cameras to photograph the same action from different angles. Rebuilding the building you have just blown up for take two is very time-consuming and expensive. Sometimes it pays to rent or purchase a small camera to be inside a car which is wrecked, knowing that the camera might be destroyed, but the film can usually be salvaged.

In case we need an extra camera, we will add an allowance of $10,000 to cover the cost of just the body and a few lenses for the few days.

Videotap/Video Assist Operator

Many feature directors expect and demand a *videotap/video assist* along with a *video assist operator.* This is accomplished through a special connection which directs part of the light coming through the film camera's lens to a video monitor for viewing. It can also be recorded to recording and playback devices. Video assists permit any director to *see* what the camera operator sees. On stunt sequences involving several cameras, additional monitors permit the action to be viewed from several angles simultaneously. Costs for a video assist operator should be included in this account.

Steadicam Package

As noted most Steadicam operators will rent you a package.

Special Equipment

Always check with your DP regarding any preferences for special photography. Your own DP might be an excellent underwater photographer and would be happy to save you the money of hiring an outside specialist, for a small extra fee. Or there might be a particular specialist who has worked well and often with your DP on past productions, and it is always preferable to hire a familiar person than an unknown quantity.

Hi-speed cameras

Sync speed cameras—those used for dialogue scenes—expose films at the rate of 24 frames per second (fps). Sound cameras have a quartz-controlled or crystal motor to ensure that they do not vary from this speed. While vari-speed motors which can be used with most cameras, allow them to run faster and yield a slow motion result. Their mechanisms do not permit ultrahigh speed or anything over 120 fps. It is customary to use vari-speed motors while filming scenes involving stunts and special effects. These scenes seem to have more impact when shown in slow motion than when they flash past the eyes of the audience at regular speed. Speeds above this are very specialized, used to capture bullets going though apples and the like, and seldom used on normal production days.

40: Purchases

You will need film cans, cores, filter gels, marking pens, and many other supplies. For *The Conversation* we will allow $5,000 which should cover the costs.

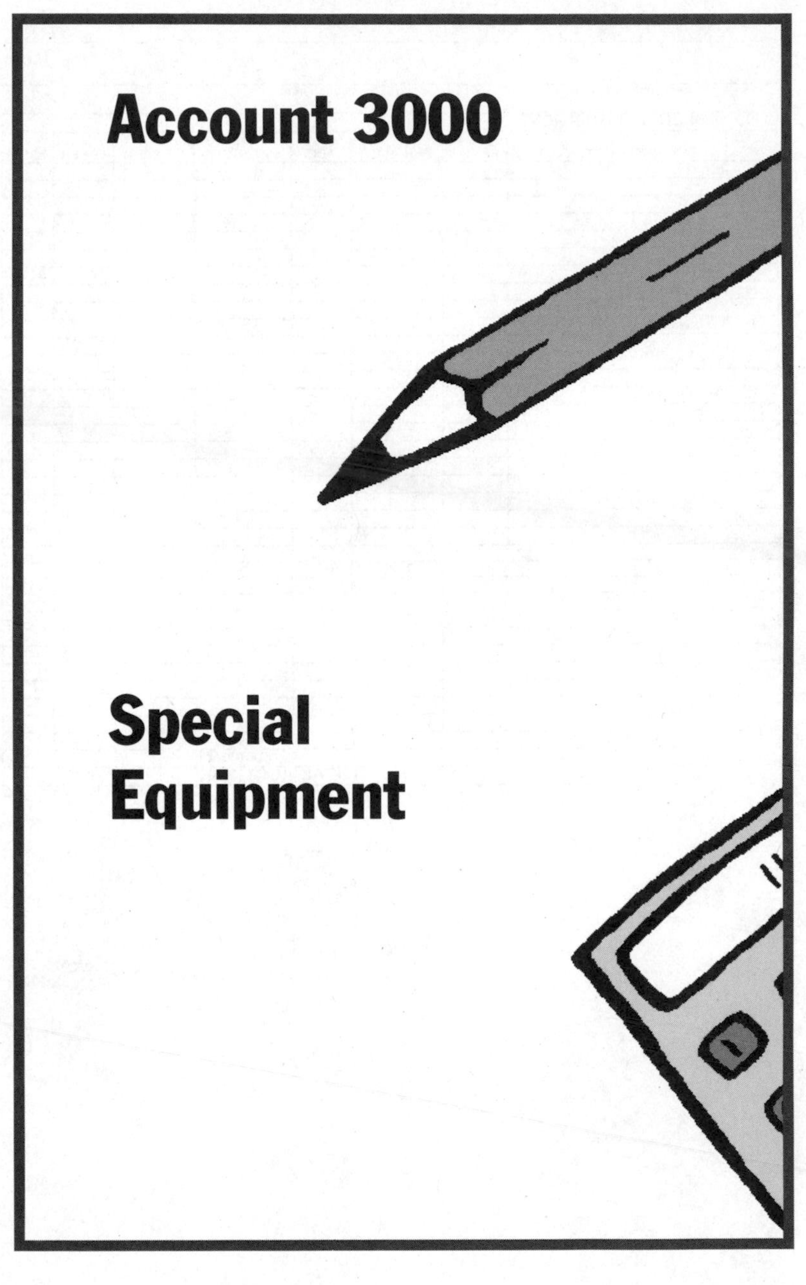

Account 3000

Special Equipment

PAGE NO. 19

PRODUCTION NUMBER | PRODUCTION TITLE | DATE

3000 SPECIAL EQUIPMENT

ACCT NO.	DESCRIPTION/SCENE NO.	RENTAL	PURCHASE	LABOR	FUEL/ MATERIALS	PICK-UP DELIVERY	OTHER	TOTAL
01	Helicopter							
05	Plane							
10	Train							
15	Boat							
20	Underwater Equipment							
25	Industrial Carne							
31	Scissors Lift							
35	Cherry Picker							
	Hand Held Camera							
	(See Camera Dept. Act. 2800)							
42	Wind Machine							
45	Low Boy							
	Additional Equipment							
							SUBTOTAL	

		TIME	RATE	AMOUNT	SUBTOTALS A	B	C
	Per Diem (List on Page 30C)						
	Travel (List on Page 30C)						
85	Additional Expenses						
95	Miscellaneous						
99	Loss, Damage, Repair						
				SUBTOTALS			
				TOTAL ACCT 3000		*0.00*	

A = Fringeable/Taxable
B = Non-Fringeable/Taxable
C = Non-Taxable

3000–SPECIAL EQUIPMENT

01: Helicopter

HELICOPTER MOUNTS ARE SPECIFICALLY DESIGNED DEVICES which isolate the camera from the vibrations of the helicopter, while at the same time providing a steady platform from which to film. The most commonly used is the Tyler Mount but there are several clones available.

A Bell Jet Ranger helicopter costs about $450 per hour with a three-hour minimum. The pilot usually charges $750 to $1,000 per day. Add to this the cost of the camera operator, assistant, camera package, mount rental, and so forth. It is very expensive, but well worth it for the spectacular shots you can get for action films.

20: Underwater Equipment

If your script calls for underwater filming you might hire a specialist. As with most technical specialists, underwater photographers usually have their own packages or people and equipment.

No special photography was needed for *The Conversation*.

—— *Notes* ——

Account 3100

Sound Department

PAGE NO.20

PRODUCTION NUMBER | PRODUCTION TITLE | DATE

3100	SOUND DEPARTMENT – 12 HR. DY.									
ACCT.		LOCAL/	DAYS/WEEKS					SUBTOTALS		
NO.	DESCRIPTION	On Loc.	PREP	SHOOT	WRAP	TOTAL	RATE	A	B	C
01	Mixer	Local	.2	8.2	.2	8.6	2951	25,380		
	42.16 p. hr.	On Loc.								
		Local								
		On Loc.								
02	Mike Boom Oper.	Local	.2	8.2	.2	8.6	2276	19,571		
	32.51 p. hr.	On Loc.								
		Local								
		On Loc.								
03	Cable Puller	Local		8.2		8.2	1991	16,325		
	28.44 p. hr.	On Loc.								
		Local								
		On Loc.								
04	Playback Operator	Local		.4		.4	2276	910		
		On Loc.								
		Local								
		On Loc.								
05	P.A. Operator	Local								
		On Loc.								
		Local								
		On Loc.								
	Additional Hire	Local								
		On Loc.								
		Local								
		On Loc.								
06	Daily Transfers	Local								
	(Labor)	On Loc.								
30	Equipment Rentals									
	Basic Sound Package 8.2 wks. x 1,750/wk.									14,350
	Radio Mikes 8.2 wks. x 75/wk.									615
	Walkie-Talkies 8.2 wks. x 1,250/wk. (25 units per week)									10,250
	Playback									
	Beepers 3 mos. x 600/mo.									1,800
	Special Boom									
	Bullhorn									
40	Equipment Purchases ALLOW									1,500
	1/4" Audiotape – Batteries (See Prod. Rawstock Acct. 4700)									
85	Additional Expense									
95	Miscellaneous ALLOW									2,500
99	Loss, Damage, Repair									
							SUBTOTALS	62,186		31,015
							TOTAL ACCT 3100	93,201		

A = Fringeable/Taxable
B = Non-Fringeable/Taxable
C = Non-Taxable

3100–SOUND DEPARTMENT

IT IS NOT UNCOMMON TO HEAR, *"We'll fix it in post,"* when referring to problems that have occurred in production. It is undeniably true that filmmakers can fix sound in post much more readily than they can alter or manipulate the picture; but the best concept is to get all the elements done right the first time. All productions will rerecord some dialogue and add more audio effects and/or music to the final soundtrack. The cleaner and less noisy production track that you can provide can only make this post-production process go faster and cost less.

The Conversation is an excellent example. The major character, HARRY CAUL, is an expert in surveillance. He mixes recordings of a single event recorded by several different sources, to make a single, cohesive, comprehensive sound track of *the conversation* in question. We hear what he hears, and in so doing, come to an understanding of his problems, his solutions, and his character. The soundtrack is like another character, a very important character, in the show.

01: Mixer

Having a usable production track for most of your dialogue not only ensures that the director has the needed audio performance but can also save you a lot of money in ADR recording time and actor fees in post-production. Don't skimp here. Suppose by spending an extra $100 per week over the eight weeks of filming we can eliminate $10,000 to $15,000 worth of ADR. An expense of $800 to offset $10,000 is a very good deal in anyone's book.

A *mixer*'s equipment does not take up a tremendous amount of space. The boxes for the wireless microphones are not bulky and the portable mixing board and Nagra or digital audio tape (DAT) recorder are not large. The little cart that the mixer uses to carry his equipment is smaller than a shopping cart in your supermarket. The mixer does not need much preparation for a picture except to load equipment on the truck. Even on a movie as sound-heavy as *The Conversation*, the mixer only needs one day to prep.

Immediately after filming a scene, you should always allow your mixer tine to record about 30 or 40 seconds of *room tone.* This gives your sound editor the tape necessary to equalize the fact that in any one scene you might have had microphones pointing in several different directions and the ambient sound in each will be different.

02: Boom Operator

Almost all *boom operators* use a *fish-pole*—or hand-held—extension rod to suspend a *shotgun* or directional microphone over the actors in the set. They place the wireless mikes on your actors in wide shots and other scenes where a boom is not feasible. These omnidirectional mikes are worn concealed in the clothing and do pick up fabric rustling and more ambient sounds.

In years past, boom operators used a sound boom—a large, platform device with wheeled devices similarly to those on a camera head to allow for quickly extension and rotation the microphone at its tip. Except in multi-camera television shows, is seldom used nowadays, even on stage, as the same quality sound can be achieved with lighter, easier to use equipment that doesn't take as much time to set up and move.

03: Cable Puller

The *cable puller* feeds out and pulls back the cable that connects the microphone to the mixer's cart. Wireless mikes do not require cable pullers; and even IA shows no longer require a three-person sound crew.

Depending on your budget it may be useful to include a cable puller or sound utility person, who helps transport and set up equipment, including the production walkie-talkies, and pull cable or handle a second boom. Such a person needs minimal or no prep or wrap time.

04: Playback Operator

The *playback operator* is in charge of playing back of any recorded sound during a take. The most common usage occurs when a performer lip-syncs words to prerecorded song in order to appear to be singing live while cameras are rolling. Playback is audible to the recording microphones which can cause a problem when performers are expected to continue from playback to dialogue in the same scene Therefore to eliminate this problem, performers are often fitted with wireless receivers (such as those used by newscasters) concealed *earwigs* so that only they can hear the playback.

In *The Conversation* we have scenes of some of the characters dancing so we will need audio playback. We also will need video playback for a few days. We have put the video playback equipment and crew in this department because in many cases the local sound union of the IATSE has jurisdiction.

30: Equipment Rentals–Basic Sound Package

The basic *sound package*, also known as a sound channel, is composed of mix board, recorder(s) and microphones. The usual practice has been to rent this, and even walkie-talkies, from the mixer. Mixers maintain their own equipment properly; their income depends on it. Some mixers have rebuilt their recorders to their own spec—some in stereo—and most own their own wireless mikes as well.

Most television shows as well as an increasing number of features are being edited on a nonlinear or digital system, such as Avid, Lightworks or D-Vision. These systems use time-code or the video system of measuring in minutes, seconds, and fields as a common reference between sound and picture elements. These devices also requires a time-code slate which uses an electronic LED device to display the start code on the sound recording as well as standard scene and take numbers. While most mixers probably plan on acquiring time-code Nagras or DAT recorders, they are less commonplace now. They are also costlier to rent, so if you plan on nonlinear editing add 50 percent (50%) to the cost of the sound channel.

30: Equipment Rentals–Walkie-Talkies

Walkie-talkies are used by crew members to communicate. Be sure when you rent yours that they have several channels. Then each department can be assigned discrete channels to minimize confusion. In Los Angeles, where many productions may be at work using walkie-talkies from the same rental house or studio department, you can avoid cross-talk with other companies. Be sure to have a safe place either on stage or in a locked camera/sound van to recharge the walkie-talkie batteries every night. Many shows add headsets and extra batteries to their package. The rates for walkie-talkies have come down to under $25 per week per unit depending on power and accessories.

[Note: Walkie-talkies and other radio-transmitting devices, including remote controls, should be used with great care. Too much power can cause interference with military and police users who have restricted frequencies. Construction sites using explosives are likely to detonate their devices via radio signals. Before shooting effects scenes with any explosives that are triggered wirelessly, safety officers will automatically call for all walkie-talkies to be turned off.]

30: Equipment Rentals–Beepers/Pagers

If key personnel don't already wear them, *beepers* or *pagers* can be rented on a monthly basis. The low cost and time savings have led to crew lists that feature dozens of pager numbers, one or more for a person in every department.

30: Equipment Rentals–Cellular Phones

Cellular phones can save many times their cost to the company, in giving you the ability to communicate about and solve problems the instant they occur.

Since so many crew members have their own cellular phones, it is not uncommon for the company to rent the use of those phones. The owner is reimbursed for the *air time* and a sometimes a prorata of the basic service charges. Since they are responsible for the usage, many owners will ask for a deposit from the production company. As with pagers, many companies rent phones on anything from a daily to multi-year basis.

Rates for *airtime* on rental phones can vary tremendously, from as little as $.20 per minute to $1.20 a minute. This all adds up quickly, so log each phone call as to destination and purpose and/or to restrict phone use to numbers pre-approved by the UPM. It is not unusual for a set phone(s) to cost several thousand dollars per month in air time, and your budget must allow for that.

Account 3200

Grip Department

PAGE NO.21

PRODUCTION NUMBER | PRODUCTION TITLE | DATE

ACCT. NO.	3200 GRIP DEPARTMENT DESCRIPTION	LOCAL/ On Loc.	DAYS/WEEKS PREP	SHOOT	WRAP	TOTAL	RATE	SUBTOTALS A	B	C
01	Key Grip	Local	3	8.2	1	12.2	1,910	23,314		
	27.30 p. hr.	On Loc.								
		Local								
		On Loc.								
02	Best Boy/2nd Co.	Local	3	8.2	1	12.2	1778	21,692		
	Grip 25.40 p. hr.	On Loc.								
		Local								
		On Loc.								
03	Dolly Grip	Local	.2	8.2		8.4	1778	14,930		
	25.40 p. hr.	On Loc.								
04	Crane Grip	Local		5 dys		5 dys	356	1,778		
	25.40 p. hr.	On Loc.								
05	Company Grip (x2)	Local	.2	8.2	.2	8.6	1645	28,294		
	23.50 p. hr.	On Loc.								
		Local								
		On Loc.								
		Local								
		On Loc.								
	Additional Hire	Local		15 dys		15 dys	329	4,935		
	23.50 p. Hr. ALLOW	On Loc.								
	2nd Dolly Grip	Local		2		2	1778	3,556		
	25.40 p. hr.	On Loc.								
06	Rigging & Striking	Local								
	See also Acct 2300)	On Loc.								
		Local								
		On Loc.								
30	Rentals (Car Mounts) ALLOW									1,000
	Dolly 8.2 wks. x 500/wk.									4,100
	Dolly Track Box Rental: 8.2 wks. x 300/wk.									2,460
	Crane Titan 585/dy. Apollo 435/dy. ALLOW									10,000
	Grip Package 8.2 wks. x 3,500/wk.									28,700
	2nd Dolly (1st 2 wks.): 10 dys. x 100/dy.									1,000
40	Purchases ALLOW									15,000
	Gels, Tarping, Diffusion ALLOW									15,000
85	Additional Expense: Condors 20 dys. x 125/dy.									2,500
95	Miscellaneous									
99	Loss, Damage, Repair									
	SUBTOTALS							98,499		79,760
	TOTAL ACCT 3200							178,259		

A = Fringeable/Taxable
B = Non-Fringeable/Taxable
C = Non-Taxable

3200—GRIP DEPARTMENT

In the simplest terms, electricians make light and grips make shadows. Grips also carry hammers and use saws to make changes to sets from moving *wild* (moveable) walls in and out, to bracing furniture. Specialized grips handle crab dollies, cranes, and other wheeled camera mounts.

01: Key Grip

With the gaffer, or chief lighting technician, the *key grip* is the DP's main assistant when fine tuning the lighting of any sequence. It is common practice to give the grips the same working arrangement as the electricians. One usually offers the same prep and wrap times, same salaries, same working conditions all around.

We are giving our *key grip* three weeks of prep for *The Conversation*, and the same wrap time (one week) as the chief lighting technician.

02: Second Grip

The number two grips and electricians are still referred to as the *best boy* or *best person*. In traditional studio shoots, the grip and electric departments assign as a second someone familiar with their operations. Now the department head normally sets the second, who still keeps inventory, orders and returns supplementary, equipment, and fills out time cards and other paperwork.

03: Dolly Grip

Other than the actual camera department personnel, the *dolly grip is* the only crew member directly involved in camera moves. Even when the dolly is not working in the shot, it is more convenient on most sound stage and many location sites, to keep the camera mounted on it during the day. The grip department lays down the tracks and/or smooth boards over which the dolly rolls and adjusts them to ensure that the track on which the dolly moves is straight and level. On most productions this is an art in itself. Dolly track has to be leveled so that the camera doesn't suddenly lean sideways during a dolly move. The camera always has to be leveled unless specifically ordered otherwise. Dolly moves must be smooth and unobtrusive. A jerky camera move is distracting and should be avoided at all costs. It is to your advantage to hire an experienced dolly grip. Most DP's have their own dolly grips with whom they work consistently. If they are available, do your best to hire them.

On *The Conversation* we will need to use two cameras on two dollies during two weeks of filming, so we will hire an extra dolly grip for the extra dolly. It is not a craft which just any grip can handle.

The dolly grip earns the same rate as the second grip.

04: Crane Grip

Camera cranes vary from small stage cranes that resemble oversized dollies to the huge remote-controlled Panavision Loumacrane that looks like an enormous praying mantis. Most are motorized and some, like the Tulip, require delicate counterbalancing or else they may easily tip over. All are best handled by experienced operators for the smoothest and safest result. All cranes are very heavy objects and have considerable inertia, so that starting and stopping its motion must be done carefully. Balance is also of great concern. A crane must be counterbalanced for the weight of the people who are riding it. If you lower the crane platform to the ground and the director or DP steps off before the weights have been shifted appropriately, the boom will fly suddenly up into the air with very dangerous results to the camera and assistant cameraman. An experienced crane grip knows how to prevent these things from happening.

Your director will have a good idea as to when a crane is needed during shooting, so check with him for the number of days you should budget for this item and its crew.

Crane Driver

The *crane driver* who manages such large cranes as the Apollos and Titans made by Chapman is also an experienced craftsperson.

TRACKING SHOTS made with a crane must also be done smoothly and unobtrusively. Instead of a using a small dolly, you now have a huge truck which must be maneuvered with elegance and grace.

The crane driver is usually a Teamster and will who drive the crane both to location and during a shot. As a result, the crane driver appears under the Transportation Account. In some budgets, so does the crane. We have allowed $10,000 to cover the use of a crane and driver under Account 3200.

05: Company Grips

Company grips—or *hammers* as they are sometimes called—do a lot of the heavy carrying work on stage. By using wedges, braces, and sandbags they make sure that whatever platform on which the camera is mounted is stable and level. They erect and breakdown the parallels used for both camera and light placement. Outdoors they are also needed to focus the reflectors or *shiny boards* used to bounce sunlight into shadow areas or to assemble and bring out on oversized *high rollers* the huge *silks* or frames of white-fabric that shade actors and soften harsh sunlight. Just as extra electricians may be needed to handle extra lights for exterior night scenes, extra grips will often be needed for exterior day scenes. But above all, their art lies in shading the light cast by the electricians.

06: Rigging Crew

A *grip rigging crew* may be a timesaving shortcut on both stage work and locations. On a sound stage, special riggers may work the high grids—often 40 feet above the floor—or on narrow platforms around the set walls in order to hang *greens* or place lights. On locations, other riggers may build frames around exterior doors. The riggers then drape those doors and windows with black cloth so that *night interiors* may be filmed during the day.

It takes far less time to remove the black covering from windows than it does to install it, so shoot your night interiors before your day interiors. That way your rigging crew can black out the windows the day prior to filming, and your electricians can run the cables and sketch in the lighting. You will arrive at the location in the morning with just a little lighting to touch up. Shoot the interior night scenes, remove the black coverings, shoot the interior day scenes. Your pre-rig has paid for itself in shooting time.

30: Rentals—Grip Package

Most rental companies offer not only combined *grip and electric packages* but also the production vans also. If the package prices are broken out, the equipment is budgeted here and under the l*ighting account*, while the vehicles are in the *transportation accoun*t. While the differences are not as great as with lighting equipment, the grip package used on a sound stage may vary considerably from what is needed on location. Additionally, some studios require that you rent the grip and electric equipment used on their stages from their grip and electric departments.

Schedule so that there is as little overlap or situations when you use both packages in the same week and budget accordingly. As with the camera and sound packages, your grip package should be rented for no longer than the production time. You should not pay for prep or wrap on these items unless it is more than a day or two. If you spend a week pre-rigging a large set or location, allow additional rental.

It is useful to bargain for an all-in weekly rental for grip and electric packages. First, the UPM and department heads should bargain the rate down to the lowest possible price. The daily rate is used as the base, so that a weekly price ranges from an exorbitant *four-day week* to as little as a *one-half day week.* Your rental house should have most of what you need and not have to *sub* or rent a lot of items from others to fill out your package. Then offer your sales rep to pay the rental house an extra $50 or $100 per week to cover any incidental charges. A few extra *century stands* or *apple boxes* or *barndoors* for a day or two should be given as part of that extra overage. In this way either side won't have to track extra paperwork for the few add-ons here and there. Most rental houses don't need the hassle anyway, and neither does your company. The savings in time and clerical labor alone is worth the extra few dollars.

We are allowing $3,500 per week for the grip rental package. Low budget features with pared-down packages can usually get by with half that.

30: Rentals—Car Mounts

Car mounts are the small platform devices which attach to car doors, hood rear decks, roofs, to hold a camera and lights to photograph the people in the car while the car is moving. One of the simplest side-mount is called a *hostess tray* due to its resemblance drive-in serving trays.

Some key grips own a set of car mounts. It is possible to attach a side-mount to a car and let the actor drive it. The safest way, however, to do any running shots is with an *insert* or *camera car* that tows the picture vehicle directly or on a process trailer during filming. Budget the car mounts here and an insert car and its specialized driver under the Transportation Account.

Since they will be used briefly during the filming we estimate around $1,000.

30: Rentals—Remote Mounts

These are used when it is determined that you will need to watch some optical special effects to be added later. These *computer-controlled remote mounts* were used, for example, on *Independence Day* to match camera movements done with live actors and *blue screen* to the post-production shots of the miniature spaceship.

30: Rentals—Dolly Rental

While there are other brands such as Stindt and McCallister, most DP's on feature and television shows insist on using either Fisher or Chapman crab dollies. Since neither Fisher nor Chapman sells their equipment, your grip supplier must *sub* from them or you must rent directly from them or, outside Los Angeles, from a licensed representative. As with Panavision cameras (or any widely used brand name equipment), bear in mind that dolly suppliers will rent to anyone on a first-come, first-served basis. During the television production season, they may not have enough dollies when you need them for your show. As soon as you know what kind you want, call the supplier and reserve it for your production. Your DP will tell you which kinds and sizes of dollies are going to be used, and when.

40: Equipment Purchase

The Grip Department uses a lot of material. Battens, cloth, scrims, etc. Much of it can be recycled. We have allotted $30,000 for *The Conversation* for expendables and will probably use the entire amount.

85: Additional Expense—Condor

A *condor* is a motorized moveable platform on which you can place people, lighting equipment, cameras, and other objects which have to be raised high above the ground. They are easier to use, however are more expensive than *using parallels*. A large light can be placed on one—raised from 20 to 60 feet—to provide instant moonlight. As with many items in this category, some budget forms place these under the *transportation account*. Wherever they are budgeted, the transportation coordinator is usually responsible for them.

Account 3300

Lighting Department

PAGE NO.22

PRODUCTION NUMBER | PRODUCTION TITLE | DATE

3300	LIGHTING DEPARTMENT – 12 HR. DY.									
ACCT.		LOCAL/	DAYS/WEEKS					SUBTOTALS		
NO.	DESCRIPTION	On Loc.	PREP	SHOOT	WRAP	TOTAL	RATE	A	B	C
01	Gaffer	Local	3	8.2	1	12.2	1911	23,314		
	27.30 p. hr.	On Loc.								
03	Best Boy	Local	3	8.2	1	12.2	1780	21,692		
	25.40 p. hr.	On Loc.								
04	Generator Oper.	Local		8.2		8.2	1745	14,309		
	24.90 p. hr.	On Loc.								
05	Electricians x 2	Local	.6	8.2	.4	9.2	1645	28,294		
	23.50 p. hr.	On Loc.								
	Additional Hire	Local		30 dys			317	9,500		
		On Loc.								
		Local								
		On Loc.								
06	Rigging & Striking	Local								
	(See Also Acct 2300)	On Loc.								
		Local								
		On Loc.								
		Local								
		On Loc.								
30	Equipment Rentals									
	Generator (A.C./D.C. Power) 8.2 wks. x 1,590/wk.									13,041
	Equipment Package 8.2 wks. x 7,500/wk.									61,500
	Lamps, Arc Lights (D.C. Power)									
	Dimmers/Cables, Connectors									
	H.J.I. Lights (A.C. Power0									
	H.M.I. Bulb Time									
	Box Rental 8.2 wks. x 350/wk.									2,870
	Musco Lights 12,000/wk. (for your info).									
40	Equipment Purchases									
	Globes and Carbons ALLOW									20,000
	Fuses, Plugs, Tapes, Other Expendables ALLOW									12,500
	Generator Gas & Oil (see Acct. 4655)									
85	Additional Expense									
	Allow extra genny days: 15 dys. x 450/dy.									6,750
95	Miscellaneous									2,500
99	Loss, Damage, Repair									2,000
							SUBTOTALS	97,109		121,161
							TOTAL ACCT 3300	218,270		

A = Fringeable/Taxable
B = Non-Fringeable/Taxable
C = Non-Taxable

3300—LIGHTING DEPARTMENT

01: Chief Lighting Technician (Gaffer)

The *chief lighting technician*, an IATSE term, is the head electrician. Some chief lighting technicians also have cards in the camera union and are qualified DP's. The progression from chief lighting technician to DP may be a natural one, but less common than it is for camera operators.

For *The Conversation*, we will hire our chief lighting technician three weeks ahead of shooting so that he and the DP can scout the locations and discuss lighting plans. More time will be allotted if there are many sets or plans to film in more than one city. This will make our rental of electric equipment far more efficient and less expensive. The gaffer can also supervise the arrangement of shelving in the production van or electric truck, tailoring it to suit his exact needs. He will also have one week of wrap to supervise the return of the electric equipment.

02: Best Boy (or Assistant Chief Lighting Technician)

Assistant Chief Lighting Technician is the official IATSE title, but *best boy* is still the more commonly used term. Like the *second grip*, this person will, prior to filming, scout locations and help determine the equipment needed.

04: Generator Operator

Local 40 of the International Brotherhood of Electrical Workers (IBEW) represents union *generator operators* in Hollywood (sometimes referred to as *40-men.*) On studio lots, the power plants are operated by members of Local 40. When you shoot on a sound stage the cost of a standby generator operator is charged to you for the entire time that you require high amperage power for your lights. On location shows, a Local 40 person may be required to handle the *wet-cells* or batteries sometimes used with car mount lights.

[Note: This Local 40 is not affiliated with the IATSE except through a common association with the AFL/CIO, as are SAG, the Teamsters, and many other Hollywood labor organizations.] On local or distant location, the generator operator is a member of the teamsters union, usually the driver of the production van. Even on non-union productions the driver responsible for getting the generator to location will also function as its operator. If not, the best boy can handle it.

Even on a major union show, the current popularity of *HMI lights* and AC-power plants on location where amperage and cycles are critical to proper functioning, the best boy will help meter and monitor the generator output.

For *The Conversation* we need a generator operator for the days we are filming but not for prep or wrap.

05: Electricians

Electricians or lamp operators handle the lights. They run cables, plug in bulbs, aim lamps, temper the quality of light, etc. There should be at least two electricians besides the gaffer and best boy. A minimum crew for features one-one-two: i.e., one gaffer, one best boy and two lamp operators.

Local Hires

When you are on distant location where an IATSE local exists, you will have to hire IATSE local resident members. In the major production centers—Los Angeles, New York, Houston, San Francisco, Chicago—places where movies are made often, there will be a pool of experienced crew people for you to draw on. Common practice is to take your chief lighting technician, best boy, and rigging gaffer from Hollywood, and hire everyone else locally. Sometimes, when you find yourself in a distant location with no experienced crew in residence, you will bring in your own, or hire inexperienced local crewpersons for on-the-job training.

06: Rigging and Striking

Knowing the best time for *rigging and striking* can save a production time (which equals money) and money. On a major pre-light while the show is in production, a rigging gaffer working at some other location will consult with and report back to the DP on the set.

We will hire a pre-rig crew to go to the next location on *The Conversation*, run the cables and basically set the lighting equipment in place. This will save us time during shooting. This crew consists of a rigging gaffer and three or four extra crew, depending on the amount of work. There is a little extra money in there in case we need an extra person or two to help handle heavier equipment. We have also left in that account a little extra money in case we run late on a few days and we need to send out a crew the next day to strike the location lights, rather than ask our shooting crew, tired at the end of a long day, to start hauling lights around. Go over your schedule carefully to determine where a rigging or striking crew would be needed. Grips will also be part of this crew. This cost is covered under Account 2355.

30: Equipment Rentals—Generator Rental

If your generator is not mounted behind the tractor that tows your production van trailer (and part of that package price), you could budget an individual *tow plant* (on its own trailer and *towed* by some production vehicle) here. Or, you may need extra generators in addition to your shooting crew's power plant.

For building sets on location, such as *Harry's Apartment* or the *Warehouse*, the location probably can not supply enough power to run all the machine tools. When the pre-rig crew arrives to light the set they will need even more power to rig all the lights and test them. On large night exteriors, it may save many hours to have added generators at various locations over the time spent and the amperage lost in long cable runs from the main plant. So we must rent extra generators to supply our needs.

30: Equipment Rentals—Equipment Package
Studios renting stages will also want you to use their lights as part of an *equipment package.* Many studio departments can also arrange for grip and electric rigging crews. However, many DPs will want to use *daylight-balanced HMI's* (i.e., with a color temperature that matches sunlight) both on location and in the studio, and will want to use the same lampheads throughout. Since HMI lights have an individual ballast mechanism which helps regulate power flow and color temperature, this is not merely an aesthetic preference. Be as aware of all these requirements as you fine tune your budget.

30: Equipment Rentals—HMI Bulbtime
When HMI lights were first introduced, they were quite expensive to manufacture and to rent. Additionally, because their small, compact heads used a costly quartz-envelope bulb that was much more fragile and shorter lived than tungsten globes, renters were changed not only for burned out bulbs but for any usage based on a metered burn time. Nowadays with HMIs as the prevailing method of lighting, most rental companies factor burn time into their rental price and eliminate the trouble of metering use.

30: Equipment Rentals—Extra Night Package
Night exteriors requires extra people and equipment. If you are somewhere for a period of time with or without pre-rigging, you may want to construct a separate *extra night package* for that night work.

30: Equipment Rentals—Electric Box Rental
The gaffer or best boy will need tools from light meters to frames for holding gels that are easier and cheaper to rent from them. This is paid in the form of an *electric box rental.*

30: Equipment Rentals—Musco Lights
Musco Lights are a particular brand name describing a self-contained unit that works as a light bank, truck, generator, and Condor rolled into one piece of equipment. While they are more expensive, such devices consisting of a truck with a power plant and one or

more powerful lights on a scissors and boom-type lift, can be a timesaving alternative condors or platforms and running cable or extra *tow plants*.

40: Purchases—Burnouts

As with HMI burn time many renters now factor burned-out globes into their rental price.

40: Purchases—Expendables

Expendables are all the *use-one-time-only* items, excluding light bulbs. They range from to clothes pins, rolls of transparent gel (cut up and to place over windows or lamps to control color temperature and/orintensity). Oh, and don't forget the all-important *gaffer's tape.*

Account 3400

Wardrobe Department

PAGE NO. 23

PRODUCTION NUMBER	PRODUCTION TITLE	DATE

3400 WARDROBE DEPARTMENT – 12 HR. DY.

ACCT NO.	DESCRIPTION	LOCAL/ ON LOC.	DAYS/WEEKS PREP	SHOOT	WRAP	TOTAL	RATE	SUBTOTALS A	B	C
01	Costume Designer	Local	6	6		12	3500	42,000		
	*1492.63 /wk.	On Loc.								
02	Asst. to Costume	Local								
	Designer	On Loc.								
		Local								
		On Loc.								
05	Women's Costumer	Local	3	8.2	2	13.2	1833	24,193		
	22.91 p.hr.	On Loc.								
06	Women's Costumer	Local		8.2		8.2	1681	13,783		
	–Set 22.01 p.hr.	On Loc.								
		Local								
		On Loc.								
		Local								
		On Loc.								
07	Men's Costumer	Local	6	8.2	2	16.2	1833	29,695		
	22.91 p.hr.	On Loc.								
08	Men's Costumer–	Local	1	8.2	.4	9.6	1681	16,136		
	Set 21.01 p.hr.	On Loc.								
09	Tailor	Local								
		On Loc.								
10	Seamstress	Local								
		On Loc.								
		Local								
		On Loc.								
	Additional Hire	Local								
		On Loc.								
30	Rentals (See Wardrobe Detail Page 23A)									21,200
	Box Rental Women's Costumer 13. wks. x 150/wk.									1,950
	Men's Costumer 14.2 wks. x 150/wk.									2,130
40	Purchases (See Wardrobe Detail Page 23A)									28,100
	Manufacturing (MOS** Meredith's Yellow Outfit)									1,000
	Equipment									
	Alteration Material (10% of purchases or rentals)									5,000
	Ageing & Dyeing									500
45	Dry Cleaning and Laundry (100/shoot dy. x 42 dys., based upon									
	$6 per shirt or per pants)									4,200
85	Additional Expense									
95	Miscellaneous (10% unknown or changes on Accts. 3430-3445)									10,000
99	Loss, Damage, Repair (approx. 2 % of purchases & rentals)									
							SUBTOTALS	125,807		74,080
							TOTAL ACCT 3400	199,887		

A - Fringeable/Taxes *Scale 5 day week (average salary for Costume Designer – $3,500)
B - Non-Fringeable/Taxable
C - Non-Taxable **MOS (Made to Order)

PAGE NO. 23A

PRODUCTION NUMBER | PRODUCTION TITLE | DATE

ACCTS 3430 & 3440 WARDROBE–DETAIL

CAST NO.	SCENE NAME/NO. CHARACTER	QTY	ITEM DESCRIPTION	RENTALS TIME	RENTALS RATE	RENTALS AMOUNT	PURCHASES AMOUNT	✔
A*	General Trailer Stock		Rental Deal		5,000	5,000		
A	Bus Drivers	5	to fit 3		150/per	750		
A	Uniformed Guards	15	to fit 10		150/per	2,250		
A	Hostess/Display Girls	20	to fit 15		150/per	3,000		
A	Bartenders/ Waitresses	8	to fit 6		100/per	800		
A	Janitor	1			100/per	100		
A	Ushers at Concert	12	to fit 8		150/per	1,800		
A	Municipal Band (Band Shell)	50			150/per	7,500		
1	Harry (Page 23B)	7	incl. 2 doubles		750/per		5,250	
2	Ann (Page 23D)	5	incl. 1 double		750/per		3,750	
3	Mark (Page 23C)	5	incl. 1 double		750/per		3,750	
5	Stanley (Page 23E)	4			300/per		1,200	
6	Paul	2			500/per		1,000	
9	Meredith	3			400/per		1,200	
12	Ron Keller	2			250/per		500	
14	Bob	2			250/per		500	
7	Martin	2			750/per		1,500	
20	Receptionist	3			400/per		1,200	
10	Millard	1			500/per		500	
8	William Moran	1			500/per		500	
17	Lurleen	1			500/per		500	
39	McNaught	1			750/per		750	
4	Mr. C	3	triples		750/per		2,250	
	15 Day Players	1	change each		250/per		3,750	
					SUBTOTALS	21,200	28,100	
			TOTAL DETAIL ACCTS 3430 & 3440			49,300		

A - Fringeable/Taxes
B - Non-Fringeable/Taxable
C - Non-Taxable

✔ - Recoupable (*A = Atmosphere)

PAGE NO. 23B

CHARACTER: HARRY CAUL

CHANGE #	SCENE #	D/N	T/X	SET	ACTION	CLOTHES
1	7-30 34-39 40-44 45	D1 N1	X&I. I. I. I.	Union Square Van Bus, Market, Laundry Apt. Bus	Watch Ann & Mark Neighbors, complaints Going to Amy's	
	46-47 48		X&I. I.	Amy's Bldg. Harry's Apt.	Sees Amy Plays Sax	
2	49 50-91 92 93-95	D2	X. X&I. I. X.	Harry's Apt. Bldg. Warehouse Phone Booth Law Office	Leaves for work Works on tapes Calls "Director" Harry is landlord; sees Tony	DBL.
	96-102 104-108 109-142 143-159		X&I. X&I. I. X.	Financial Bldg. Amy's Apt. Bldg. Convention Streets	Walking, no m.c. Amy's room is empty Convention Car Chase	
	160-177 178-187		I. I.	Warehouse Warehouse	Party Meredith & Harry	
3 Sunday	188-194 195-229 230-231 232-270	D3	X. X. I. X&I.	Golden Gate Park Financial District Church Motel	Meets Stanley Gives Tapes to Mr. C Confession Rents room, hears murder	
4	271-281 282-332 333-353 354	D4 N4	X&I. I&X. I. I.	Financial Bldg. Bus, streets, park Warehouse Motel Room	Wants to see Mr. C Harry follows Ann Listens to tapes again Blood	DBL.
5	367-376 377-397	D5	I. I.	Financial Bldg. Harry's Apt. Bldg.	See's Ann & Mark Call from Mark, paranoid	

PAGE NO. 23C

CHARACTER: MARK

CHANGE #	SCENE #	D/N	T/X	SET	ACTION	CLOTHES
1	9	D1	X.	Union Square	Walk & talk	
2	102	D2	I.	Financial Bldg.	Harry sees him at work	
3	356-363	D3	I.	Motel Room	Kill Mr. C	DBL.
4	371-376	D5	I.	Financial Bldg.	At work	

PAGE NO. 23D

CHARACTER: ANN

CHANGE #	SCENE #	D/N	T/X	SET	ACTION	CLOTHES
1	9	D1	X.	Union Square	Walk & talk	
2	276-281 282-331	D4	I&X. I&X.	Financial Bldg. Bus, Street, Park	Harry sees Ann Harry follows Ann	
3	356-363	D3	I.	Motel Room	Kill Mr. C	DBL.
4	371-376	D5	I.	Financial Bldg.	In mourning	

PAGE NO. 23E

CHARACTER: STANLEY

CHANGE #	SCENE #	D/N	T/X	SET	ACTION	CLOTHES
1	12,27	D1	I.	Van	Recording	
2	51-67	D2	I.	Harry's Warehouse	Talk about convention	
3	128-142 143-159 160-173	N2	I. X. I.	Convention Streets Warehouse	Working for Moran Car Chase Party	Jacket with Moran Emblem
4	188-194	D3	X.	Golden Gate Park	Harry tells Stan to stay away	Jacket & tie

3400—WARDROBE DEPARTMENT

WHETHER THE PICTURE IS PERIOD OR CONTEMPORARY, the first responsibility of the wardrobe department is to know what the clothes should look like—sometimes necessitating doing a great deal of research . The director, production designer, and director of photography may all want input with regard to style and color, but they will all rely on the *wardrobe department* for authenticity. In the studio system, wardrobe departments had not only substantial inventories of clothes but large libraries of references books on every period in history available for their designers to use.

01: Costume Designer

On smaller productions, the *costume designer* may be less of an actual *designer* than a style consultant and buyer. Just as the production designer may not actually build sets and furnishings from scratch, designer refers to conceptualizing the look as much as to creating tangible items. Except on bigger budget shows, uniforms or period clothes are rented rather than made. Contemporary clothes that look good on camera can be purchased for little more than a few week's rental price. You can pay a wardrobe allowance to an actor or an extra to *wear their own*, but be wary of loss or damage to clothing that works in several scenes and should be doubled. When you are dealing with clothes that cannot be purchased *off-the-rack*, a designer is very necessary. Even when a designer is creating new clothes for a period or futuristic setting, she is likely begin with an existing piece of clothing and modify it rather than having it made from bolts of cloth and detailed patterns.

The Conversation requires a great deal of attention to the costumes. HARRY CAUL'S rumpled look is an essential part of his personality. The common quality of the suits worn by the other cast members—e.g., the upscale clothing worn by the people in *MR. C'S* office—all are very large pieces of the intricate personality jigsaw we are building. And each must not attract undue attention as a designed piece.

The costume designer will need six weeks of prep, but does not have to stay for the entire filming. Six weeks of production will be enough time to make sure that the major characters are all wardrobed properly. Scale is $1,406.95 per week. The range for high-cost pictures as $3,500 to $6,000 per week. For lower budgets $2,500 or so is usually enough.

05: Women's Costumer

The *women's costumer* is in charge of all the clothes for the female members of the cast. On many contemporary shows, the costumer will be hired as the head of the department. If there are more females in the show than males, then the head of the costumer's department will be the women's costumer (and vice versa.)

06: Women's Costumer—Set or Assistant Costumer

Wardrobe is too large a job for one person to handle,. There will always be days when there are lots of actors who need to be dressed and ready at the same time. It is unwise to hold up the shooting crew by making them wait for everyone to be wardrobed for the first shot. That is why an assistant is necessary, and on very heavy days extra help is required.

07: Men's Costumer

Our *men's costumer* has his work cut out for him on this show. He will have six weeks of prep during which time he must work closely with the casting people. As soon as a role is set, he must contact the actor's agent and get the actor's measurements. If necessary he will meet with the actor and take measurements himself. He will then obtain two or three selections for each wardrobe change, narrowing down the choices in consultation with the director. All this is under the supervision of the costume designer.

The main costumer will stay on set during the shooting, unless an emergency arises. Then he will always be sure to leave his assistant well within shouting distance of the assistant director.

At the end of the show he will need two weeks to return the wardrobe to the rental houses and put the purchases in storage.

10: Seamstress
Sometimes things don't fit costumers do not have the time to adjust them. Hiring a seamstress for a short time to help out can save valuable shooting time. Since we have so many suits in *The Conversation* we will allow four weeks.

30: Rentals
Most major cities which support filming have rental houses (*See Account 3430, budget page 23.*) Since *The Conversation* is a contemporary film and the majority of the wardrobe consists of business suits for males we should be able to make some good rental deals.

40: Purchases—Manufacturing
Most clothes used in contemporary features and television shows are purchased. After a period in which they are stored for possible retakes or added scenes, they are sold, given away, or discarded. Many actors have clauses in their contracts either giving them or letting them purchase the wardrobe if they so desire.

The wardrobe department also spends a few dollars at the local Army-Navy supply buying a large number of cheap ponchos or raincoats. In case of a sudden rainstorm these can be handed to those cast (and crew) who left theirs at home. This is less expensive than waiting around on the set while everyone runs down to the corner raincoat store.

45: Dry Cleaning and Laundry
Whatever it may say on the manufacturer's label, most wardrobe is dry cleaned overnight. This can be hard on the fabric after several weeks and is another reason for having extra sets of key costumes. There are companies in Los Angeles and New York which cater strictly to the movie business. They will take in your actor's wardrobe at 10:00 PM and turn it back out by 5:00 AM.

95: Miscellaneous—Wardrobe Department Space
Whether on a studio lot or location, most costumers operate out of a wardrobe truck or trailer that is budgeted in transportation. On large shows there may not be room in the trailer for all the costumes at once, and an office or warehouse may be needed.

95: Miscellaneous—Polaroid Camera/Film
A *Polaroid camera and film* are essential tools for wardrobe. If during a scene one of your actors spills a bowl of soup on his lap and you need match the shot four days later, that Polaroid photograph will enable you to recreate the exact size and shape of the spill. Proper continuity demands it.

95: Miscellaneous—Costumer's Box Rental
Gaffers have light meters, Costumers have scissors and sewing machines. The cost of renting those items goes in this account.

— Notes —

Account 3500

Makeup and Hairdressing Department

PAGE NO. 24

PRODUCTION NUMBER	PRODUCTION TITLE	DATE

3500 MAKEUP AND HAIRDRESSING DEPARTMENT – 13 HR. DY.

ACCT NO.	DESCRIPTION	LOCAL/ ON LOC.	PREP	SHOOT	WRAP	TOTAL	RATE	A	B	C
01	1st Makeup Artist	Local	.4	8.2	.2	8.8	2663	23,436		
	33.29 p.hr.	On Loc.								
02	2nd Makeup Artist	Local		8.2	.2	8.4	2410	20,241		
	30.12 p.hr.	On Loc.								
03	Makeup Assistant	Local								
		On Loc.								
		Local								
		On Loc.								
05	Body Makeup	Local								
		On Loc.								
		Local								
		On Loc.								
	Additional Hire	Local								
		On Loc.								
		Local								
		On Loc.								
10	1st Hairstylist	Local	.4	8.2	.2	8.8	2387	21,007		
	29.84 p.hr.	On Loc.								
11	2nd Hairstylist	Local		8.2	.2	8.4	2096	17,606		
	26.20 p.hr.	On Loc.								
12	Hairstylist Asst.	Local								
		On Loc.								
	Additional Hire	Local								
		On Loc.								
		Local								
		On Loc.								
30	Rentals									
	Equipment, Tables, Chairs, Mirrors, Wigs				ALLOW					5,000
	Box Rentals: Makeup/Hair 250 ea./wk. x 8.2						ALLOW			4,100
	Asst. Makeup/Hair 250 ea./wk. x 8.2						ALLOW			4,100
40	Purchases									
	Lights, Bulbs									
	Makeup Supplies									
	Hairdressing Supplies						ALLOW			5,000
	Wigs and Hairpieces						ALLOW			3,500
85	Additional Expense						ALLOW			500
95	Miscellaneous						ALLOW			500
99	Loss, Damage, Repair									
							SUBTOTALS	82,290		22,700
							TOTAL ACCT 3500	104,990		

A - Fringeable/Taxes
B - Non-Fringeable/Taxable
C - Non-Taxable

PAGE NO. 24A

PRODUCTION NUMBER | PRODUCTION TITLE | DATE

ACCTS 3530 & 3540 MAKEUP AND HAIRDRESSING—DETAIL

CAST	SCENE NAME/NO.	ITEM		RENTALS			PURCHASES	
NO.	CHARACTER	QTY	DESCRIPTION	TIME	RATE	AMOUNT	AMOUNT	✔
19	Tony		INT. LAWYER'S OFFICE Sc. 94, 95 - TEARS					
					SUBTOTALS			
	TOTAL DETAIL ACCTS 3530 & 3540							

A - Fringeable/Taxes
B - Non-Fringeable/Taxable
C - Non-Taxable

3 - Recoupable

3500—MAKEUP AND HAIRDRESSING DEPARTMENT

MAKEUP IS A KEY ELEMENT IN PRODUCTION for many reasons. Usually it is the first thing that happens to a performer upon arriving for work, so generally it can set the tone for the day. It affects the way a performer looks on screen.

The time that you schedule and budget for ordinary makeup and hairstyling will depend on the individual actor's complexion and hair type, and how that relates to the desired look of the character.

01: First Makeup Artist (or Department Head)

The primarily responsibility of the *makeup artist* is to make the actor look natural under the particular lighting conditions of the scene. Motion picture film has a great latitude—it can accommodate a considerable range of color tones and exposures. Nonetheless, very light or very dark complexions present problems to the DP, as they may be either too light or too dark compared to the mid-range tone for which he is exposing.

The *makeup artist* makes as much of an adjustment as is necessary but no more. And if makeup alone cannot lighten or darken sufficiently, the DP will have to complete the process by using *key lights* on individual actors that are brighter (for dark subjects) or filtered down (for light subjects), both of which are more time-consuming and complicated than a few extra minutes in the makeup chair. Makeup artists and hairstylists can either correct nature's imperfections from scars to receding hairlines or create them. The former removes distracting features which an actor may have but a character does not need; the latter is the reverse.

Makeup artists do not need much prep time unless there are specific needs. On *The Conversation* nothing seems to be unusual, so we give our makeup artists two days to arrange the makeup trailer the way they wish to work, and to purchase supplies.

02: 2nd (or Key) Makeup Artist

If you have more than one actor in the opening scene you will need at least two *makeup artists* to prepare them. Trying to save money by cutting down on the number of makeup artists or hairstylists is extremely inefficient when there are large numbers of actors to get ready for a scene. For *The Conversation* we will carry an extra makeup artist for the length of the show.

05: Body Makeup

When anyone appears in the picture with bare torso, legs, or anything in-between, you will probably hire a body makeup specialist who can makeup large areas of skin in a very short period of time. That person will usually be of the same gender of the person whose skin is being covered. Not much skin appears in *The Conversation* so no body makeup artist will be necessary.

10: First (or Head) Hairstylist

The same comments apply to hair styling as applied to makeup with one exception: if you have a one-person show, you might consider having the same person do both makeup and hairstyling. Usually this is not a good idea. The two disciplines are quite different and require different skills.

30: Rentals

Makeup artists and hairstylists also have scissors (the former to cut up makeup sponges) and mirrors and blow dryers and so on. They will rent them to you as part of their box rental. If they don't have wigs, hairpieces, mustaches, etc., to give the actor a character look or for the stunt persons who double the main actors, these can be rented.

40: Purchases

This covers everything from stage blood to shampoo. As with the costumers, this department normally has its own room or trailers and the incidentals used to stock it from light bulbs to Kleenex are included here.

Other Charges—Makeup Tests
Except for adding the simplest item of makeup, such as a beauty mark, it is advisable to do a film test to see how it looks projected on the screen. Obviously, you must allow much more time and money for complex shows with appliances or prosthetics.

85: Additional Expense—Polaroid Camera/Film
It is absolutely essential to take Polaroid shots of all special makeup and hairstyles for matching purposes. This is especially true when there are such things as burns, scars, and other specialty items. These must be matched exactly from one day to the next.

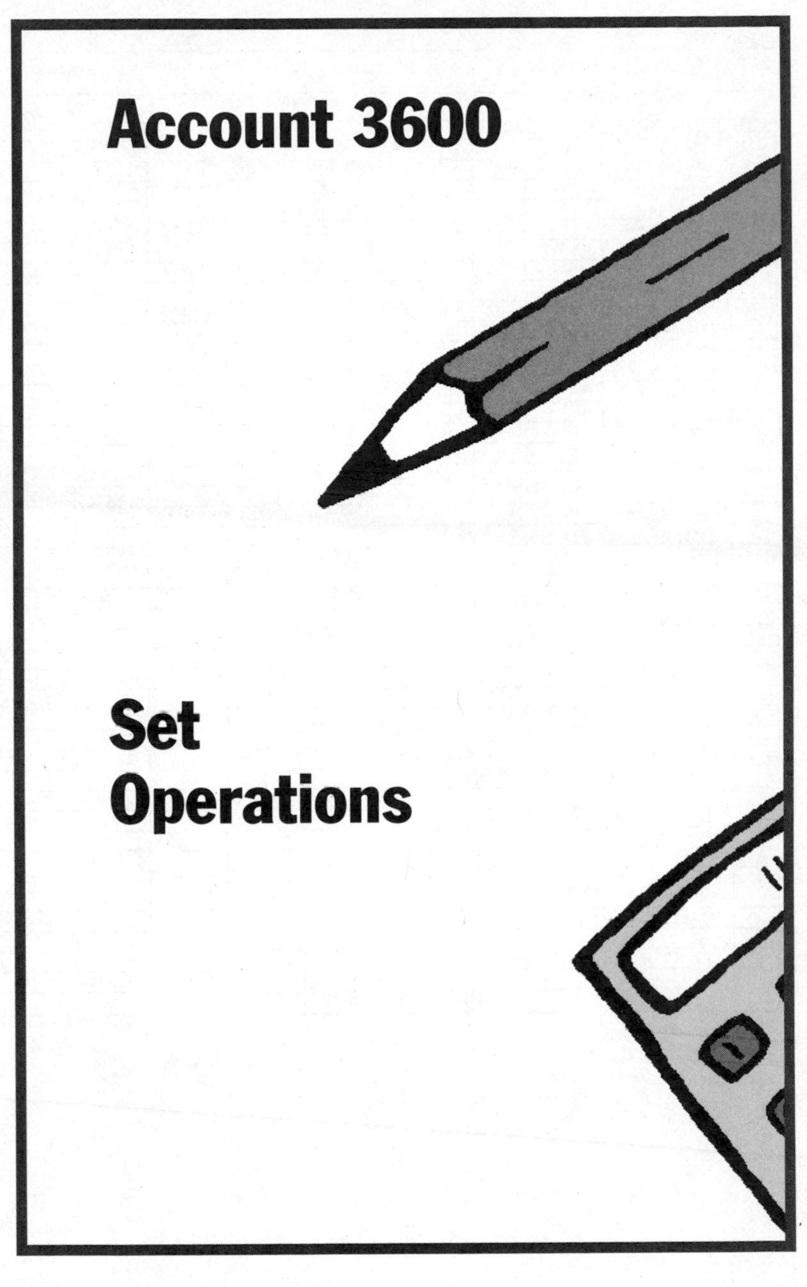

Account 3600

Set Operations

PAGE NO. 25

PRODUCTION NUMBER	PRODUCTION TITLE	DATE

3600 SET OPERATIONS – 13 HR. DY.

ACCT NO.	DESCRIPTION	LOCAL/ ON LOC.	PREP	SHOOT	WRAP	TOTAL	RATE	A	B	C
01	Caterer/Driver	Local		8.2		8.2	1663	13,638		
	20.79 p.hr.	On Loc.								
02	Caterer/Asst. x 2	Local		8.2		8.2	1000	16,400		
	200/dy.	On Loc.								
04	Craft Service	Local	.4	8.2	.2	9	1727	15,890		
	21.59 p.hr.	On Loc.								
05	First Aid/Nurse	Local	5	8.2	.2	13.4	1742	23,000		
	21.78 p.hr.	On Loc.								
06	Doctor	Local								
		On Loc.								
07	Police x 4	Local		8.2		8.2	1664		54,576	
		On Loc.								
08	Firemen	Local		8.2		8.2	2310		18,942	
		On Loc.								
09	Guards/ Watchmen	Local		8		8	490		7,840	
	x 2	On Loc.								
	Addt'l. Craft Service	Local		1.4		1.4	1727	2,418		
	21.59 p.hr	On Loc.								
		Local								
		On Loc.								
		Local								
		On Loc.								
10	Police Vehicle Expense									
11	Ambulance									
15	Fire Equipment									
20	Catering Costs (No. People x No. Days x Rate)									
	Coffee, Rolls, etc.									
	Breakfast 41 dys. x 100 m/dys. x $14/person									57,400
	Lunch Extras: 1,459 m/days x $14/person									20,426
	Dinner 2nd Meals:						ALLOW			20,000
	Soft Drinks, etc. 41 dys. x $150/day									6,150
	Tables, Chairs									
	Taxes									
	Caterer-Mileage (Travel & Living See Location Acct 4000)									
	Hotel & Restaurants Gratuities									
	Teamsters Meals						ALLOW			15,000
	SUBTOTALS THIS PAGE							71,346	81,358	118,976
	CONTINUED ON NEXT PAGE							271,680		

A - Fringeable/Taxes
B - Non-Fringeable/Taxable
C - Non-Taxable

PAGE NO. 26

PRODUCTION NUMBER	PRODUCTION TITLE	DATE

3600 SET OPERATIONS–(CONT'D)

ACCT NO.	DESCRIPTION	SUBTOTALS A	SUBTOTALS B	SUBTOTALS C
25	Courtesy Payments (see Acct. 3717)			
26	Weather Service			
27	Portable Toilets (Weeks x Rate)			
29	Transportation Fee			
30	Rentals (Weeks x Rate)			2,050
	Craftservice Box 8.2 wks. x 250/wk.			2,050
	Dolly, Dolly Track, Crane (See Grip Dept. Acct 3200)			
	Grip Package & Grip Box (See Grip Detp. Acct 3200)			
	Camera Platform, Planes, Helicopters, Trains, Boats, etc.			
	(see Special Equipment Acct 3000)			
	Paint Box (See Set Dressing Dept. Acct 2400)			
	Greens (See Set Dressing Dept. Acct 2400)			
	1st Aid Equipment Rental 13.4 wks. x 75/wk.			1,005
40	Purchases (Weeks x Rate)			
	Craftservice 8.2 wks. x 2,500/wk.			20,500
	Greens (See Set Dressing Acct 2400)			
	Paint (See Set Dressing Acct 2400)			
85	Additional Expenses ALLOW			2,500
95	Miscellaneous			
99	Loss, Damage, Repair			
	SUBTOTALS FROM PREVIOUS PAGE	71,346	81,358	118,976
	SUBTOTALS THIS PAGE			28,105
	TOTAL ACCT 3600	299,785		

A - Fringeable/Taxes
B - Non-Fringeable/Taxable
C - Non-Taxable

3600—SET OPERATIONS

ON MANY BUDGETS FORMS, SET OPERATIONS REFERS TO GRIPS and *laborers*. The categories below are included with *location expenses*. Having a separate account permits you to isolate the quantifiable costs (e.g., meals, police work hours) from the indirectly related costs of site rentals, etc., in Account 3700. There is some overlap between the two.

01: Caterer/Driver
It is a union (e.g., DGA/SAG/IATSE) requirement and accepted industry practice that hot meals must be provided on location—local or distant. On many shows your caterer is a Teamster. In any case, while similar to catering weddings or parties, motion picture catering is best done by specialists who are trained to drive to and from location, cook wholesome food in good variety for all the production personnel, and—this is critical—be ready on time. Many caterers have trucks that are mobile kitchens. They arrive for breakfast or a light first meal then cook lunch or the second meal on site. There are also many motion picture caterers who prepare both meals off site and bring them to the set in chafing dishes. Caterers usually charge per meal. Although this method may be less expensive, it requires two round trips and is less flexible. If you shoot at a studio or other facility which has a commissary or restaurant on site, you are not required to cater simply to break for lunch. This means the crew pays for its own meals. Industry practice allows that get-your-own lunch breaks are one hour long. Catered lunches can be cut down to one-half hour to 42 minutes. This ends up being a choice between giving up a certain amount of control over the meal period, breaking up the work flow for a longer period, and extending the production day. Many companies feel it is less expensive all around to provide the catered meals.

The caterer usually comes with at least one helper. On union pictures the rates of cook/driver and helpers are Teamster rates.

On *The Conversation* we will cater every day since we are spending almost every day on location and it will save time.

04: Craft Service

The position of *craft service* is covered on union films by the set laborers union (Local 727 in Los Angeles and Local 52 in New York.) The *craft service* person or set laborer is the ultimate *swing person*, who should be able to work with any other department. In practice, the craft service person prepares the coffee, stocks the cold drinks and snacks which are present on most sets, and does occasional cleanup work on spills, footprints in the sand, etc. On stage shoots there are additional esoteric tasks ranging from opening and closing stage door to answering the house phone.

A few studios ask that the crew make contributions to offset the cost of drinks and snacks; most productions don't. While it may not sound like much, a large crew on a hot day can easily consume several hundred dollars worth of soft drinks alone and bottled water. Keep that in mind when you budget that in catering costs below.

05: First Aid/Nurse

While it is not absolutely required, even in hazardous situations, industry practice had determined that a medically-trained person on the set is an economic and humanistic necessity. When a small first aid emergency arises it can be treated in the spot rather than having to transport the crewperson to the nearest emergency room—losing time and money. It makes sense in every other way also because as a conscientious employer you must care for your crew properly. Furthermore when an accident does occur a qualified first aid person should fill out all the Worker's Compensation forms and file your OSHA requirements.

07: Police

Whenever you are filming on public property, your filming permit will probably require that a member of the local Police Department be with you to keep the local populace from wreaking havoc on you and vice versa. Many cities—even New York City—charge you nothing for their police officers who stay with you on location but incorporate the cost into their permit fees. For running shots and a lot of traffic control, you should budget for motorcycle officers; their rate is the same, but they are paid a rental on their cycles.

In Los Angeles you must hire off-duty or retired police officers. The rules in the many small municipalities in the Los Angeles area vary. Your location manager and/or one of the services that specializes in securing permits and hiring police and fire officers can inform you about rules and rates.

08: Firefighters/Fire Safety Officer

Any time you are filming in a location to which the public has access or whenever there is any sort of combustible material being filmed, be it just a lighted fireplace or candles on a dinner table, you may also be legally required to have a *firefighter* or *fire safety officer* (FSO) with you. In the Los Angeles area, many FSOs are retired firefighters and, unlike police, their rate is lower.

We will have one for the entire filming of *The Conversation*.

09: Guards/Watchmen

Sound stages may be hot locked or secured and guarded by the studio security force (*guards/watchmen*) until an authorized person calls for it to be opened. The risk on locations varies depending on type of site and the cost of the set dressing, etc. involved. Even a cheap but unusual key item can become a costly headache if it somehow walks away.

We are allowing eight weeks at $98.00 per day times possibly two people, for a total of $16,000.

Most union contracts require that cars for the crew and cast be parked in a guarded lot. If you are on a major studio lot there is no problem. If you are on location, as we will be on *The Conversation*, the company must provide the guards. There are companies which provide parking guards, or you can hire your own.

Additional Hire

On days with a lot of actors or extras, an additional craft service person may be helpful.

On *The Conversation* we allowed 1.4 weeks.

20: Catering Costs

Detail the cost of meals here.

Teamsters Meals

Because they start earlier and finish later than the rest of the crew, there should be an allowance for teamster breakfasts and dinners. The Teamsters will usually purchase these meals at a local restaurant.

Account 3700

Local Site Rental

PAGE NO. 27

PRODUCTION NUMBER	PRODUCTION TITLE	DATE

3700 LOCAL SITE RENTAL EXPENSE

ACCT NO.	DESCRIPTION		SUBTOTALS A	B	C
01	Site Contact/Broker				
	Location Manager (See Acct 2000)				
03	Site Rental (See Detail Page 27A)				365,500
04	Survey Costs — Scouting	ALLOW			10,000
	Mileage				
	Gas/Oil				
08	Gratuities	ALLOW			2,500
09	Meals				
17	Courtesy Payments (See also Accts 6204 and 3625)	ALLOW			5,000
25	Permits, Fees, etc. (See Detail Page 27A)				1,000
27	Parking (Crew and Equipment) Local: 37 dys. x 1,000/dy.				37,000
	Extra Local: 15 dys. x 400/dy.				6,000
	Police, Fire Safety Officers, etc. (See Set Operations Acct 3600)				
32	Messenger Service				
35	Janitorial ALLOW 41 dys. x 50/dy.				2,050
	Additional Hire	ALLOW			2,500
85	Additional Expenses	ALLOW			2,500
95	Miscellaneous	ALLOW			5,000
99	Loss, Damage, Repair				
		SUBTOTALS			439,050
		TOTAL ACCT 3700	439,050		

A - Fringeable/Taxes
B - Non-Fringeable/Taxable
C - Non-Taxable

PAGE NO. 27A

PRODUCTION NUMBER | PRODUCTION TITLE | DATE

3703 LOCAL SITE RENTAL—DETAIL												
SET NO.	SCENE NAME/NO.	PREP			SHOOT			STRIKE			PERMITS, FEES	TOTALS
		TIME	RATE	AMT.	TIME	RATE	AMT.	TIME	RATE	AMT.		
DAY 1 1	EXT. FIN. DIST. Scn. 195-198	1 dy.	2000	2000	1/2 dy.	4000	4000	1/2 dy.				6,000
2	EXT. Phone Booth Scn. 226-229	1 dy.	500	500	1 dy.	500	500					1,000
3	EXT. Golden GT. PK. Scn. 188-194	1 dy.	1500	1500	1/2 dy.	1500	1500	1/2 dy.	500	500		3,500
DAY 2 4	EXT. ST. ELEC. BUS/ Neighborhd Scn. 34, 36, 37	1 dy.	2000	2000	1/2 dy.	3000	3000	1/2 dy.	500	500		5,500
5	INT. ELECT. BUS Scn. 35	1 dy.			1/4 dy.			1/4 dy.				
6	INT. MARKET Scn. 38	1 dy.	500	500	1/4 dy.	1500	1500	1/4 dy.	500	500		2,500
DAY 3 7	EXT. STREET (burning car) Scn. 365	1 dy.	500	500	1/2 dy.	2000	2000	1/2 dy.	1000	1000		3,500
8	INT./EXT. ELECT. BUS & STREET Scn. 45	1 dy.	1500	1500	1/2 dy.	1500	1500	1/2 dy.	500	500		3,500
DAY 4 1	EXT. FIN. DIST. Scn. 96, 97	1/4 dy.	2000	500	1/2 dy.	4000	4000	1/2 dy.	500	500		5,000
1	EXT. FIN. PLAZA Scn. 271, 272	1/2 dy.	500	500	1/2 dy.	1000	1000	1/2 dy.				1,500
9	EXT. DIRECTOR BLDG (bus 1&2)	1/2 dy.	1500	750	1/2 dy.	4000	4000	1/2 dy.	2000	2000		6,750
DAY 5 &6	EXT. UNION SQ. Scn. 1-9	1 dy.	2000	2000	1 dy.	4000	4000	1 dy.	500	500		6,500
10	Scn. 58, 62, 64, 66, 68, 71, 87, 107	1 dy.	1000	1000	1 dy.	4000	4000	1 dy.	1000	1000		6,000
DAY 7 10	EXT. UNION SQ. Scn. 19-22, 81, 28, 33, 182, 185, 222	1 dy.	1750	1750	1 dy.	4000	4000					5,750
DAY 8 &9 11	EXT. EIFFEL TOWER ROOF Scn. 10.11, 25, 26, 17.31	1 dy.	1000	1000	1/2 dy.	3000	3000	1/2 dy.	500	500		4,500
12	EXT. TOP of BLDG. Window & SO. Scn. 18, 23, 24, 103, 32	1 dy.	1500	1500	1 dy.	3000	3000	1/2 dy.	1500	1500		6,000
	SUBTOTALS	17,500			41,000			9,000				67,500
								TOTAL DETAIL ACCT 3703				

A - Fringeable/Taxes
B - Non-Fringeable/Taxable
C - Non-Taxable

PAGE NO. 27AA

PRODUCTION NUMBER	PRODUCTION TITLE	DATE

3703 LOCAL SITE RENTAL—DETAIL

SET NO.	SCENE NAME/NO.	PREP TIME	PREP RATE	PREP AMT.	SHOOT TIME	SHOOT RATE	SHOOT AMT.	STRIKE TIME	STRIKE RATE	STRIKE AMT.	PERMITS, FEES	TOTALS
DAY 1 1	EXT. FIN. DIST. Scn. 195-198	1 dy.	2000	2000	_dy.	4000	4000					
	SUBTOTALS											
								TOTAL DETAIL ACCT 3703				

A - Fringeable/Taxes
B - Non-Fringeable/Taxable
C - Non-Taxable

PAGE NO. 27AB

PRODUCTION NUMBER | PRODUCTION TITLE | DATE

3703 LOCAL SITE RENTAL—DETAIL

SET NO.	SCENE NAME/NO.	PREP TIME	PREP RATE	PREP AMT.	SHOOT TIME	SHOOT RATE	SHOOT AMT.	STRIKE TIME	STRIKE RATE	STRIKE AMT.	PERMITS, FEES	TOTALS
DAY 8 & 9 10	EXT. VAN - UNION SQUARE Scn. 13, 30	1/2 dy.	1000	1000	1/2 dy.	3000	3000	1/2 dy.	500	500		4,500
DAY10 13	INT. MIRROR VAN Scn. 12, 14, 15, 16, 27, 29	1/2 dy.			1 dy.	3000	3000	1/2 dy.	1000	1000		4,000
DAY11 14	INT. AMY'S APT. BLDG. Scn. 46	1 dy.	1500	1500	1/4 dy.	3500	3500	1/4 dy.	500	500		5,500
15	INT. AMY'S APT. Scn. 47	5 dys.	1500	7500	3/4 dy.	see above		2 dys.	1500	3000		10,500
DAY12 16	EXT. AMY'S APT. Scn. 104	2 dys.	2000	4000	1/4 dy.	5000	5000	1/2 dy.	1000	1000		10,000
14/15	INT. AMY'S APT. Scn. 105, 106, 108				3/4 dy.	Inc.						
DAY13 17	INT. Mr. C's BLDG Elevator Scn. 98, 199, 276, 277, 280, 281	1/2 dy.	2000	2000	1/2 dy.	5500	5500	1/2 dy.	500	500		8,000
18	INT. LOBBY - Mr. C's BLDG. Scn. 366-368	1 dy.	2000	2000	1/2 dy.	2000	2000	1/2 dy.	500	500		4,500
DAY14 19 20	INT. Mr. C's Suite/Lobby/Corridor	3 dys.	7000	7000	3/4 dy.	5500	5500	2 dys.	2500	5000		17,500
	INT. Mr. C's Suite Reception Area Scn. 273-275 369-376	2 dys.	Inc.		1/4 dy.	Inc.		2 dys.	2500	5000		5,000
DAY15 19&20	INT. SUITE/Recep/Corr./Office Scn. 99-102				1 dy.	5500	5500					5,500
DAY16 19	INT. Mr. C's Off. Scn. 206-225	3 dys.	7000	7000	1 dy.	5500	5500	2 dys.	2500	5000		17,500
DAY17	INT. Lawyer's Office Scn. 93-95	2 dys.	2500	5000	1 dy.	5000	5000	2 dys.	2500	5000		15,000
DAY18 19&20	INT. HARRY'S APT.		"S E T"									
	SUBTOTALS	37,000			43,500			27,000				107,500
								TOTAL DETAIL ACCT 3703				

A - Fringeable/Taxes
B - Non-Fringeable/Taxable
C - Non-Taxable

PAGE NO. 27AC

PRODUCTION NUMBER | PRODUCTION TITLE | DATE

3703 LOCAL SITE RENTAL—DETAIL

SET NO.	SCENE NAME/NO.	PREP TIME	PREP RATE	PREP AMT.	SHOOT TIME	SHOOT RATE	SHOOT AMT.	STRIKE TIME	STRIKE RATE	STRIKE AMT.	PERMITS, FEES	TOTALS
DAY21 22	EXT. Phone Booth Scn. 92	1/2 dy.	1000	1000	1/4 dy.	1000	1000	1/2 dy.	500	500		2,500
23	INT. Catholic Church Confessional Scn. 230, 231	1 dy.	1000	1000	1/4 dy.	1000	1000	1/2 dy.	1000	1000		3,000
24	INT. Laundry Scn. 39	1 dy.	1000	1000	1/4 dy.	1000	1000	1/2 dy.	1000	1000		3,000
25	INT. AUD/Slides Scn. 120, 123, 125	1 dy.	2000	2000	1/4 dy.	4000	4000	1/2 dy.	2000	2000		8,000
DAY2 2 26	EXT. Continental Lodge Scn. 232-236	1 dy.	1000	1000	1/2 dy.	1000	1000	1/2 dy.	2500	2500		7,500
27	INT. Continental Lodge - Lobby	1 dy.	1000	1000	1/4 dy.	1000	1000	1/2 dy.	Inc.			2,000
28	INT. Continental Corridor Scn. 238-254	1/2 dy.	Inc.		1/4 dy.	Inc.		1/2 dy.	Inc.			
DAY2 3 29	INT. MOTEL RM. B-5 Harry's Scn. 239-250 251-253	3 dys.	3000	3000	1 dy.	4000	4000	2 dys.	4000	4000		11,000
DAY2 4 30	INT. MOTEL RM. B-7 Scn.255-260	3 dys.	3000	3000	1/4 dy.	4000	4000	2 dys.	4000	4000		11,000
31	INT. Bathrm. B-7 Scn. 261-270	2 dys.	3000	3000	1/2 dy.	Inc.		1 dy.	2000	2000		5,000
30	INT. Motel Rm & Bathrm Scn. 354	-						-				
32	EXT. Motel Window B-7 Scn. 269	1/2 dy.	Inc.		1/4 dy.	Inc.						
DAY2 5 30& 31	INT. B-7 Motel Rm. & Bath Scn. 363, 359, 360, 361, 356	-			1 dy.	4000	4000	-				4,000
DAYS 26/27 33	EXT./INT. Bus #1 Scn. 284, 285 289, 291	1 dy.	1000	1000	1/2 dy.	1000	1000					2,000
33&34	INT. Bus #1 Scn. 298, 300-302				1/2 dy.	Inc.						
34	EXT. Bus #1 Scn. 299											
34	EXT. Bus #1 (N) Scn. 303, 304	1/2 dy.	500	500	1/4 dy.	1000	1000	-	Ligh i	ng:P 4	ep & Shoot	1,500
34	INT. Bus #1 (N) Scn. 305, 306				1/2 dy.	Inc.						
	SUBTOTALS	17,500			26,000			17,000				60,500
								TOTAL DETAIL ACCT 3703				

A - Fringeable/Taxes
B - Non-Fringeable/Taxable
C - Non-Taxable

PAGE NO. 27AD

PRODUCTION NUMBER | PRODUCTION TITLE | DATE

3703 LOCAL SITE RENTAL—DETAIL												
SET		PREP			SHOOT			STRIKE			PERMITS,	
NO.	SCENE NAME/NO.	TIME	RATE	AMT.	TIME	RATE	AMT.	TIME	RATE	AMT.	FEES	TOTALS
DAY26 & 27 (cont) 35	EXT. Poles & Lines (inserts) Scn. 286, 290, 294	1 dy.	1000	1000				1 dy.	1000	1000		2,000
36	EXT. Street & Harry's Bus - Scn. 297				1 dy.	1000	1000	1 dy.	1000	1000		2,000
37	INT. BUS #2 Steet Scn. 287, 288, 292, 293, 295, 296											
38	EXT. BUS & Street (N) Scn. 307, 308	1 dy.	2000	2000	1/4 dy.	2000	2000	1 dy.	1000	1000		5,000
DAY28 39	EXT. Stepped Street Scn. 309-316	1 dy.			1/2 dy.			1/2 dy.	1000	1000		1,000
40	EXT. PARK (N) Scn. 317-319, 321-332	1 dy.	1000	1000	1/2 dy.	2500	2500	1/2 dy.	1000	1000		4,500
DAY29	INT. HARRY'S RM. Scn. 380-397		" S E	T "								
DAY30 & 31 41	EXT. HARRY'S Warehouse Scn. 50	1 dy.	1000	1000	1/4 dy.	*9000	9000	1 dy.				10,000
42	INT. WAREHOUSE Scn. 51-57, 59-61, 63, 65, 67, 69, 70, 72-80, 82-86, 88-91	5dys.	1000	5000	1 3/4 dys.	4000	4000	5dys.	1000	5000		14,000
DAYS 32-34	INT. WAREHOUSE Scn. 160-173	-			3dys.	4000	12000	-				12,000
DAYS 35-36 42	INT. WAREHOUSE Scn. 174-181 357, 358, 362, 364	-			2dys.	4000	8000	-				8,000
DAY37 42	INT. WAREHOUSE Scn. 337-353, 355, 357, 358, 362, 364	-			3/4 dy.	4000	4000	-				4,000
43	EXT. WAREHOUSE ALLEY Scn. 333-336	1 dy.	1000	1000	1/4 dy.	Inc.		1 dy.	1000	1000		2,000
DAY38 44	INT. CAR (Traveling) Scn. 144, 146-149 151-153, 155, 157-159	1 dy.	1000	1000	1/2 dy.	4000	4000	1 dy.	1000	1000		6,000
45	EXT. STREET-Sedan & Mustang Scn. 145, 150, 154, 156	1 dy.	1000	1000	1/2 dy.	Inc.		1 dy.	1000	1000		2,000
	SUBTOTALS		13,000			46,500			13,000			72,500
* includes 5000 pymt. to rail road									TOTAL DETAIL ACCT 3703			

A - Fringeable/Taxes
B - Non-Fringeable/Taxable
C - Non-Taxable

PAGE NO. 27AE

PRODUCTION NUMBER | PRODUCTION TITLE | DATE

3703 LOCAL SITE RENTAL—DETAIL

SET NO.	SCENE NAME/NO.	PREP TIME	PREP RATE	PREP AMT.	SHOOT TIME	SHOOT RATE	SHOOT AMT.	STRIKE TIME	STRIKE RATE	STRIKE AMT.	PERMITS, FEES	TOTALS
DAY39 46	INT. Convention Bar Scn. 133-136	1 dy.	3000	3000	1/4 dy.	5000-10000	10000	1 dy.	500	500		13,500
47	INT. Convention Booth Area Scn. 137-142	5dys.	3000	15000				3dys.	8000	8000		23,000
48	EXT. Parking Lot Scn. 143	1/2 dy.	500	500	1/4 dy.	see above		1/4 dy.	500	500		1,000
DAY40 47 49	INT. Convention Lobby/Booth Area Scn. 109-117, 119				1/2 dy.	5000-10000	10000	-				10,000
50	INT. Convention Auditorium Scn. 120 (pt.), 121-124				1/2 dy.	see above		-				
DAY41 47	INT. Convention Booth Area Scn. 126-128				1 dy.	5000-10000	10000					10,000
	SUBTOTALS		18,500			30,000			9,000			57,500
								TOTAL DETAIL ACCT 3703				365,500

A - Fringeable/Taxes
B - Non-Fringeable/Taxable
C - Non-Taxable

3700—LOCAL SITE RENTAL

From the creation of the first studios in New York and Los Angeles early in the 20th century, filmmakers discovered the advantages of total control over their environment. With the arrival of sound and the bulky, unsophisticated equipment used to record it, the vast majority of productions were restricted to sound stages and backlots for the first decade. Actors went on location for ESTABLISHING SHOTS at the beginning and/or end of scenes then reconvened on a sound stage in front of a rear projection of the location and spoke their lines.

After World War II, a host of technological innovations made or perfected during the war became available to producers: portable generators; higher speed film and lenses; compact, lighter weight lamps and dollies; and more sensitive, directional microphones which would not pick up every ambient sound. Today most production days, interior or exterior are filmed on local or distant locations.

01: Site Contact

Your local *site contact* is usually a real estate broker or other local person who is familiar with the commercial and/or residential buildings in the area planned for filming.

03: Site Rentals

This is the cost of *renting* a location. Just as your locations may vary from small apartments to nightclubs, so will the costs. In New York and Los Angeles where filming is more commonplace, most owners are too sophisticated to offer you a bargain. Of course, owners there do understand the concept of a reduced rate for prep and strike time.

An average figure of $6,500 per day is not unlikely, considering the magnitude of our filming for *The Conversation*. It is normal for a location to ask for $2,000 to $3,000 a day for a location, and we might be filming two or three locations in any one day.

Lunch Site

Once you bring food to location you will need a place to serve it—a sheltered space if the weather conditions are inhospitable. Space should be arranged for not only the tables and chairs, but also the catering truck, salad tables, and other necessary catering equipment. After lunch is over and the entire company has been properly fed, find a local charity which can distribute your unserved food (you have paid for it anyway) to the homeless in the neighborhood.

Repair

This is the location equivalent of lost or damaged equipment. You can imagine how building walls, tacking up blacking, or taping gels can damage paint and floor coverings. Many owners are also savvy enough to ask for large deposits and to be named as *additionally insured* on your production policies.

04: Survey Costs

All the states as well as many cities and other attractions in the U.S. and many foreign locations have film offices or commissions set up to provide information and encourage filmmakers to bring their cast, crew, and money to their area. They have 800 numbers, brochures, videos, data bases of local hires, and will provide them on request at little or no cost to you. Many of them have web sites. Photos are helpful, but ultimately you will have to see the site in person. And when you go, you need to provide money for travel, rooms, meals, driving when there, and taking and keeping pictures of what you have seen. Be sure to budget enough money for the number of people going. Location scouting happens in several stages:

1. The location manager and/or production designer probably will travel for a few days to find areas in which to search, then narrow down the choices to a few good possibilities.
2. The director, producer and production manager will join the location manager and/or production designer on the site(s) when the choices have been narrowed to the very best possibilities.
3. After the decisions have been made as to where filming will happen, the location manager obtains the necessary clearances

from the proper authorities. The department heads who must see the location are then taken on a crew survey. These should include the first AD and sometimes the second AD, DP, chief lighting technician, key grip, stunt gaffer, special effects coordinator, construction coordinator, transportation captain, and anyone else whose presence will add and whose absence may cost.

08: Gratuities
If someone is extremely helpful in aiding you with a location you should acknowledge this help by paying a small fee. We will allow a total of $2,500 here.

17: Courtesy Payments
A *courtesy payment* is another form of gratuity. You never know when you will someone's help or permission to get a switch turned on, have a car moved, or permission to gain access to someone's roof.

25: Permits
Wherever you film, there are local authorities who will issue you permits to film on public property. There are also permits for parking your vehicles in the streets. These permits vary in price from free to thousands of dollars, depending on your location.

To combat *runaway productions*—productions which go to the other cities and states instead of staying in Los Angeles—there is now a central film permit office in Hollywood which supplies you with all the information you will need about filming on LA streets. This information includes street permit fees, police requirements, and so forth. Wherever you are, local or distant, it is important to check with the local authorities to see what permits may be necessary. You will need to obtain those permits in order to film legally.

We will allow $1,000 to cover any paperwork and fees in San Francisco.

27: Parking (Crew and Equipment)

On *The Conversation,* we are figuring 37 days on local location and four days on stage. Union contracts require that a company provide secure crew parking while on location. Common sense tells you to provide secure parking even if the crew is nonunion. Few things can cost you so much filming time (and money) as having a crew member running around complaining that the radio was stolen from his car. The rest of the crew becomes nervous and people start disappearing from the set to check their own cars.

And don't forget to plan for parking for the extras. The extras breakdown tells us that we will need parking for about 15 days. This will cost around $300 to $400 per day. If the crew parking is more than a block or two from the set, you should allow for maxivans and drivers under transportation to shuttle personnel.

Your permit should allow your location manager to post *no parking* signs for the days of location filming, so that the most-needed vehicles can be parked near the set.

35: Janitorial

As with sound stages, locations need to be left clean and in good repair. It makes for a better working environment to do this on a daily or weekly basis. On *The Conversation*, we budgeted a daily service fee of $50.

Additional Hire

Many locations that are often used for filming may require you to hire one or more of their staff for a variety of standby tasks. You may allow for that here.

Government Representative

This was discussed under Account 2000. It can also be budgeted here.

95: Miscellaneous

Something always comes up in the 3700 account which you won't expect. Allow yourself a little breathing space by adding $5,000 here.

Account 3800

Stage Rental and Expense

PAGE NO. 28

PRODUCTION NUMBER | PRODUCTION TITLE | DATE

3800 STAGE RENTAL AND EXPENSE

ACCT NO.	DESCRIPTION	TIME	RATE	AMT.	SUBTOTALS A	B	C
01	Guards						
02	Lot Person (Local 40)	6	1633.10	9799	9,799		
	23.33						
	12 hrs.						
03	Utility Person						
	Additional Hire						
05	Power 4 dys. shoot	4 dys.	900/dy	3600			3,600
	25 dys. construction/strike	25 dys.	300/dy	7500			7,500
06	Equipment Package						
	Grip	5	3500	17500			17,500
	Electrical	5	12000	60000			60,000
	Cherry Picker						
	Forklift, etc.						
30	Rental						
	(See Detail Page 28A)	9	see 28A	52800			52,800
65	Office Rental						
70	Telephone ALLOW			2000			2,000
85	Additional Expenses						
	Mill	15 dys.	500/dy	7500			7,500
95	Miscellaneous						
99	Loss, Damage, Repair						
				SUBTOTALS	9,799		150,900
				TOTAL ACCT 3800	160,699		

A - Fringeable/Taxes
B - Non-Fringeable/Taxable
C - Non-Taxable

PAGE NO. 28A

PRODUCTION NUMBER ____ PRODUCTION TITLE ____ DATE ____

3830 STAGE RENTAL—DETAIL

SET NO.	SCENE NAME/NUMBER	CONSTRUCTION		REHEARSAL		HOLD		TEST		SHOOT		STRIKE		TOTAL	
		TIME	RATE	TIME	RATE	TIME	RATE	TIME	RATE	TIME	RATE	TIME	RATE	TIME	AMOUNT
1	Harry's Apartment Scn. 40-44, 48, 377, 379-397	20 dys.	1,100/ dy.	2 dys.	N/C for Dressing	15 dys.	1,100/ dy.	--	1,100/ dy.	4 dys.	2,200/ dy.	5 dys.	1,100/ dy.	29 dys.	52,800
	SUBTOTALS														
														TOTAL DETAIL ACCT 3830	52,800

A - Fringeable/Taxes
B - Non-Fringeable/Taxable
C - Non-Taxable

3800–STAGE RENTAL AND EXPENSE

RENTING SOUND STAGES—FROM A SINGLE, independently run stage to one of many on a major studio lot—involves many ancillary charges. The rates to rent the stage itself is usually quoted as one fee for prep and strike and a higher fee for lighting and shooting. Do not include the numerous other potential charges which are detailed here. Be aware that all these charges are negotiable and ascertain which if not all of them will apply to your agreement.

01: Guards

Studios have guards present on a 24-hour basis. They check everyone coming onto the lot and issue **DRIVE-ON PASSES**. However, from evening until morning, many will curtail operations and close some of their gates or entrances. If you are shooting past that time, you may be charged for a standby guard. These charges will usually end when your ADs call for the stage to be locked after wrap. The same may apply to work beginning very early. Early stage openings and other special requirements may be requested through studio operations via your **CALL SHEET**.

If there is another company shooting, many studios will allow all or some of the standby charges to be split between the production companies.

02: Lot Person (Local 40)

We are employing a Local 40 person for the length of *The Conversation*. This crew member belongs to the International Brotherhood of Electrical Workers (IBEW), not to IATSE. (*See Account 3304.*)

04: Utility Person

Many studios and stand-alone stages will require a stage manager to work with you during your entire rental period.

05: Power

Some stages include normal AC or *house power* in the cost of rental; others have a flat charge of $50 to $100 per day. As mentioned in the Lighting Account, the high amperage power used for lights is typically charged on an hourly basis. There are two charges: for the power itself and for the lot person.

On some stages which are actually converted warehouses, the power supply may be inadequate to your needs and require you to bring in a portable generator. Your power on a sound stage will cost about $300 per day for construction and strike. This figure can go up to $900 per shooting day.

30: Equipment Package

Separate *grip* and *electric packages* for stage work, as was the case on *The Conversation* are detailed here.

30: Rental—Rehearsal Stage

Most large cities have rehearsal stages or rooms available for stage or dance work that will also serve for rehearsing movie scenes. Major studios also have several of these rooms though they are not always available.

30: Rental—Shooting Stage

For *The Conversation* we will need to film in a studio for four days. So the shooting crew is not standing around watching the construction crew put up walls, we are budgeting for 20 days of construction. Additionally, we are adding fifteen *hold* days, during which we are renting the studio with the standing set, but during which we will not film. This gives us a **COVER SET**. In a production with this number of exteriors a cover set like this is a good idea. It is especially wise when filming in San Francisco where it often rains.

A stage for a small set like *Harry's Apartment* will cost $1,100 per day for construction and strike, and $2,200 per day for shooting.

30: Rental—Backlot

Most backlots and ranches where the major studios kept standing outdoor sets of Western streets or tenement blocks have long since been converted to offices. (Long before serving as a backdrop in *Die Hard,* Century City was the Fox backlot) or condominiums (the fate of the old MGM lots). Of the few that remain, fewer have power, commissaries or other services.

Rates vary, but $10,000 per day plus $2,000 for backlot security, Local 40 person, etc., should suffice for major studio lots.

65: Office Rental

Stage rental normally entitles you to rent a certain number of offices and parking spaces. This varies with each place you speak to. Some facilities can also rent you furnishings.

70: Telephone

Most facilities require you to use their phone system and voice mail. The advantage is that it is in place and your extensions can be immediately connected; the disadvantage is that there may be surcharges on all calls. If no phone system exists, you will need to make arrangements as soon as possible. Phone installations always take more time than expected.

85: Additional Expenses

Charges vary with the facility. Typical charges are trash removal, cast breakfasts purchased from a commissary, storage rooms, use of pieces from the scene dock, etc.

85: Additional Expenses—Construction

Large studios have scene docks and mills or shops to make or alter set pieces.

The Conversation will rent the mill for 15 days to construct the sets for the studio filming.

85: Additional Expenses—Dressing Rooms

For the studio filming, the actors in *The Conversation* will have separate, private dressing rooms supplied by the studio and charged to our production. Most permanent dressing rooms and bungalows have long since been converted to offices. The ones offered today are small, wheeled cabins with window air conditioners and electric area heaters. Most studios which cannot offer *star* rooms will allow you to bring motor homes or trailers on the lot.

Account 4000

Location Expense

PAGE NO. 29

PRODUCTION NUMBER	PRODUCTION TITLE	DATE

4000 LOCATION EXPENSE

ACCT NO.	DESCRIPTION	TIME	RATE	AMT.	SUBTOTALS A	SUBTOTALS B	SUBTOTALS C
01	Location Contact/Broker						
	Location Mgr. (See Acct 2000)						
	Interpreters (See Acct 2000)						
02	Location Site Rental (See Detail 30A)						
03	Permits						
04	Scouting Costs (See Detail 30B)						
	Travel and Living (See Detail Page 30B)						
	Local Contact						
	Vehicle Rentals						
	Additional Expenses						
05	Transportation to Location						
	(See Detail 30C)						
06	Flight Insurance						
07	Passports, Visas and Work Permits						
08	Travel Gratuities & Excess Baggage						
09	Travel and Living (See Detail Page 30C)						
	Travel						
	Lodging						
	Meals						
	Catering Costs						
	(See Set Operations Acct 3600)						
10	Shipping Costs (Also See Acct 6205)						
	Custom and Brokerage Fees						
	Export Taxes						
	Equipment Shipment						
	Loading and Unloading Crates						
	Packing/Crating, Labor & Materials						
	Film Shipments ALLOW						500
	Air Freight						5,000
	Airport Pickups & Deliveries						
				SUBTOTALS			5,000
	CONTINUED ON NEXT PAGE				5,500		

A - Fringeable/Taxes
B - Non-Fringeable/Taxable
C - Non-Taxable

ACCOUNT 4000—Location Expense

PAGE NO. 30

PRODUCTION NUMBER	PRODUCTION TITLE	DATE

4000 LOCATION EXPENSE—(CONT'D)

ACCT NO.	DESCRIPTION	SUBTOTALS A	B	C
11	Postage (Also See Acct 6240)			
12	Office Supplies (Also See Acct 6240)			
13	Office Rental (Also See Acct 6230)			
14	Office Equipment and Furniture Rental (Also See Acct 6230)			
15	Special Equipment			
16	Telephone and Telegraph (Also See Acct 6230)			
	Installation Charges			
17	Courtesy Payments (Also See Acct 6204 & 3625)			
18	Government Censors			
19	Location Weather Service			
22	Local Projection Service			
25	Permits (Props and Special Effects)			
26	Storage/Working Space Rental			
	Wardrobe			
	Makeup/Hair			
	Carpentry			
	Prop			
	Set Dressing			
	Special Effects			
	General Storage			
	Vehicles (See Transportation Acct 4600)			
27	Parking			
	Location Medical, Police, Fireman			
	Watchmen (See Set Operations Acct 3600)			
28	Messenger Service			
29	Janitorial/Cleaning			
35	Hotel and Restaurant Gratuities			
85	Additional Expenses			
95	Miscellanous			500
99	Loss, Damage, Repair			
	SUBTOTALS FROM PREVIOUS PAGE			5,000
	SUBTOTALS THIS PAGE			500
	TOTAL ACCT 4000	5,500		

A - Fringeable/Taxes
B - Non-Fringeable/Taxable
C - Non-Taxable

PAGE NO. 30A

PRODUCTION NUMBER | PRODUCTION TITLE | DATE

4002 LOCATION SITE RENTAL—DETAIL													
SET NO.	SCENE NAME/NO.	PREP			SHOOT			STRIKE			PERMITS, FEES	TOTALS
		TIME	RATE	AMT.	TIME	RATE	AMT.	TIME	RATE	AMT.		
	SUBTOTALS											
										TOTAL DETAIL ACCT 4002		*0*

A - Fringeable/Taxes
B - Non-Fringeable/Taxable
C - Non-Taxable

PAGE NO. 30B

PRODUCTION NUMBER | PRODUCTION TITLE | DATE

4004 SCOUTING COSTS—TRAVEL AND LIVING

POSITION/NAME	DESTINATION (RT)	AIRFARES			LODGING (PER DIEM)			MEALS (PER DIEM)				TOTALS
		NO. FLIGHTS	RATE	SUBTOTAL	NO.DAYS	RATE	SUBTOTAL	NO.DAYS		RATE	SUBTOTAL	
									B			
									L			
									D			
									B			
									L			
									D			
									B			
									L			
									D			
									B			
									L			
									D			
									B			
									L			
									D			
									B			
									L			
									D			
									B			
									L			
									D			
									B			
									L			
									D			
									B			
									L			
									D			
									B			
									L			
									D			
			SUBTOTALS									
								TOTAL DETAIL ACCT 4004				0

A - Fringeable/Taxes
B - Non-Fringeable/Taxable
C - Non-Taxable

PAGE NO. 30C

PRODUCTION NUMBER | PRODUCTION TITLE | DATE

4005 ON LOCATION—TRAVEL AND LIVING

POSITION/NAME	DESTINATION (RT)	AIRFARES			LODGING (PER DIEM)			MEALS (PER DIEM)				TOTALS
		NO.FLIGHTS	RATE	SUBTOTAL	NO.DAYS	RATE	SUBTOTAL	NO.DAYS		RATE	SUBTOTAL	
									B			
									L			
									D			
									B			
									L			
									D			
									B			
									L			
									D			
									B			
									L			
									D			
									B			
									L			
									D			
									B			
									L			
									D			
									B			
									L			
									D			
									B			
									L			
									D			
									B			
									L			
									D			
									B			
									L			
									D			
			SUBTOTALS									
											TOTAL DETAIL ACCT 4005	0

A - Fringeable/Taxes
B - Non-Fringeable/Taxable
C - Non-Taxable

4000–LOCATION EXPENSE

MANY PICTURES ARE SHOT ENTIRELY ON DISTANT location these days. Those expenses related to shooting on location are budgeted here. It has been broken out in order to more easily pinpoint areas/costs which vary from normal costs of shooting in town. Since *The Conversation* was shot on a *local hire basis* in the San Francisco and no crew members were brought in from another area, we will have no costs in this account. For *The Conversation* all location expenses are found under the *site rental expense* budget, Account 3700. Even when you are not on distant location, if any of your crew members is brought in from elsewhere, the costs of maintaining them while they work for you should go into this 4000 account.

02: Location Site Rental

Local location site rentals are budgeted in Account 3700. *Distant location* site rentals appear here.

05: Transportation to Location

The cost of driving, or otherwise transporting, equipment to location can also be budgeted here.

06: Flight Insurance

SAG and DGA contracts require first class tickets where available and special insurance. That may be included either in this account or in the *insurance account.*

07: Passports, Visas, and Work Permits

Requirements for work outside the U.S. vary considerably. You may use an allowance, but if you are going to shoot in a foreign country, you should research the costs and other constraints through its film commission or nearest consulate. *[Note: Also make sure someone checks any tax ramifications which may apply, especially to those people who use loan-out companies. In many cases, those who per-*

form in front of the camera have stiffer, non-waivable penalties than other crew members. Check to see whether the production company will need to indemnify the performer for the tax amount.

[If the foreign country in which you are shooting has a reciprocal tax agreement with the USA, then in many cases the taxes paid to the foreign country can be credited against the taxes due in the USA.]

09: Travel and Living

There are several travel agencies in Los Angeles with experience making production arrangements. They advertise in many trade publications, and there is no cost to you for their services. They can book airfares, rooms, rental cars, etc. Remember that star actors may have provisions in their contracts for extra fares, higher per diem, and better accommodations.

09: Travel and Living—Travel

Put all charges for transporting any out of town crew members to your local location in this account. As all crew members on *The Conversation* were local hires, we have incurred no charges in this account. If you had any cast members coming from out of town, you would put their travel and living expenses under the *cast budget, Account 1400*—not here.

09: Travel and Living—Lodging

You are also required to house your cast and crew when on location overnight. Unless there are not enough rooms in the hotels and motels in the area, doubling up is not permitted under many union contracts. You can usually negotiate a lower room rate based on the large number of rooms you are renting and the length of the stay. If possible putting everyone in the same hotel makes the logistics of location that much simpler.

09: Travel and Living—Apartment/Condo Rental

When a show will be out of town several months, it may be cheaper and more comfortable to find apartments or condominiums. Again film commissions and local brokers can help with rates.

09: Travel and Living—Meals/Per Diem
Per diem is the money paid to your crew for their daily meals and/or living expenses. In larger, more expensive cities such as New York and Los Angeles, per diem will be more than in small inexpensive towns. The Screen Actors Guild has a list of such cities. In any case, per diem must be reasonable. In small towns, will limited facilities, you might pre-purchase meals from local restaurants and issue meal vouchers rather than giving cash. To find a workable figure, check with film commissions or other companies which have shot in the area recently. *[Note: In recent years,* per diem *income has been made taxable over a certain amount (very low.)]*

95: Shipping Costs
If you are filming in a distant city, you will probably have to ship your film from the location to the lab in Hollywood and back daily. We have allowed for that as *The Conversation* is filming in San Francisco and not using a local lab.

13: Office Rental—Location
Most productions on distant location who are staying in a hotel, find it convenient to convert several of the rooms into offices. Some hotels will provide additional rooms at no extra charge as part of a package deal, or offer you rooms at reduced rate.

Give yourself enough time prior to setting up the office to get your local utilities in place, especially if filming outside the U.S. Local telephone companies generally do not understand the life-or-death urgency of show business, and might not be prepared to install ten telephone lines on one day's notice. The same goes for the water and power company. If you are going to be in a city for a period of time, you may wish to establish credit with local merchants. Most production open a bank account at a local bank. It will take the bank a and few days to perform or all their routine credit checks. All those setup costs should be allowed for in this account.

85: Additional Fees—Customs Fees
Many brokers specialize in helping production companies get personnel and equipment in and out of foreign countries. They can advise on those costs and their fees for coordinating the process.

95: Miscellaneous
Allow $500 to cover any forgotten expenses.

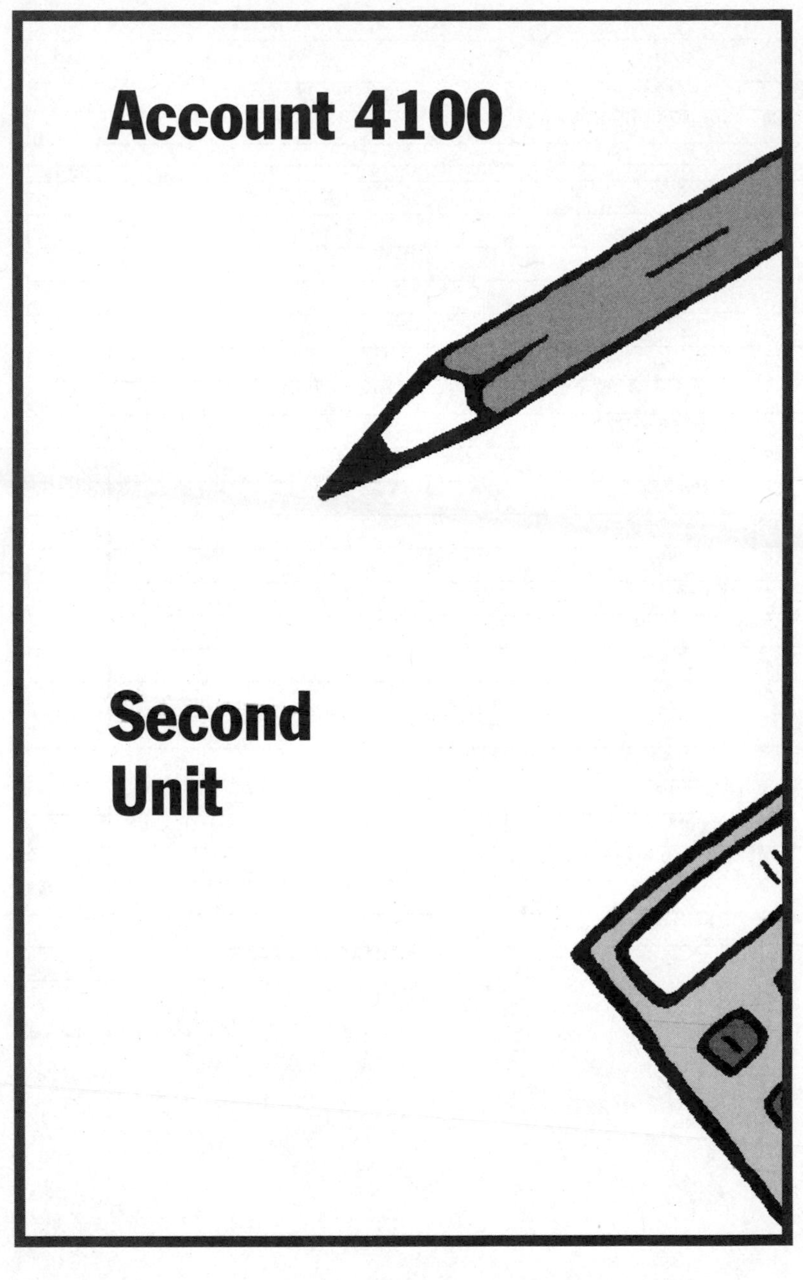
Account 4100
Second
Unit

PAGE NO. 31

PRODUCTION NUMBER | PRODUCTION TITLE | DATE

4100 SECOND UNIT—SUMMARY

ACCT NO.	DESCRIPTION	PAGE NO.	BUDGET	TOTALS
01	Director (See Acct 1202)	32A		
02	Choreographer	32A		
03	Dialogue Director	32A		
04	Cast	32A		
19	Fringe Benefits & Payroll Taxes	32A		
	TOTAL SECOND UNIT ABOVE THE LINE			
20	Production Department	32A		
21	Extra Talent	32B		
22	Art Department	32B		
23	Set Construction	32B		
24	Set Dressing	32B		
25	Prop Department	32B		
26	Picture Vehicles	32B		
27	Special Effects	32B		
28	Camera Department	32B		
31	Sound Department	32C		
32	Grip Department	32C		
33	Lighting Department	32C		
34	Wardrobe	32C		
35	Makeup & Hair Dressing	32C		
36	Set Operations	32C		
40	Location Expenses	32D		
	SUBTOTAL THIS PAGE		0	

(CONTINUED ON NEXT PAGE)

PAGE NO. 32

PRODUCTION NUMBER | PRODUCTION TITLE | DATE

4100 SECOND UNIT—SUMMARY (CONT'D)

ACCT NO.	DESCRIPTION	PAGE NO.	BUDGET	TOTALS
45	Animals	32D		
46	Transportation	32E		
47	Film/Sound & Lab	32E		
48	Expenses (Rentals & Purchases)	32F		
49	Fringe Benefits & Payroll Taxes	32G		
85	Additional Expenses	32G		
95	Miscellaneous	32G		
99	Loss, Damage & Repair	32G		

SUBTOTALS THIS PAGE	
SUBTOTALS FROM PREVIOUS PAGE	
TOTAL SECOND UNIT BELOW THE LINE	
TOTAL SECOND UNIT ABOVE THE LINE	0

TOTAL ACCOUNT 4100 | 0

PAGE NO. 32A

PRODUCTION NUMBER | PRODUCTION TITLE | DATE

4100 SECOND UNIT

NO.	TITLE	DAYS PREP	SHOOT	WRAP	TOTAL	RATE	SUBTOTALS A	B	C
01	Director								
02	Choreographer								
03	Dialogue Director								
								TOTAL	0

04	CAST NAME & STUNTS	DAYS PREP	SHOOT	WRAP	TOTAL	RATE	SUBTOTALS A	B	C
	Welfare Worker/Teacher								
								TOTAL	0

19	FRINGE BENEFITS & PAYROLL TAXES/ABOVE-THE-LINE SECOND UNIT	AMOUNT	TOTALS
	Payroll Taxes & Comp. Ins.		
	Pension		
	Health & Welfare		

TOTAL SECOND UNIT ABOVE THE LINE	0

20	PRODUCTION DEPARTMENT	DAYS PREP	SHOOT	WRAP	TOTAL	RATE	SUBTOTALS A	B	C
	Production Mgr.								
	1st Asst. Director								
	2nd Asst. Director								
	Location Mgr.								
	Production Acct.								
	D.G.A Trainee								
	P.A.'s								
	Script Supervisor								
	Prod. Office Coord.								
	Additional Clerical								
	Technical Advisor								
								TOTAL	0

TOTAL	0

PAGE NO. 32B

PRODUCTION NUMBER	PRODUCTION TITLE	DATE

4100 SECOND UNIT–(CONT'T)

	EXTRA TALENT									SUBTOTALS		
21	DAY NO.	NO.	RATE	DAY NO.	NO.	RATE	DAY NO.	NO.	RATE	A	B	C
	1			4			7					
	2			5			8					
	3			6			9					
										TOTAL	0	

		DAYS					SUBTOTALS		
22	ART DEPARTMENT	PREP	SHOOT	WRAP	TOTAL	RATE	A	B	C
	Prod. Designer								
	Art Director								
							TOTAL	0	

		DAYS					SUBTOTALS		
23	SET CONSTRUCTION	PREP	SHOOT	WRAP	TOTAL	RATE	A	B	C
	Const. Coordinator								
	Const. Labor								
							TOTAL	0	

		DAYS					SUBTOTALS		
24	SET DRESSING	PREP	SHOOT	WRAP	TOTAL	RATE	A	B	C
	Set Decorator								
	Swing Gang-Leadman								
							TOTAL	0	

		DAYS					SUBTOTALS		
25	PROP DEPARTMNET	PREP	SHOOT	WRAP	TOTAL	RATE	A	B	C
	Prop Master								
	Asst. Propmaster								
							TOTAL	0	

		DAYS					SUBTOTALS		
26	PICTURE VEHICLES	PREP	SHOOT	WRAP	TOTAL	RATE	A	B	C
	Vehicle #1 Driver/Owner								
	Vehicle #2 Driver/Owner								
	Vehicle #3 Driver/Owner								
							TOTAL	0	

		DAYS					SUBTOTALS		
27	SPECIAL EFFECTS DEPT.	PREP	SHOOT	WRAP	TOTAL	RATE	A	B	C
	Special Effects Man								
							TOTAL	0	

		DAYS					SUBTOTALS		
28	CAMERA DEPARTMENT	PREP	SHOOT	WRAP	TOTAL	RATE	A	B	C
	Director of Photography								
	Camera Operator								
	1st A.C.								
	2nd A.C.								
							TOTAL	0	

PAGE NO. 32C

PRODUCTION NUMBER	PRODUCTION TITLE	DATE

4100 SECOND UNIT—(CONT'D)

		DAYS					SUBTOTALS		
31	SOUND DEPARTMENT	PREP	SHOOT	WRAP	TOTAL	RATE	A	B	C
	Mixer								
	Boom Operator								
								TOTAL	0

		DAYS					SUBTOTALS		
32	GRIP DEPARTMENT	PREP	SHOOT	WRAP	TOTAL	RATE	A	B	C
	Key Grip								
	2nd Company Grip								
	Company Grip								
								TOTAL	0

		DAYS					SUBTOTALS		
33	LIGHTING DEPARTMENT	PREP	SHOOT	WRAP	TOTAL	RATE	A	B	C
	Gaffer								
	Best Boy								
	Electrician								
								TOTAL	0

		DAYS					SUBTOTALS		
34	WARDROBE DEPARTMNET	PREP	SHOOT	WRAP	TOTAL	RATE	A	B	C
	Designer								
	Wardrobe Woman								
	Wardrobe Man								
								TOTAL	0

		DAYS					SUBTOTALS		
35	MAKE-UP and HAIRDRESSING	PREP	SHOOT	WRAP	TOTAL	RATE	A	B	C
	Make-up Artist								
	Hair Stylist								
								TOTAL	0

		DAYS					SUBTOTALS		
36	SET OPERATIONS	PREP	SHOOT	WRAP	TOTAL	RATE	A	B	C
	Craft Serviceman								
	Policeman								
	Fireman								
	Watchman								
	First Aid/Nurse								
	Doctor								
								TOTAL	0

PAGE NO. 32D

PRODUCTION NUMBER	PRODUCTION TITLE	DATE

4100 SECOND UNIT—(CONT'T)

		DAYS					SUBTOTALS		
40	SOUND DEPARTMENT	PREP	SHOOT	WRAP	TOTAL	RATE	A	B	C
	Location Contact								
	Interpreters								
	Location Site Rental								
								TOTAL	0

		DAYS					SUBTOTALS		
45	ANIMALS	PREP	SHOOT	WRAP	TOTAL	RATE	A	B	C
	Animals								
	Wrangler/Trainer								
								TOTAL	0

		DAYS					SUBTOTALS		
46A	TRANSPORTATION (LABOR)	PREP	SHOOT	WRAP	TOTAL	RATE	A	B	C
	Driver 1								
	Driver 2								
	Driver 3								
	Driver 4								
	Driver 5								
	Driver 6								
	Driver 7								
	Driver 8								
								TOTAL	0

PAGE NO. 32E

PRODUCTION NUMBER ______ PRODUCTION TITLE ______ DATE ______

46 TRANSPORTATION, LODGING, MEALS—SECOND UNIT

POSITION/ NAME	DESTINATION (RT)	AIRFARES			LODGING (PER DIEM)			MEALS (PER DIEM)				TOTALS
		NO. FLIGHTS	RATE	SUB-TOTAL	NO.DAYS	RATE	SUB-TOTAL	NO.DAYS		RATE	SUB-TOTAL	
									B			
									L			
									D			
									B			
									L			
									D			
									B			
									L			
									D			
									B			
									L			
									D			
									B			
									L			
									D			
									B			
									L			
									D			
									B			
									L			
									D			
									B			
									L			
									D			
									B			
									L			
									D			
									B			
									L			
									D			
			SUBTOTALS									
								TOTAL DETAIL ACCT 46				0

A - Fringeable/Taxes
B - Non-Fringeable/Taxable
C - Non-Taxable

PAGE NO. 32F

PRODUCTION NUMBER | PRODUCTION TITLE | DATE

4100 SECOND UNIT–(CONT'D)

48A	EQUIPMENT AND MATERIALS/RENTALS		
	DEPARTMENT	DESCRIPTION	SUBTOTAL
		TOTAL	0

48B	EQUIPMENT AND MATERIALS/PURCHASES		
	DEPARTMENT	DESCRIPTION	SUBTOTAL
		TOTAL	0

PAGE NO. 32G

PRODUCTION NUMBER | PRODUCTION TITLE | DATE

4100 SECOND UNIT—(CONT'D)

49	FRINGE BENEFITS AND PAYROLL TAXES (2ND UNIT)				
	DESCRIPTION	PAYROLL	PENSION	HEALTH & WELFARE	TOTALS
	DGA $	%	%	%	
	PGA $	%	%	%	
	WGA $	%	%	%	
	SAG $	%	%	%	
	IATSE $	%	%	%	
	NABET $	%	%	%	
	OTHER OR ALLOW $	%	%	%	
	SUBTOTALS				0

85	ADDITIONAL EXPENSES	
	TOTAL	
95	MISCELLANEOUS	
	TOTAL	
99	LOSS, DAMAGE, REPAIR	
	TOTAL	

TOTAL SECOND UNIT BELOW-THE-LINE	0
TOTAL SECOND UNIT ABOVE-THE-LINE	0

TOTAL ACCT 4100	0

4100–SECOND UNIT

THERE ARE MANY TYPES OF SECOND UNITS as we discussed under the *second unit director budget*. All those costs, including second unit director, may be budgeted in this account. If you plan on having a **SECOND UNIT**, you may begin with a *general allowance* and add more details as they becomes known. A fairly common second unit that shoots either in pre-production or in post-production involves either the director or a director and background extras. The unit usually shoots *establishing shots* for a day or two, sometimes in another city. If you bring along actors, your second unit has now become a modified *first unit*. You may simply wish to add days to the time already allocated for all the people involved and use this account only for transportation, local hires, etc.

A simultaneous second unit or any one that has its own crew and equipment should be budgeted here using as much of the account details as appropriate.

There was no need for a second unit on *The Conversation,* so the budget has nothing in this account.

[Note: Smaller productions such as student films, music videos or even commercials have often used the second unit *part of the budget form as their entire budget form as it is so detailed.]*

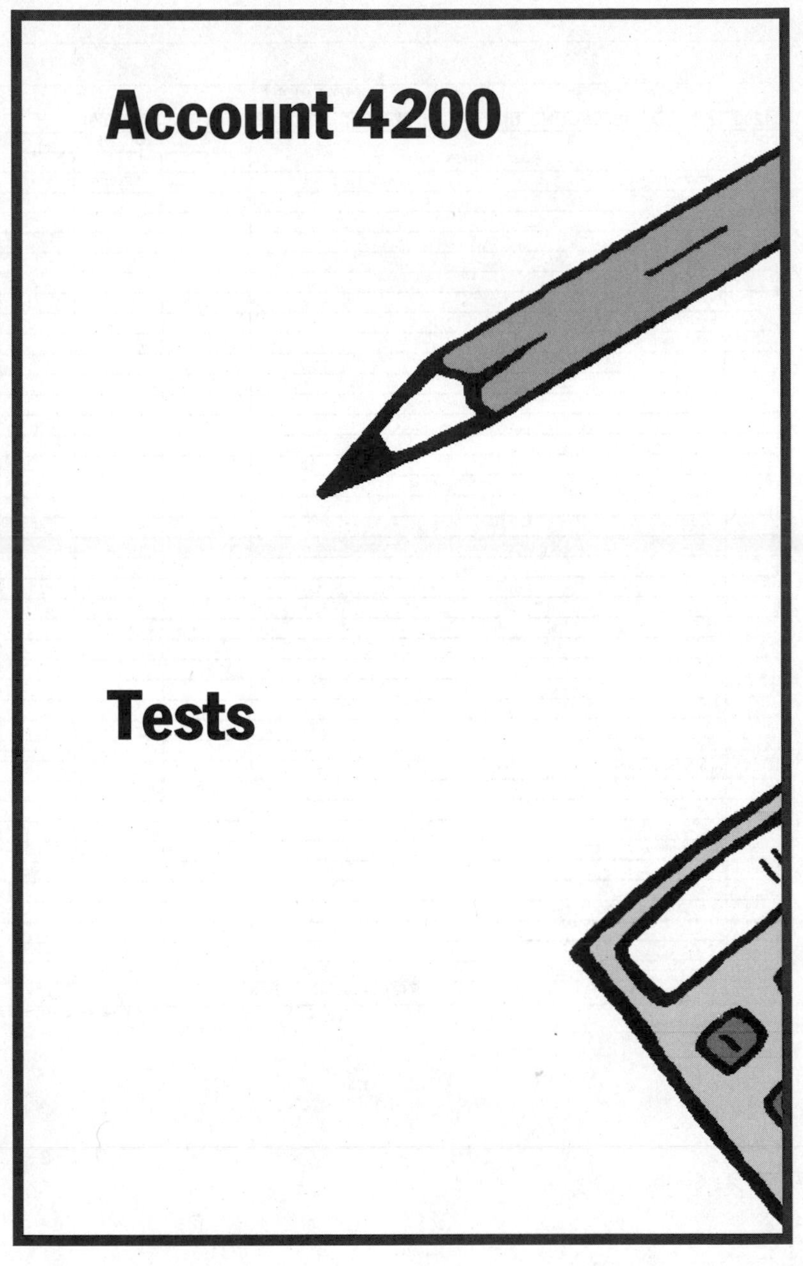

Account 4200
Tests

PAGE NO. 33

PRODUCTION NUMBER	PRODUCTION TITLE	DATE

4200 TESTS (USE SECOND UNIT FOR DETAILED TEST BUDGET—ACCT 4100)

ACCT NO.	DESCRIPTION		SUBTOTALS A	SUBTOTALS B	SUBTOTALS C
47	Film/Sound Lab	ALLOW		25,000	
	Negative Film				
	Sound Negative				
	Film Negative Develop				
	Film One Light Print				
	Color Corrected Dailies				
	Sound Transfers—Stock				
	Sound Transfers—Labor				
85	Additional Expenses				
95	Miscellaneous				
99	Loss, Damage, Repair				
		SUBTOTALS		25,000	
		TOTAL ACCT 4200		25,000	

A - Fringeable/Taxes
B - Non-Fringeable/Taxable
C - Non-Taxable

4200—TESTS

TESTS ARE DONE FOR SEVERAL REASONS: TECHNICAL REASONS, to check out the camera and lenses or a film stock's reaction to specific lighting; or for aesthetic reasons, to see how an actor looks in particular makeup and costumes. **SCREEN TESTS** are very rarely done these days. A video reference from casting sessions is usually sufficient. The overall allowance of $25,000 should cover all tests. We have put some money in other accounts for *screen tests* and **WARDROBE TESTS** as part of the overall budget.

Account 4300
Miniature Department

PAGE NO. 34

PRODUCTION NUMBER	PRODUCTION TITLE	DATE

4300 MINIATURE DEPARTMENT

ACCT			LOCAL/	DAYS/WEEKS					SUBTOTALS		
NO.	DESCRIPTION		ON LOC.	PREP	SHOOT	WRAP	TOTAL	RATE	A	B	C
			Local								
01	Supervisor		On Loc.								
			Local								
	Labor	No.	On Loc.								
			Local								
05	Painters		On Loc.								
			Local								
			On Loc.								
			Local								
06	Scenic Artists		On Loc.								
			Local								
			On Loc.								
			Local								
07	Carpenters		On Loc.								
			Local								
			On Loc.								
			Local								
08	Propmakers		On Loc.								
			Local								
			On Loc.								
			Local								
			On Loc.								
			Local								
			On Loc.								
			Local								
	Additional Hire		On Loc.								
15	Labor (See Detail Page 34A)										
20	Materials (See Detail Page 34A)										
22	Rigging (See Detail Page 34A)										
24	Striking (See Detail Page 34A)										
30	Rentals (See Detail Page 34B)										
40	Purchases (See Detail Page 34B)										
85	Additional Expense										
95	Miscellaneous										
99	Loss, Damage, Repair										
								SUBTOTALS			
								TOTAL ACCT 4300		0	

A - Fringeable/Taxes
B - Non-Fringeable/Taxable
C - Non-Taxable

PAGE NO. 34A

PRODUCTION NUMBER | PRODUCTION TITLE | DATE

4315, 4320, 4322, 4324 MINIATURES—DETAIL

SET NO.	SCREEN NAME/NO. DESCRIPTION	(4315) LABOR	(4320) MATERIALS	(4322) RIGGING	(4324) STRIKING	SUBTOTALS A	B	C
	SUBTOTALS							
	TOTAL DETAIL ACCT 4315, 4320, 4322, 4324						0	

A - Fringeable/Taxes
B - Non-Fringeable/Taxable
C - Non-Taxable

PAGE NO. 34B

PRODUCTION NUMBER | PRODUCTION TITLE | DATE

ACCTS 4330 & 4340 MINIATURES—DETAIL

SET	SCENE NAME/NO.	ITEM		RENTALS			PURCHASES	
NO.	DESCRIPTION	QTY	DESCRIPTION	TIME	RATE	AMOUNT	AMOUNT	✔
					SUBTOTALS			
	TOTAL DETAIL ACCTS 4330 & 4340						0	

A - Fringeable/Taxes
B - Non-Fringeable/Taxable
C - Non-Taxable

3 - Recoupable

4300–MINIATURE DEPARTMENT

MINIATURES COMPRISE A WHOLE SEPARATE ART. At times it is far more economical to construct a miniature set of a building or a town and use forced perspective to make it appear as if your actors are actually standing in it, than to build the full-size set. No matter how it is accomplished, however, your set must appear realistic. This can be done simply by having smoke rising from miniature chimneys, or using toy electric trains to chug through a town.

Some films will build miniature sets to test out special effects photographic shots.

The Conversation was a psychological study which dealt with HARRY CAUL and his demons. Miniatures were not necessary in the telling of this story.

Account 4400
Process
Department

PAGE NO. 35

PRODUCTION NUMBER	PRODUCTION TITLE	DATE

4400 PROCESS DEPARTMENT

ACCT NO.	DESCRIPTION	LOCAL/ ON LOC.	PREP	SHOOT	WRAP	TOTAL	RATE	SUBTOTALS A	B	C
01	Projectionist	Local								
		On Loc.								
		Local								
		On Loc.								
02	Camera Man	Local								
		On Loc.								
		Local								
		On Loc.								
03	Camera Operator	Local								
		On Loc.								
		Local								
		On Loc.								
04	Asst. Camera Man	Local								
		On Loc.								
		Local								
		On Loc.								
05	Electrical	Local								
		On Loc.								
06	Grip	Local								
		On Loc.								
07	Matte Artist	Local								
		On Loc.								
08	Matte Crew	Local								
		On Loc.								
		Local								
		On Loc.								
09	Rear Screen									
10	Front Screen									
12	Mock Up									
30	Rentals									
40	Purchases									
85	Additional Expense									
95	Miscellaneous									
99	Loss, Damage, Repair									
							SUBTOTALS			
							TOTAL ACCT 4400		*0*	

A - Fringeable/Taxes
B - Non-Fringeable/Taxable
C - Non-Taxable

4400—PROCESS DEPARTMENT

We mentioned **REAR SCREEN PROJECTION** (also known as *Process Photography* or *Front Projection*) in the introductory comments to Account 3700. *Rear Projection* uses a *plate* or shot of a location and combines it with actors on a sound stage. For instance, a shot of the Eiffel Tower may be a stock image or specially shot for you by a cameraperson in France. That film is processed and projected on a screen in the *process studio*. Your actors stand in front of the screen. The projector and the camera are mechanically locked into sync, and actors then appear to be standing in front of the Eiffel Tower, when in fact they are standing on a set in front of a projection of the Eiffel Tower.

Today's films can achieve the same effect by using a blue screen process adapted from video instead a projection. If your project requires this effect, it can be budgeted here; but only the costs of shooting in front of the blue screen are actual productions costs. The images are combined in post-production and those costs belong in the *film effects budget*, Account 5200.

There will be no process photography in *The Conversation*, so we will leave the account blank.

Account 4500

Animals

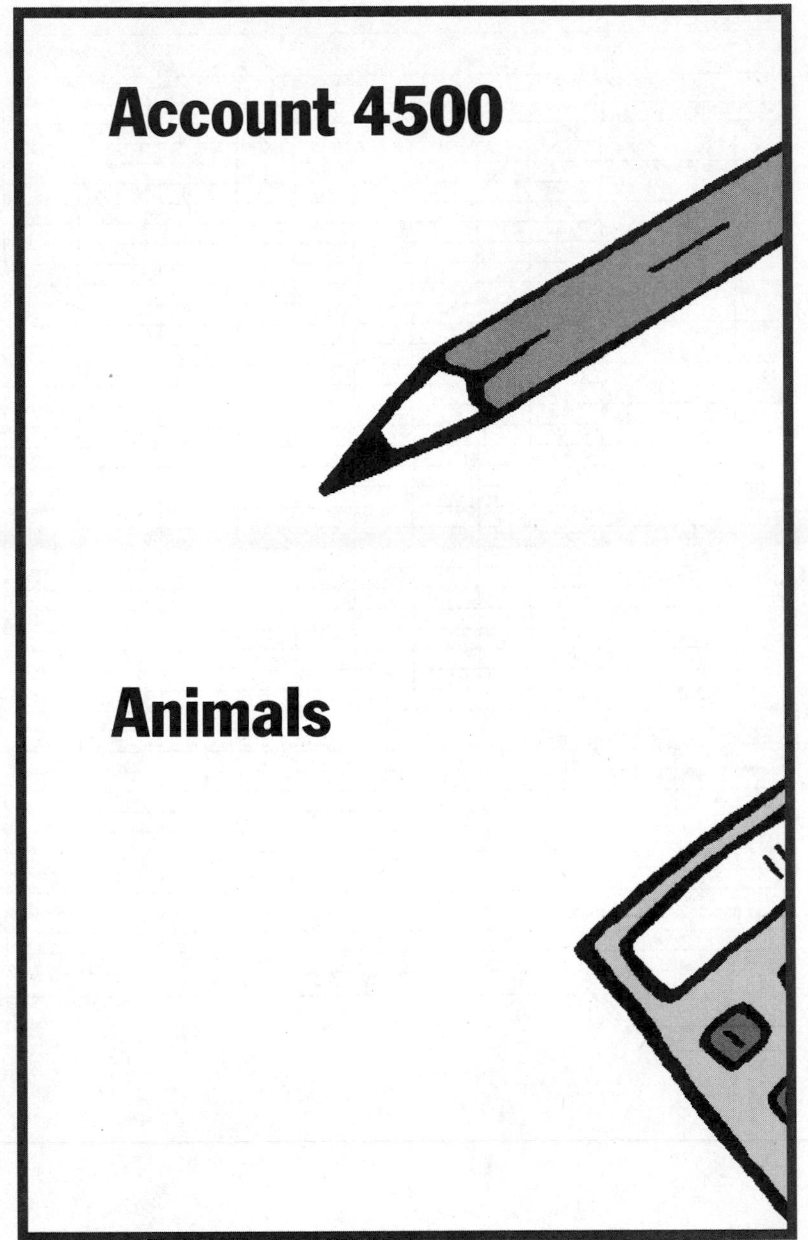

PAGE NO. 36

PRODUCTION NUMBER | PRODUCTION TITLE | DATE

4500 ANIMALS – 12 HR. DYS.

ACCT NO.	DESCRIPTION	LOCAL/ ON LOC.	PREP	SHOOT	WRAP	TOTAL	RATE	A	B	C
			DAYS/WEEKS					SUBTOTALS		
01	Head Wrangler	Local	5 dys.	4 dys.	--	9 dys.	306.18	2,756		
	21.87	On Loc.								
02	Addtional	Local								
	Wrangler	On Loc.								
03	Trainers	Local								
		On Loc.								
		Local								
		On Loc.								
04	Handlers	Local								
		On Loc.								
		Local								
		On Loc.								
		Local								
		On Loc.								
		Local								
		On Loc.								
		Local								
		On Loc.								
		Local								
		On Loc.								
		Local								
		On Loc.								
		Local								
		On Loc.								
	Additional Hire	Local								
		On Loc.								
30	Rentals (See Detail Page 36A)				ALLOW					1,750
40	Purchases (See Detail Page 36A)									
50	Animal Maintenance									
60	Special Transportation									
75	Travel and Living (List on Acct 4005)									
85	Additional Expense									
95	Miscellaneous									
99	Loss, Damage, Repair									
							SUBTOTALS	2,756		1,750
							TOTAL ACCT 4400	4,506		

A - Fringeable/Taxes
B - Non-Fringeable/Taxable
C - Non-Taxable

PAGE NO. 36A

PRODUCTION NUMBER | PRODUCTION TITLE | DATE

ACCTS 4530 & 4540 ANIMALS—DETAIL

SET NO.	SCENE NAME/NO. DESCRIPTION	ANIMALS QTY	ANIMALS DESCRIPTION	RENTALS W/H/L	RENTALS RATE	RENTALS AMOUNT	PURCHASES AMOUNT	✔
	Sc. 200-205							
	Int. Mr. C's Suite							
	Lobby & Corridor	1	Doberman Pinscher	1	250/dy.	250		
	(2 handlers at 23.41/hr. each)							
	Sc. 206-225							
	Int. Mr. C's Office	1	Doberman Pinscher	1	250/dy.	250		
	Sc. 40							
	Int. Harry's Apt.							
	Building	1	Dog	1	250/dy.	250		
	Sc. 44							
	Int. Harry's Apt.							
	Living Room/ Kitchen	1	Dog	1	250/dy.	250		
	Sc. 1-9							
	Ext. Union Square	3	N.D. Dogs		250/dy.	750		
					SUBTOTALS	1,750		
	TOTAL DETAIL ACCTS NO. 4530 & 4540				1,750			

A - Fringeable/Taxes   3 - Recoupable
B - Non-Fringeable/Taxable   W/H/T - Wrangler, Handler or Trainer
C - Non-Taxable

4500–ANIMALS

WHETHER FEATURED OR IN BACKGROUND, ANIMALS and their handlers are sometimes a subaccount under the *property budget.* In this account, budget the rentals on the animals themselves, the salaries for their handlers, and associated costs such food and transportation. Horses and other livestock require wranglers—usually Teamsters—who preferably are specialists in motion picture work. Dogs, cats, birds, fish, etc., may or may not have union handlers depending on the rental company. Propmasters often arrange for such rentals. Exotic animals from snakes to tigers require specialized handlers and are almost always a package deal with specialty companies.

The Conversation calls for a Doberman. This dog has to be trained before the picture starts. Once hired for the show, the has to be cared for, kenneled, and kept photogenic. The **WRANGLER** does this unless some specialized training is necessary.

It also is necessary to submit a script to the American Society for the Prevention of Cruelty to Animals (ASPCA) prior to filming. Part of the paperwork process that you will go through on your project with SAG will include answering their query on behalf of the ASPCA, and they will notify the ASPCA for you if animals are to be used. The ASPCA will review your script and decide if it is necessary for you to have a representative of theirs on the set to watch after the animals' welfare. The ASPCA does not charge for its representative. So when you have an animal, you could also have the animal's owner, its trainer, a wrangler and an ASPCA representative in attendance.

Account 4600

Transportation

PAGE NO. 37

PRODUCTION NUMBER | PRODUCTION TITLE | DATE

4600 TRANSPORTATION DEPARTMENT

ACCT NO.	DESCRIPTION	SUBTOTALS A	SUBTOTALS B	SUBTOTALS C
01	Coordinator	36,400		
	Rental:			3,822
02	Drivers—Captain and Co-Captain (See Detail Pages 37A & B)	32,999		
	Rental:			3,402
03	Drivers (See Detail Pages 37A & B)	421,825		
30	Vehicles—Rentals/Local (See Detail Pages 37A & B)			131,215
35	Vehicles—Rentals/Location (See Detail Pages 37A & B)		N/A	
50	Gas and Oil Allow:			40,000
55	Gas and Oil—Generator #1: 100 gals/day x $1.6 p.			
	gal. x 41 days			6,560
	Gen. #2: 15 days			2,400
57	Messenger Service Allow			35,000
59	Deliveries and Pick-Ups			
60	Pick-Up—Dailies (Also See Location Acct 4000) Covered by		N/A	
	transportation dept.			
61	Taxis and Limos Allow			7,500
63	Car Allowances (See Detail Page 37D) Allow			5,000
65	Vehicle Mileage (See Detail Page 37B)			
67	Mileage Allowances—Crew and Cast (See Detail Page 37E)			
	Allow			24,600
69	Permits, Tolls, Parking and Fees (See Detail Page 37B)			
70	Maintenance (See Detail Page 37B)			
71	Storage Allow			5,000
73	Trucks to Distant Location—Expenses			
75	Truck Rigging/Shelving Allow			3,000
85	Additional Expenses			
95	Miscellaneous Allow			25,000
99	Loss, Damage, Repair Allow			5,000
	SUBTOTALS	491,224		302,499
	TOTAL ACCT 4600	793,723		

A - Fringeable/Taxes
B - Non-Fringeable/Taxable
C - Non-Taxable

PAGE NO. 37A

TRANSPORTATION—DETAIL (14 HR. DYS.)

P:Prep, S:Shoot, W:Wrap
NOTE: For varying times and rates indicate PREP/SHOOT/WRAP

	DRIVERS					EQUIPMENT				
	P/S/W LOCAL		LOCATION			P/S/W LOCAL		LOCATION		
DESCRIPTION	WEEKS	RATE	WEEKS	RATE	TOTAL	WEEKS	RATE	WEEKS	RATE	TOTAL
Coordinator	8/8.2/2	2,000			36,400	18.2	210			3,822
				4601 Total	40,222					
Captain 23.96	6/8.2/2	2,037			32,999	16.2	210			3,402
Co-Captain										
Dispatcher										
				4602 Total	36,401					
Mechanic 16.61	1	1,412			1,412					
Production Van (Grip/Electric) 24.46	2/8.2/1	2,079			23,285	2/8.2/1	1,500			16,800
Camera/Sound Truck 19.24	1/8.2/.4	1,635			15,696	1/8.2/.4	475			4,560
Prop Truck 19.24	3/8.2/2	1,635			21,582	3/8.2/2	450			5,940
Special Effects Truck/sm. truck 19.24	1/8.2/.2	1,635			15,369	1/8.2/.2	400			3,760
Wardrobe Truck 19.24	1/8.2/1	1,635			16,677	1/8.2/1	300			3,060
Wardrobe Trailer						1/8.2/1	750			7,650
Makeup/Hair Truck										
Makeup/Hair Trailer	-	-	-	-	-	.4/8.2/.2	500			4,400
Set Dressing Truck 19.24	5/8.2/2	1,635			24,852	5/8.2/2	400			6,080
Set Dressing Wagon/crew cab 17.61	6/8.2/2	1,497			24,251	6/8.2/2	300			4,860
Construction Truck 19.24	4	1,635			6,540	4	325			1,300
Construction Crew Cab 19.24	4	1,635			6,540	4	425			1,700
Star Wagons : 2						5	500			5,000
Honeywagons 20.79	.2/8.2/.2	1,767			15,196	.2/8.2/.2	1,400			12,040
Station Wagon #3 16.61	8.2	1,412			11,578	8.2	210			1,722
Moter Homes : 2 20.79	.2/8.2/.2	1,767			30,392	.2/8.2/.2	750			12.900
(2) Crew Cabs trans. trailers 20.79	2/8.2/.4	1,767			37,460	2/8.2/.4	300			3,180
Station Wagons : 2 16.61	3/8.2/2	1,412			37,277	3/8.2/2	210			5,544
Crew Bus 19.24	4	1,635			6,540	4	750			3,000
Extra Bus										
Mini Vans/Crew Cab : 2 17.61	2/8.2/.4	1,497			31,736	2/8.2/.4	325			3,445
People Mover										
Catering Truck (Fee): See Acct 3601										
				4603 Total	326,383	4630 Total	106,941	4635 Total	N/A	

CONTINUED ON NEXT PAGE

CONTINUED ON NEXT PAGE

PAGE NO. 37B

TRANSPORTATION—DETAIL (CONT'D)

NOTE: For varying times and rates indicate PREP/SHOOT/WRAP

DESCRIPTION	DRIVERS LOCAL WEEKS	DRIVERS LOCAL RATE	DRIVERS LOCATION WEEKS	DRIVERS LOCATION RATE	DRIVERS TOTAL	EQUIPMENT LOCAL WEEKS	EQUIPMENT LOCAL RATE	EQUIPMENT LOCATION WEEKS	EQUIPMENT LOCATION RATE	EQUIPMENT TOTAL
Limo										
Camera Car/Insert Car 20.79	1	1,767			1,767	1	750			750
Car Carrier										
Water Wagon 20.79	1.6	1,767			2,827	1.6	1,500			2,400
Pick-up Trucks										
Crane Driver										
Fuel Truck										
Ambulance (See Location Acct 4000)										
Fork Lift										
Tow Trucks										
Generator										
Other Production Cars										
Crew Cab - Props 17.61	7/8.2/2	1,497			25,748	7/8.2/2	300			5,160
Wardrobe Wagon 16.61	6/8.2/2	1,412			22,874	6/8.2/2	210			3,402
Additional Hire										
Extra O.T.	Allow	25,000			25,000					
Director's Car 16.61	4/8.2	1,412			17,226	4/8.2	210			2,562
Cast Car(s) self drives	N/A				N/A	Allow	10,000			10,000
				Subtotal From Previous Page	326,383		**	see Acct.	#4635	106,941
				TOTAL DETAIL 4603	421,825		Total Det. 4630		Total Det. 4635	131,215
65 Vehicle Mileage										
69 Permits, Tolls, Parking and Fees										
70 Maintenance		Allow			5,000					
71 Storage		Allow			5,000					

** Acct. #4630 put in Acct. # due to space

PAGE NO. 37C

TRANSPORTATION—DETAIL

NOTE: For varying times and rates indicate PREP/SHOOT/WRAP

DESCRIPTION	DRIVERS					EQUIPMENT				
	LOCAL		LOCATION			LOCAL		LOCATION		
	WEEKS	RATE	WEEKS	RATE	TOTAL	WEEKS	RATE	WEEKS	RATE	TOTAL
										0

PAGE NO. 37D

PRODUCTION NUMBER	PRODUCTION TITLE	DATE

4663 CAR ALLOWANCES—DETAIL

DEPARTMENT	POSITION/NAME	WEEKS/DAYS	RATE	TOTAL
	Miscellaneous Rentals		Allow	5,000
	TOTAL DETAIL ACCT 4663	5,000		

A - Fringeable/Taxes
B - Non-Fringeable/Taxable
C - Non-Taxable

PAGE NO. 37E

PRODUCTION NUMBER | PRODUCTION TITLE | DATE

4667 MILEAGE—DETAIL					
DAY NO.	NO. PEOPLE	SET NO./LOCATION	MILES	RATE	TOTAL
41 dys.	100 p. dy.	Various locations in and around San Francisco	20 mi. p. dy.	.30□	24,600
		TOTAL DETAIL ACCT 4667	24,600		

A - Fringeable/Taxes
B - Non-Fringeable/Taxable
C - Non-Taxable

4600–TRANSPORTATION

UNLESS YOUR ENTIRE SHOW WILL BE SHOT ON a sound stage, the *transportation department* will be one of the most important in the entire production unit. Moving anything with wheelas well as many things with four legs is the province of the *transportation department*. In Los Angeles, cooks, wranglers, location managers, some generator operators as all drivers are members of Local 399. On a Teamster show, union members do all the driving. No one else on the crew can transport equipment or material. Cast and crew can report to a specific location in their own cars, but once there, any further movement of personnel must be done in Teamster operated vehicles. There are some lower budget production companies doing shows with non-Teamster crews. In major cities doing this automatically means you will experience difficulty renting some equipment; union organizers will visit your sets and possibly set up picket lines. Unlike SAG, the DGA, and the IATSE, the Teamsters have no low-budget contract or side-letter. In Los Angeles, they will negotiate *special deals*. There are also new restrictions and requirements on commercial drivers. In California, all those who drive trucks, haul trailers, or transport others should have a chauffeurs or Class One (also known as Class A) license. In the long run, coming to terms with the Teamsters Union may be the least troublesome and costly solution.

01: Transportation Coordinator

The *transportation coordinator* is the right arm of the production manager. It the coordinator's responsibility to obtain the proper *rolling stock* of all kinds such as picture vehicles and equipment trucks. At times this job can be difficult as many of the cars that the director has specified cannot be located. Period cars, special models, certain color combinations are especially difficult.

Our coordinator for *The Conversation* will come in at the beginning of prep for eight weeks. Under the Teamster's agreement, the coordinator's rate is negotiable and can make a *flat deal* for unlimited hours.

02: Transportation Captain

The *transportation captain* is the main assistant to the transportation coordinator. If your show has locations in several different cities you will probably have a captain for every city, each captain reporting to the coordinator.

30: Vehicles—Rentals/Local

If you rent or lease vehicles for more than four months, you are responsible for making sure they conform to Department of Transportation and, in California, local environmental standards. If a vehicle is not in good running order, there is the risk of being fined and/or having it taken out of service by a government inspector.

30: Vehicles—Production Van (Grip/Electric)

The *production van* usually consists of a 40-foot trailer which tows a tractor. The trailer houses the electrical and grip packages. The tractor has two 750-amp generators mounted on it. When the van arrives at location, the tractor is removed from the trailer and placed as near to the set as possible. The trailer is left up on jacks. The generators are specially built to be as quiet as possible so as not to disturb sound recording.

30: Vehicles—Camera/Sound Truck

The camera and sound equipment are kept on the *camera/sound truck*. Some trucks are compact step-vans. Others are five or ten-ton trucks rigged with work tables, power strips, air tanks for cleaning, and a small darkroom.

30: Vehicles—Prop Truck
This five or ten-ton truck holds the propmaster's boxes and the props. Most of the department trucks with have side-doors, lift gates, and ramps so that boxes and carts may easily loaded and unloaded. Depending on the show requirements set dressing, special effects, wardrobe, and makeup/hair will have its own truck or trailer, and sometimes more than one each depending on the needs of the show.

30: Vehicles—Honeywagons
These are small, portable dressing rooms and restrooms for cast and crew. Screen Actors Guild requires that each actor be given a separate room. The DGA requires the same for the director. Other rooms may be needed for a production office, schoolroom, etc. Large shows may have two or three honeywagons.

In addition, some performers may require, and insist upon via a contract clause, slightly better dressing rooms. Roomier trailers with two or three larger rooms, often equipped with TVs, VCRs, and small refrigerators are the next step up. Many performers are on a **FAVORED NATIONS** basis for rooms—they receive no less than anyone else. This can quickly add up to a fleet of motor homes.

30: Vehicles—Multiple-Unit Trailers
Several firms in Los Angeles (Star Waggons for one, owned by actor Lyle Waggoner) offer towable *multiple unit trailers* with anywhere from two to five dressing rooms each. The advantage is that these units can be towed by a general use pickup truck and do not need separate drivers.

30: Vehicles—Motor Homes
Regular *motor homes*, just like RVs, are much easier to park and maintain. Major stars are likely to have one in their contract, or may even have their own which you will be required to rent from them for their use. To avoid paying for additional drivers, try to use trailers which can be towed by a multipurpose transportation vehicle.

30: Vehicles—Crew Bus
When a large number of cast or crew members need to report to a studio, you will need to charter a *bus* (or more) to get every one to location.

30: Vehicles—Vans/Crew Cabs
Vans (mini and maxi) or crew cabs, sometimes called people movers, have a few more seats than standard vehicles and cost just a little more per week. One or two will be needed during prep for location scouts.

You will also need a mixture of station wagons, crew cabs, ordinary pickup trucks, and maybe a large sedan or a limousine to drive actors, director, or others to the set. Insert cars or camera cars also appear in the vehicles detail.

50: Gas and Oil
Costs for *gas and oil* for all vehicles is listed here. The diesel for the generator goes into Account 4655. Remember trucks get poor mileage. Base your allowance by factoring number of vehicles, miles to and from expected location, and days worked with average miles and price per gallon. The result may be much higher than you expected.

57: Messenger Service
We will need a *messenger service*, and might hire an extra driver or two from time to time to handle that chore. *[Note: Many productions spend way too much money on messenger services and/or overnight deliveries. Some think the only way to send anything is by messenger or overnight delivery. If it is not urgent, UPS can deliver local packages by the next day for a fraction of the cost of messengers and/or overnight delivery.]*

63: Car Allowances
If the film is being shot on location, be careful not to duplicate these costs that have already been recorded in the *location budget.* Usually when you are filming in Los Angeles, you will not need to rent cars.

There may be times, however, when you will need to arrange for a rental car for a person. An actor who is from out of town is an example.

Sometimes, it is more advantageous to lease a car on a long-term basis, as opposed to paying someone mileage or renting their own car from them. If the car rental/mileage bill works out to more than $500 per month and it would cost you $450 to lease them a car and pay their gasoline, lease the car.

67: Mileage Allowances

All the production *mileage* payments you expect to make to cast and crew for reporting to location should be detailed here.

85: Additional Expenses—Mechanic

A *mechanic* can suddenly become a key member of your crew especially if you are using cars for stunts. If the car doesn't work, your crew will stand around waiting for it to be fixed.

Since *The Conversation* has a short car chase, allow one week for a mechanic to ensure that all vehicles are in top running condition. List this expense under *Drivers—Account 3603*.

Account 4700

Production Rawstock and Lab

PAGE NO. 38

PRODUCTION NUMBER | PRODUCTION TITLE | DATE

ACCT NO.	DESCRIPTION	FOOTAGE	RATE	AMOUNT	SUBTOTALS A	B	C
4700 PRODUCTION RAWSTOCK AND LABORATORY							
01	Picture Negative Rawstock	5,000	.51	41 dys.			104,550
	1/4" Audio Tape Rawstock	6 reels	$12.00	41 dys.			2,952
	Second Camera Rawstock	5,000	.51	10 dys.			25,500
	Total Rawstock - 255,000'						
10	Picture Negative Developing 90%	230,000	$.2211				50,853
	(90% of Rawstock)						
	Forced Developing 1 stop		$.2837				
	2 stop		$.313				
20	Picture Negative Print						
	One Lite Print (65% of 230,000)	149,500	$.4013				59,994
	Color Corrected Dailies						
35	Sound Transfer						
	Stock	230,000	$.09				20,700
	Labor						
	(same as develop)						
45	Video ALLOW						10,000
	Video Tape Rawstock						
	Film to Tape Transfer						
	3/4" Tape Time Code Copies		145/hr.				
	1/2" Dailies		85/hr.				
	VCR/Monitor Rental		125/mo.				
50	Special Lab Work						
85	Additional Expenses						
90	Sales Tax on Acct. 4700						
95	Miscellaneous ALLOW						5,000
	Reels, Cases, Boxes, Etc.						
	Picture Leader						
99	Loss, Damage Repair						
				SUBTOTALS			279,549
				TOTAL ACCT 4700	279,549		

A - Fringeable/Taxes
B - Non-Fringeable/Taxable
C - Non-Taxable

4700–PRODUCTION RAWSTOCK AND LAB

WHEN YOU BEGIN BUDGETING A PROJECT, check current prices on rawstock—unexposed film—and lab fees. Only the lab costs of processing the camera negative into a work print are entered in this budget section.

01: Picture Negative

Most cinematographers prefer using Eastman (Kodak) stock. Whatever brand film you choose to use (Fuji, Agfa, Kodak), Eastman has four different film types on which the price varies by as much as $.08 per foot. The same is true for the other brands.

If this is a lower budget show you may want to consider buying your stock through a *rawstock exchange*. They offer previously purchased stock which was not consumed by the original buyer. Prices are lower based on several conditions: *unopened* or still factory sealed; *re-canned full rolls* or film which was put into a camera magazine but never loaded into the camera; or *long* and *short ends*— partial rolls left in a magazine when the assistants sent a given day's work into the lab. Rawstock exchanges usually *slop test* or process part of the ends and, on request, the full loads to ascertain that they have not been *flashed* or exposed to light; but there is no guarantee that other problems may not exist. Unless your budget is very low, any film that has been out of the can represents a risk you should not take. Even *unopened* rolls that were not properly stored could be a problem. While modern production techniques mean that the emulsions of the same type are unlikely to vary much, many DPs still prefer to have all the raw stock from the same batch number, that is manufactured at the same time.

The normal allowance is 5,000 feet of film per day per camera. You may budget slightly less for a second camera, but to cover ourselves in *The Conversation* we will budget the full 5,000 feet for each camera.

10: Picture Negative Developing

Some of the negative, such as the *short ends*, will not be processed. It is typical to allow for 90 percent (90%) of the rawstock which you purchase to be developed. Every film lab has its own set of rates. The ones here are above average; lower budget shows can find rates of $.10 to $.16 per foot. Labs will bid a picture. It is always a good idea to get bids from competing labs. If you are working at a major studio the lab probably already has a special deal for you.

20: Picture Negative Print

Many television programs and more features are using nonlinear editing systems. On features, it is still advisable to print and sync up film for dailies. If you make video transfers of production film, either directly from negative or from work print, that cost should be budgeted in this account.

Since only circled takes are printed, not all 90 percent (90%) of the footage processed needs to be included. The lab will use the camera reports to *pull*—or select—your circled takes from the camera negative and create *lab rolls*.

The range of process to print is 50 percent (50%) to 75 percent (75%.) On *The Conversation*, we allowed 65 percent (65%.)

35: Sound Transfer

Your production sound must be transferred for editing. For dailies and editing purposes, the transfer will be to 35mm film stock with a **MAG STRIPE** for audio. Estimate the cost of stock here. The labor may be built into the price per foot or detailed by the hour. If the transfers are being done by the same company contracted for your final mix, the cost may appear either here or in *Post-Production Sound budget account.*

45: Video—Half-Inch Dailies

Even if you are cutting on film, you will probably want to have your dailies transferred to half-inch video for the director, the studio and selected other people. Rates are for transfer to a **MASTER** with VHS **DUBS** (copies.) These rates are for straight transfers. For nonlinear editing which requires several times of code and edge numbers to be recorded in *windows* or on overlays on the image and on a computer diskette, the cost is $250 to $350 per hour. For each hour of film, allow four to six hours of transfer time.

85: Additional Expense—Projection

Normally the printed film **DAILIES** are screened each day of production for the director, producer, editor, DP and others, either at lunch or in the evening after wrap. Most labs have their own screening rooms where you can view dailies during normal office hours at no charge, but it may be more convenient to use a room closer to the studio and/or location. Budget that cost or the cost of having a projectionist standby after hours at the lab in this account.

Account 4900

Fringe Benefits and Payroll Taxes

PAGE NO. 39

PRODUCTION NUMBER | PRODUCTION TITLE | DATE

4900 FRINGE BENEFITS AND PAYROLL TAXES—BELOW-THE-LINE

ACCT NO.	DESCRIPTION	PAYROLL	VACATION HOLIDAY & PENSION	HEALTH & WELFARE	TOTALS
01	DGA $ 136,519	% 16	% 13.22	% 7.01	49,461
02	PGA $	%	%	%	
03	WGA $	%	%	%	
04	Extras SAG $ 83,247	% 16	% 12.5	% Inc.	23,725
05	IATSE $ 1,900,790	% 16	% 11.72*	% 4*	602,930
06	NABET $	%	%	%	
07	NON-UNION OTHER $ 247,604	% 16	%	%	39,617
10	TEAMSTERS $ 552,795	% 16	% 11.72	% 4	175,347
	SIDELINE MUSICIANS AFM $ 4,620	% 16	% 13	% 4	1,525
	FICA - 7.65% FUI - .8% SUI - 5.4% W.C. - 2.15%	% 16			

	PAYROLL	VACATION HOLIDAY & PENSION	HEALTH & WELFARE	TOTALS
SUBTOTALS				

TOTAL ACCT 4900 892,605

TOTAL COST BELOW-THE-LINE 5,723,706

A - Fringeable/Taxes
B - Non-Fringeable/Taxable
C - Non-Taxable

* – Approximate

Note – Above figures will decrease as individuals make more money.

4900–FRINGE BENEFITS AND PAYROLL TAXES

THIS ACCOUNT IS FOR *BELOW-THE-LINE* PERSONNEL. Calculate fringes here as you did for above-the-line fringes in Account 1900. Remember that fringes on below-the-line DGA personnel is 13 percent (13%)—one-half of one percent (.5%) being added for the costs of administering the **DGA TRAINING PROGRAM** and *qualification lists*. There are additional below-the-line DGA fringes: *vacation pay* (4 %) and *unworked holiday* pay (3.719%.) The latter is an allowance for DGA freelancers who may not be on payroll when holidays occur. If you do have DGA members on payroll for holidays, you may deduct what they receive for holidays from the *unworked holiday* total. Trainees do not receive this, but they do get the four percent (4%) *vacation pay*.

After this account enter the sub-total for the entire *Below-The-Line*. This now completes the Below-the-Line section.

Post Production

POST-PRODUCTION

Now you have finished production and all the film is *in the can*. It is time for the editor to connect the pieces. The process began after the first day of filming when your editor started a rough assembly of the first scenes that you shot.

After the picture is *locked* or the final decision is made on the visual content, the sound and music editing work will begin in earnest, leading up to the mix. When that is completed, the original camera negative will be cut to conform to the *locked* work print. The result is the *answer print* will eventually will yield the finished product.

Account 5000

Film Editing Department

PAGE NO. 40

PRODUCTION NUMBER	PRODUCTION TITLE	DATE

5000 FILM EDITING DEPARTMENT – 10 HR. DYS.

ACCT		LOCAL/	DAYS/WEEKS					SUBTOTALS		
NO.	DESCRIPTION	ON LOC.	PREP	SHOOT	WRAP	TOTAL	RATE	A	B	C
01	Post Production	Local	.2	8.2	21	29.4	1,500		44,100	
	Supervisor	On Loc.								
		Local								
		On Loc.								
02	Editor*	Local	.2	8.2	21	29.4	1,870.92	55,005		
		On Loc.								
		Local								
		On Loc.								
03	Asst. Editors	Local	.4	8.2	21	29.6	1,354.10	40,081		
	24.62/hr.	On Loc.								
		Local								
		On Loc.								
04	Apprentice Editor	Local	.2	8.2	21	29.4	1,138.50	33,472		
	20.70/hr.	On Loc.								
		Local								
		On Loc.								
05	Looping Editors	Local				90 hrs	400/hr	36,000		
		On Loc.								
06	Asst.	Local								
	Looping Editor	On Loc.								
		Local								
		On Loc.								
08	Music Editor	Local			12	12	2,500	30,000		
	Allow O.T.	On Loc.						3,000		
09	Asst.	Local								
	Music Editor	On Loc.								
							SUBTOTALS THIS PAGE	197,558	44,100	

CONTINUED ON NEXT PAGE

A - Fringeable/Taxes
B - Non-Fringeable/Taxable
C - Non-Taxable * – Scale for editor. Aug. salary for editor is 3500/wk.

ACCOUNT 5000– *Film Editing Department*

PAGE NO. 41

PRODUCTION NUMBER	PRODUCTION TITLE	DATE

5000 FILM EDITING DEPARTMENT–(CONT'D)										
ACCT		LOCAL/	DAYS/WEEKS					SUBTOTALS		
NO.	DESCRIPTION	ON LOC.	PREP	SHOOT	WRAP	TOTAL	RATE	A	B	C
07	Sound Effects	Local				ALLOW	185,000	185,000		
	Editor & Asst.	On Loc.								
		Local								
		On Loc.								
08	Projection Labor	Local				ALLOW	30,000	30,000		
		On Loc.								
		Local								
		On Loc.								
09	Dialogue	Local								
	Transcription	On Loc.								
11	Off Line	Local								
	Editing - Labor	On Loc.								
12	Cutting Continuity	Local			12 R	OLLS	300/roll			3,600
		On Loc.	1 B/W	DUPE	1,300;	1 SING	LE STRIPE	1,200		2,500
13	Secretary	Local								
		On Loc.								
14	Librarian	Local								
		On Loc.								
		Local								
		On Loc.								
15	Coding	Local				8 mos.	500			4,000
	Maintenance	On Loc.								
16	Shipping &	Local								
	Messengers	On Loc.								
30	Rentals SFX ROOMS: 10 wks. x 8 x 200									16,000
	Cutting Room 30 wks. x 3 x 250									22,500
	Editing Equipment KEM 8 mos. x 1,750; Jr. KEM 8 mos. x 1,350									24,800
	Projection Room									
	Music & Effects									
	Off-Line Editing									
40	Purchases									
	Supplies						ALLOW			5,000
	Video Transfers 15 rolls x 10; 150 hrs. x 12,000									13,500
80	Preview Expenses									
85	Additional Expenses									
95	Miscellaneous						ALLOW			5,000
99	Loss, Damage, Repair									
	SUBTOTALS FROM PREVIOUS PAGE							197,558	44,100	
	SUBTOTALS THIS PAGE							216,200		96,900
	TOTAL ACCT 5000							554,758		

A - Fringeable/Taxes
B - Non-Fringeable/Taxable
C - Non-Taxable

5000–FILM EDITING DEPARTMENT

WHETHER YOU ARE CUTTING ON FILM or using a video format, you will need an *editor* (or several) to physically make the cuts. Large budget shows needing to make tight delivery dates may put teams of editors on a project. Your director might be putting in as much time supervising the editing process as he when directing. When you budget for a short and/or intense post-production, remember that there are physical limits to what one person can do.

01: Post Production Supervisor

If you must work quickly because of time constraints, you should consider using a nonlinear system. Its speed will mostly offset the added costs of transfers and pricier rentals. Also consider hiring a *post production supervisor* (the UPM's counterpart in post-production.) The post production supervisor should be thoroughly familiar with all editing and post production sound methods you have decided to use. She will then be prepared to administer your budget and coordinate all the post production elements to finish on schedule.

02: Editor

The rates for editors vary tremendously. A higher weekly rate for an editor working on a nonlinear system actually ends up being less costly when you factor in the reduced number and time required of assistants.

Extra Editors

When necessary, you may hire extra editors for all or part of the post production period. It is possible to bring in additional editors for a few weeks to cut specific sequences only.

03: Assistant Editor(s)

Major features often have several assistant editors, classified as *first assistant editors, second assistant editors*, etc., as ADs are on production. The first assistant editor (or *key assistant editor*) keeps the logs which are vital both to making changes during the editing process and conforming all the elements when the picture is locked. Other duties vary from recording the director's notes during dailies to cleaning the work print.

04: Apprentice Editor

The IATSE formalized the concept of *apprentice editors* in the cutting room many years ago. Apprentices work at a reduced rate to learn the job of the assistant.

05: Looping Editor

Dialogue replacement is a very special form of editing in which the dialogue track alone must be replaced with one which has been rerecorded with better quality on the ADR stage.

For pictures cut on non-film systems and mixed using a video work print and 24-track audio tape, many of these sound-related editorial functions are performed as part of the sound package.

07: Music Editor

A traditional *music editor* syncs up the recorded and transferred cues created by the *music composer*. On non-film systems, music editors may work for the post-production sound facility. Also when a composer scores a picture electronically and delivers the music on a time-coded DAT, the syncing is done via computer.

07: Sound Effects Editor and Assistant

Whether *sound effects editing* is done using digital media, 24-track tape as part of the sound package or is cut on the film, it is almost always bid as a complete package. Working on either film or tape, sound effects facilities will bid all the finishing sound work on your locked picture.

15: Coding
Once the dailies are in sync, matching numbers—*code*—are printed every foot along both strips of film as a permanent reference. The dailies can be sent out for this procedure; but most editors prefer to have a coding machine rented so that the assistants can code the film in the cutting room.

30: Rentals—Editing Rooms/Rentals
For a film edit, you will need two or more cutting rooms and bulky equipment. If you are at a studio, the room and equipment rentals are separate. As with production equipment, however, some studios require that you rent editing equipment from them. Many independent facilities have full or partially equipped rooms for rent. If you rent flatbed editors, Moviolas, rack, bins, tables etc., make sure that delivery charges are included or allow additionally for them.

Video systems, linear or not, are much more compact and readily available in rooms at standing facilities.

30: Rentals—Projection Room
As sequences are first assembled and then fine tuned, the director, editor, etc., may want to see them projected on screen.

When the picture is **LOCKED,** the director will **SPOT** it, or discuss the music, sound effects, looping, and other requirements with the composer, etc.

40: Purchases—Supplies
Whether you are editing by splicing film or tape, or on computer, all methods require that you budget an allowance for expendables.

40: Purchases—Video Transfer
On a film cut, you may also want to transfer assembled sequences for the director or other to review on video. You should also budget to make video transfers of certain sequences as well as the entire *locked picture* for the composers, sound editors, et al. Those related costs are listed here.

Account 5100

Music

PAGE NO. 42

PRODUCTION NUMBER	PRODUCTION TITLE	DATE

5100 MUSIC

ACCT NO.	DESCRIPTION	TIME	RATE	AMT.	SUBTOTALS A	B	C
01	Composer		ALLOW		125,000		
02	Lyricist						
03	Music Coordinator						
04	Arrangers and Orchestrators		ALLOW		12,500		
05	Director/Conductor						
06	Copyists and Proof Readers		ALLOW		10,000		
07	Musicians		ALLOW		75,000		
08	Singers						
09	Rehearsal Pianist						
10	Coaches—Instrumental/Vocal						
11	Labor on Music Stage						
12	Labor Moving Instruments						
13	Cartage						
14	Sync Rights/Music License Fees		ALLOW				10,000
15	Original Songs Purchased Master Music Lic.		ALLOW				45,000
	Music Publishing Licenses		ALLOW				55,000
30	Rentals						
	Instruments		ALLOW				5,000
	Studio—Rehearsal		ALLOW				5,000
	Studio—Recording Facilities		ALLOW				35,000
40	Purchases—Equipment Rental		ALLOW				7,500
	Research Reports		ALLOW				1,500
85	Additional Expenses						
95	Miscellaneous		ALLOW				1,500
99	Loss, Damage, Repair						
				SUBTOTALS	222,500		165,500
				TOTAL ACCT 5100	388,000		

A - Fringeable/Taxes
B - Non-Fringeable/Taxable
C - Non-Taxable

5100–MUSIC

THERE ARE MANY TYPES OF MUSIC POSSIBLE IN A MOVIE. The most basic is the *underscore*, music that comes from nowhere and helps set the mood—from suspense to slapstick. There is also *source music*: songs or symphonies that appear to be coming from a radio or TV on in the background. Songs can also be part of the underscore. Whether songs are existing recordings licensed for use in a movie, new recordings made for the same purpose, or new songs written for your show, there are *use fees* and/or *production costs* that must be budgeted here.

With the exception of the musicians who usually get AFM (American Federation of Musicians) union salaries, the other people involved in the production of music can be paid in as many different ways and with as many pay scales as can actors or writers.

It is not uncommon for the music to be contracted at an all-in package price paid to the composer and/or a music coordinator. This arrangement will relieve you of all the financial and technical details of music production, from having the score copied to paying the musicians. On all but the smallest ensembles, music contractors are used to hire the players. With increasing frequency, there are persons working as *music producers* for hire by movie producers who for a contracted fee will provide you with an entire music track.

On *The Conversation*, various costs were somewhat detailed.

01: Composer

Except for the music which appears in the film, such as that which HARRY CAUL and his friends dance at the party in *The Warehouse*, we will want to have music composed specifically for this movie. The composer will be given copies of each reel when editing is complete. It will be viewed several times for rhythm and emotional content. Then the music will be composed to fit the emotional content of the piece.

04: Arrangers and Orchestrators

When time is short, it can help to have an **ARRANGER** handle the nuts and bolts of music writing, much as a sketch artist does the renderings for the art director in the *art department.*

05: Director/Conductor

When the composer does not conduct the musicians, you will need a **CONDUCTOR**.

07: Musicians

Unless your composer is using a synthesizer, you will need to hire musicians who will paid at AFM union rates. Musicians will need instruments to play, usually their own. You will have to pay for *cartage* —which is the cost of transporting the instruments to and from the music recording studio.

14: Sync Rights (Royalties)/Music License Fees

If you are using music which was not specifically composed for your show (e.g., such as popular songs from the Top 40) you will need to buy the rights to use that music on your production. There are two types of rights. Any music which is under copyright requires payment of *sync rights* or a negotiated *music publishing license* fee for the music itself. Public domain works by Mozart or the like are free. To use an existing recording a *master use* or *master music license* must also be purchased from the owners of the recording. Although Mozart's actual compositions are in the public domain, few of the actual recordings of Mozart or anyone else's music are. Sometimes it is not obvious who owns the rights, and it will take some research to find out. Take nothing for granted; even the song *Happy Birthday To You* was owned by someone until the copyright expired last year!

Account 5200

Film Effects

PAGE NO. 43

PRODUCTION NUMBER	PRODUCTION TITLE	DATE

5200 FILM EFFECTS

ACCT NO.	DESCRIPTION	QTY.	RATE	AMT.	SUBTOTALS A	SUBTOTALS B	SUBTOTALS C
01	Consultants						
02	Opticals						
	Fades, Dissolves, etc.		ALLOW				30,000
	Special Opticals - Montages,						
	Split Screen, Computer Graphics, etc.						
	Backgrounds for Process						
03	Matte Shots (Also See Process Acct 4400)						
04	Inserts						
05	Animation						
06	Process Plates						
30	Rentals						
	Equipment						
40	Purchases						
	Film and Lab Charges						
	Materials and Supplies						
	Film-Picture Negative						
	Film-Interpositive						
	Film-Positive Print Negative						
85	Additional Expenses						
90	Sales Tax						
95	Miscellaneous						
99	Loss, Damage, Repair						
				SUBTOTALS			30,000
				TOTAL ACCT 5200	30,000		

A - Fringeable/Taxes
B - Non-Fringeable/Taxable
C - Non-Taxable

5200—FILM EFFECTS

OPTICAL EFFECTS REFER TO THE PHOTOGRAPHY OF THINGS that are not actually there. Many books have been written about the art of *optical effects*. A large supporting industry has sprung up in Hollywood and in Northern California (e.g., George Lucas' company, Industrial Light and Magic—ILM). Whole series of pictures such as *James Bond* or *Star Wars*, as well as the spectacular effects in *Independence Day, Jurassic Park, Twister*, would not have been possible without the magicians in the optical effects department.

02: Opticals—Fades, Dissolves

Fades, *dissolves*, and old-fashioned wipes—still used to achieve a certain campy effect—can all be done now by film labs. (Many of you can even do them on your home video cameras.) Budget a general allowance.

02: Opticals—Special Opticals

The advent of computer-generated graphics has made California the center for such *special opticals*. For complex work, companies such as ILM, Digital Domain, V.I.F.X., will review your script and give you a bid for all the effects contained therein.

03: Matte Shots

Matte shots normally require interaction with the production unit. The live action and/or location *establishing shots* that will be embellished by combining them with **MATTE PAINTINGS** may need to be photographed with special cameras that have finer registration or alignment of each frame than a normal Panaflex or Arri. Budget that cost in production and the rest of the matte process here.

Account 5300

Titles Department

PAGE NO. 44

PRODUCTION NUMBER | PRODUCTION TITLE | DATE

ACCT NO.	DESCRIPTION	QTY.	RATE	AMT.	SUBTOTALS A	B	C
5300	**TITLES DEPARTMENT**						
01	Title Design (includes Title Filming)		ALLOW				45,000
	Art, Lettering						
02	Title Filming (see Title Design)						
03	Sub Titles						
30	Rentals						
	Equipment						
40	Purchases						
	Film and Lab Charges						
85	Additional Expenses						
90	Sales Tax						
95	Miscellaneous						
99	Loss, Damage, Repair						
				SUBTOTALS			45,000
				TOTAL ACCT 5300	45,000		

A - Fringeable/Taxes
B - Non-Fringeable/Taxable
C - Non-Taxable

5300—TITLES DEPARTMENT

SINCE THE CONFIGURATION OF THE TITLES IS NOT usually determined until after production is finished, it is common to budget an allowance—as opposed to exact numbers—for the title area. A complicated sequence of animated graphics in the title will cost a bit more than simple white letters on a black background.

01: Title Design

There are main titles—usually at the beginning of the picture—and end titles—at the end of the picture. No matter what the design, the required position and size of credits are often affected in detail by cast and crew employment contracts. When the picture credits are designed the result should be reviewed by the production attorneys for approval prior to the picture's release. You will bid for a package deal so the total goes into Column C not into Column A as the fringes on the labor are figured in.

02: Title Filming

This section is used only if you have a special cameraperson hired to photograph the background scenery for your titles. On *The Conversation* this is incorporated into *title design.*

Textless Titles

In anticipation of selling the foreign rights to your picture, you may wish to budget for *textless titles*, which shows just the background of the front and end titles so that the production credits translated into other languages can be superimposed.

Account 5400

Post-Production Sound

PAGE NO. 45

PRODUCTION NUMBER	PRODUCTION TITLE	DATE

5400 POST-PRODUCTION SOUND

ACCT NO.	DESCRIPTION	QTY.	RATE	AMT.	SUBTOTALS A	B	C
01	Sound Transfers—Labor/Facilities						
	Daily Reprints						
	Narration/Loops						
	Sound Effects						
	Music						
	Mix						
02	Magnetic Film						
	Narration/Loop Recording Masters						
	Narration/Loop Transfers						
	Sound Effects Recording Masters						
	Sound Effects Transfers						
	Music Recording Masters						
	Music Dub-Down Masters						
	Music Transfers						
	Dupe Work Track Transfers						
	Dubbing Masters						
	Dub Transfers						
	Music File Copy						
03	Sound Effects Recording ADR	90 hrs.	400	36,000			36,000
04	Dolby		ALLOW	7,500			7,500
05	Foley	90 hrs.	400	36,000			36,000
06	Dialogue Replacement						
	Looping/Narration						
07	Vocals Walla Crew		ALLOW	8,000	8,000		
08	Music Recording						
09	Dub Downs						
10	Re-Recording (Pre-Dubbing) MIXER	45 hrs.	850	38,250	38,250		
	MIXERS	135hrs.	850	see A	114,750		
11	Miscellaneous Labor O.T. MIXERS		ALLOW		10,000		
	Set Up Scoring Dubbing						
12	Sound Negative Raw Stock						
	35mm						
13	Foreign Delivery Requirements						
	Music Tracks						
14	Playback Preparation—Labor						
15	Daily Transfers—Material (incl. 16 & 17)		ALLOW	90,000			90,000
16	Reprint Transfers						
17	Playback Preparation—Material						
30	Rentals						
	Facilities (Post Production)						
40	Purchases		ALLOW				3,000
85	Additional Expenses						
95	Miscellaneous		ALLOW				50,000
99	Loss, Damage, Repair						
				SUBTOTALS	171,000		222,50
				TOTAL ACCT 5400		393,500	

A - Fringeable/Taxes
B - Non-Fringeable/Taxable
C - Non-Taxable

5400–POST-PRODUCTION SOUND

ALL SOUNDTRACKS HAVE THREE MAIN ELEMENTS: *music, sound effects,* and *dialogue*. Many of elements are recorded on the set, on a music stage, or simply borrowed as part of a package from a sound effects library. The cost of recording other elements such as the ADR dialogue and *foley effects* (*see below*) is detailed in this account. Finally all these elements are equalized, mixed and rerecorded in the *master dub*.

Most sound houses will give you a package bid on your project, no matter what combination of elements you need from them, and on what medium. For example, your mix of music, sound and dialogue can be a sprocket film-based mix where the perforations on the edge of the picture and sound elements hold them in sync. Or, they can be a combination of *multitrack, magnetic media interlocked with time-code.* Those bids are based on *their* estimate of how many hours and days of each facility you will use. If you end up using more time it will cost more money.

Many time-code based sound houses can also do the music and effects editing. The latter can be accomplished in a fraction of the time by a single person using a vast library of sounds stored on and accessed via computer. All the rates include the basic hourly cost of their mixers, engineers, and other staff. If you work long hours, your average hourly rate will go up due to overtime. People not on their payroll, such as **FOLEY ARTISTS** or **DOLBY** *engineers*, will incur additional costs. You should make a package deal so that their fringes are part of the deal.

01: Sound Transfers
02: Magnetic Film

If you are mixing on film, the costs involved in transferring post elements such as music and library effects to mag stripe film are budgeted here. *Sound transfer* time costs in hours goes in

Account 5401. Stock footage of *magnetic film* chargeable in feet goes in Account 5402.

03: Sound Effects Recording ADR

The costs of renting an ADR studio goes into this account. The costs of paying the actors to record the additional dialogue should be placed in the *cast account budget*.

04: Dolby

Using Dolby (or Ultra-Stereo, the main Dolby alternative) Noise Reduction system requires paying a licensing fee. Currently the Ultra-Stereo system costs half as much. The fee here is $7,500.

05: Foley

Just as actors add or replace dialogue to played back loops of scenes, *foley artists* add or replace sounds. Using props and a variety of hard surfaces they add or embellish everything from footsteps to rustling clothes. Even if these sounds are on the production track under dialogue, they may need to be recorded so that you have a *fully-filled* or clean, separate effects track available for use with dubs into foreign languages. Foley artists usually work on a daily basis and should be budgeted as a separate line item.

The soundtrack is so vital to *The Conversation* as to almost be a separate character. Our *foley crew* and *walla group* will be putting in long hard hours to make sure that the soundtrack is as realistic as possible, giving as much life to the film as Coppola wants.

07 Vocals

Your *loop group* or *walla crew* are budgeted here. They will fill in crowd scenes with a background of murmurs and other sounds to the effect of indecipherable conversations. In Hollywood you can hire a company to provide you with specialized actors for this purpose.

09: Dub Downs

When the quality of sound is as important as it is in *The Conversation,* it will take a great deal of time and care to perform the mix. The sound track should highlight whatever activity is being portrayed on the screen at any one time. When there is a close-up of HARRY CAUL speaking in the Convention Center Scene, there will be an effects track of the murmur of voices and some electronic sounds in the background, but HARRY'S voice track will be raised for his close-up. If we cut away to an overall view of the convention we will lower the volume on HARRY'S voice and raise the murmur and FX (sound effects) level. If there is a band playing in the background, we may have the music faintly audible mixed in with the murmur. If the director then decides to have HARRY walk past the band, we would lower the murmur track and raise the volume of the band to show our proximity.

All this is an art in itself. The director, editor and sound editor might spend hours just mixing the sound of one vital scene until it exactly suits the mood of the piece. They will try different volume levels for the various elements show on the screen, mixing them in a way that will give the audience impression that they are really in the same room with the performers.

13: Foreign Delivery Requirements

Both *foreign* and *domestic distribution contracts* may contain extensive schedules or lists of delivery items—their *foreign delivery requirements*. Many of these are directly related to making foreign versions. A dialogue continuity, or *script* of the finished film with footage and time-code reference marks for all the lines, will be used both for subtitles and to dub into other languages.

For these dubs to be seamless, each foreign distributor will require a *M&E* or *music and effects track*. Using the dialogue continuity and a *cue track* of the English, a foreign actors will dub all the lines. That dub will be combined with the music and effects to create a finished foreign soundtrack. Budget the M&E here.

15: Daily Transfers

The stock for your *film transfers* of dailies may be detailed here or in Account 4700. Additional transfers to magnetic film or video should be detailed in this account.

85: Additional Expenses—TV Version Dub

This category can be used for budgeting a *TV version dub*, in which words unacceptable on television are replaced. Most domestic distribution contracts call for delivery of a TV version.

Account 5500

Post-Production
Film and Lab

PAGE NO. 46

PRODUCTION NUMBER | PRODUCTION TITLE | DATE

5500 POST-PRODUCTION FILM AND LAB

ACCT NO.	DESCRIPTION	QTY.	RATE	AMT.	SUBTOTALS A	SUBTOTALS B	SUBTOTALS C
01	Editorial Reprints—1 Lite Color		ALLOW	8,000			8,000
02	35mm Silent Timing Print						
03	35mm Composite Answer Print						
04	35mm Release Prints		1.6082	12,000ft			19,298
05	35mm Interpositive or C.R.I. (Prot. Master)	3		12,000ft			36,000
06	35mm Internegatives						
07	1st Trial Composite Answer Print		1.6082	12,000ft			19,298
08	16mm Release Prints						
09	16mm Protective Master						
10	Reversal Prints Black & White						
11	35mm Sound Negative Dev. & Print		ALLOW	3,000			3,000
12	16mm Sound Negative Dev. & Print						
13	Stock Footage—License Fees		ALLOW	15,000			15,000
14	Stock Footage—Processing						
15	Negative Cutting	12rolls	700	8,400	8,400		
16	Outside Lab Charges						
17	Transfer to Cassette						
18	Shipping Charges						
19	Network Requirements						
	Cutting (Post Prev. Print)		ALLOW	3,000			3,000
	Recuts		ALLOW	7,500			7,500
30	Rentals						
	Vault Rental						
40	Purchases						
	Picture Leader (Positive & Negative)		ALLOW	5,000			5,000
	Reels						
	Cans						
	Video Cassettes						
	Videotape Dupes						
	Film Charges						
	Laboratory Charges						
85	Additional Expenses						
95	Miscellaneous						
99	Loss, Damage, Repair						
				SUBTOTALS	8,400		116,096
				TOTAL ACCT 5500	124,496		

A - Fringeable/Taxes
B - Non-Fringeable/Taxable
C - Non-Taxable

5500—POST-PRODUCTION FILM AND LAB

THIS ACCOUNT CONTAINS ALL THE COSTS NEEDED to purchase the necessary stock as well as pay for all the lab work required to finish the film. As with the *post production sound account*, if your project has (or anticipates) domestic or foreign distribution contracts, many of the delivery items will be budgeted here. Just as the price of the film stock is included in the rates per foot for printing dailies, most of the lab work here includes both stock and labor in the price.

01: Reprints

On film edits, the physical act of running the work print repeatedly through a **FLATBED** or **MOVIOLA** causes wear and tear and the film often tears or breaks. *Reprints* are used to replace damaged or lost pieces.

07: First Trial Composite Answer Prints

Depending upon the batch of emulsion and the exact chemical mix when it is processed, every piece of negative varies slightly in its density and color values. Prior to answer print, the lab's color timer will usually work with your DP at a *hazeltine* or other apparatus to set the correct color for each scene and each piece of film. When the answer print is screened, it will be the first time you, the director, the DP, et al, will see all the color corrections printed and projected. Until now, the picture or action has been on one piece of film (the **WORK PRINT**) and the sound on another (the **MAG STRIPE**). Although its overriding purpose is to evaluate the picture and not the sound, the answer print is also the first time that the movie's two elements will be together on the same piece of film. This is called **COMPOSITED** print.

All the subaccounts refer to particular types of prints. If you are working on a deadline, you may begin to cut the negative

(Account 5515) as soon as the picture is locked including all inserts and stock footage (Account 5513.) In film edits, the **EDGE NUMBERS** on the work print which refer back to the original negative from which it was made are the guide to cutting. In nonlinear edits, the computer generates an *edit list* from the **EDGE NUMBER** information recorded during the video transfer. Depending on how long the sound work takes, you may be ready for an answer print before the sound work is done and use a **BLACK TRACK** or *silent timing print* (Account 5502) so that both processes can proceed simultaneously.

Those parts of the answer print which are not quite right are readjusted until the entire film is acceptable. Because there is a risk of scratching, breaking or otherwise damaging the original camera negative every time it is used for printing, it should be retired from the process as soon as possible. Costs for making an **INTERPOSITIVE** (IP) or an **INTERNEGATIVE** (IN) **STAGE** are listed in Accounts 5505 and 5506. A interpositive is a copy of the finished film using the timing information from the answer print. From them enough internegatives are made to manufacture **RELEASE PRINTS**. Additional IPs, answer prints (Account 5503), normal and *low-con(trast)* prints are then made to satisfy film delivery needs, as well as for making video masters.

Other costs included here are for **DIRTY DUPES** (Account 5510.) Dirty dupes are inexpensive black and white black-and-white copies of the locked picture. These are used by the music and sound effects editors to sync up their material.

After the master dub, the print master or final master magnetic track is used to *shoot* an *optical negative* (Account 5511.) This becomes the sound equivalent of the cut picture negative.

If the director's cut or other semi-locked picture is to be previewed you must make an allowance for additional editing based on the preview results.

For *The Conversation* we have made a **MASTER POSITIVE** from the cut negative in order to strike. Once done, we can make our first answer print for delivery to the distributor. After the distributor has seen and approved it, all prints made after that are paid for by the distributor and our financial responsibility for post-production ends.

13: Stock Shots

We have made an allowance of $15,000 for *The Conversation*, to cover any stock footage we may need.

15: Negative Cutting

We are allowing $700 per reel (average amount) for our negative cutting. We are assuming the film as released to be about two hours long. Each reel equals about ten minutes of screen time, so we will need 12 reels, or 120 minutes. After the first preview we might need an additional amount of cutting, so we have allowed an extra $3,000 to cover that possibility.

Account 5900

Fringe Benefits and Payroll Taxes

PAGE NO. 47

PRODUCTION NUMBER	PRODUCTION TITLE	DATE

5900 FRINGE BENEFITS AND PAYROLL TAXES—POST PRODUCTION

ACCT NO.	DESCRIPTION		PAYROLL	PENSION	HEALTH & WELFARE	TOTALS
01	DGA	$	%	%	%	
02	PGA	$	%	%	%	
03	WGA	$	%	%	%	
04	SAG	$	%	%	%	
05	IATSE	$ 591,958	% 16	% 11.72	% 4	187,769
06	NABET	$	%	%	%	
10	OTHER	$ 44,100	% 16	%	%	7,056
	AFM	or ALLOW $ 222,500	% 16	% 13	% 4	73,425

	PAYROLL	PENSION	HEALTH & WELFARE	TOTALS
SUBTOTALS				

TOTAL ACCT 5900 268,250

TOTAL COST—POST PRODUCTION 1,804,004

A - Fringeable/Taxes
B - Non-Fringeable/Taxable
C - Non-Taxable

5900—FRINGE BENEFITS AND PAYROLL TAXES

This account is used for listing the fringe benefits and payroll taxes on personnel who are listed in the post-production subsection only.

Now enter the subtotal for the Post-Production Account.

Account 6000

Publicity

PAGE NO. 48

PRODUCTION NUMBER	PRODUCTION TITLE	DATE

6000 PUBLICITY – 12 HR. DYS.

ACCT NO.	DESCRIPTION	LOCAL/ ON LOC.	PREP	SHOOT	WRAP	TOTAL	RATE	SUBTOTALS A	B	C
01	Publicity Firm Fee	Local								
		On Loc.								
02	Unit Publicist	Local	.4	8.2	.4	9.0	1409.48	12,685		
		On Loc.								
		Local								
		On Loc.								
03	Still Photographer	Local	.2	8.2	.2	8.6	2295.30	19,740		
	32.79	On Loc.								
		Local								
		On Loc.								
04	Special Photographer	Local								
		On Loc.								
		Local								
		On Loc.								
	Additional Hire	Local								
		On Loc.								
	Secretary	Local								
		On Loc.								
		Local								
		On Loc.								
05	Trailers	Local								
		On Loc.								
10	Consulting Fees	Local								
		On Loc.								
		Local								
		On Loc.								
30	Rentals									
	Camera Equipment (8.2 WKS. X 500/WK.)									4,100
30	Purchases									
	Film									
	Processing									
	Prints									
	Lab Expense									
85	Additional Expenses									
	Entertainment						ALLOW			2,500
95	Miscellaneous									
99	Loss, Damage, Repair									
							SUBTOTALS	32,425		6,600
							TOTAL ACCT 6000	39,025		

A - Fringeable/Taxes
B - Non-Fringeable/Taxable
C - Non-Taxable

6000—PUBLICITY

THE PROCESS OF SELLING YOUR MOVIE BEGINS LONG before the cameras roll. Properly timed press announcements, called press releases, about the selection of cast, director, etc., can create interest as early as possible. Publicists can also be helpful in quashing any unwanted stories or by creating interest by not releasing any information to the press. Filmmakers want to create interest not only among future patrons and ticketbuyers, but also among potential distributors.

In *The Conversation* we have a publicist working with us during the entire production. He will keep stories flowing into the newspapers, announcing via the trade papers all the world-shaking news which happens on the set *or* keeping things quiet.

02: Unit Publicist

A *unit publicist* can either be assigned by a studio or hired as a freelancer (independent.) Often they are members of the Publicist's Guild and have established fees and rates.

Publicity is one of the least understood and most overlooked areas of filmmaking, which can sometimes be one of the most important. A well-placed article or favorable review can, many times, increase word-of-mouth more on your project than a paid ad—and the space is free! If your movie is mentioned on *Entertainment Tonight* you will reach a vast audience for literally the price of the few phone calls needed to set it up. Although it is not yet a common practice to keep a publicist on until the release of the film, I would consider it to be money well spent. Your publicist can follow up on all the interviews set up during production, and also coordinate with the studio Public Relations Department which has many other films to worry about.

03: Still Photographer

On IATSE shows the *still photographer* is a member of the same local as the *camera department* and is often budgeted there. The still photographs for publicity and distributor use will come from this person. Some lower budget shows call a *still person* in on a spot basis and/or let the publicist coordinate the days on which the still person works. If you can afford it, have the photographer on the set every day of shooting.

10: Consulting Fees

You may want to test markets, design posters, or plan previews with a specialized consultant. Public relations departments of the studios have many films to which they are attending. Many large outside public relations firm also have many clients whom they are overseeing. They will not be able to devote all their time to your project alone. Usually it is better to hire your own publicist, and use a *public relations* firm to coordinate a specific event, such as the *premiere*.

85: Additional Expense—Entertainment

The unit publicist may often arrange for cast interviews over dinner or otherwise entertain journalists. Allow for those costs here.

Account 6100

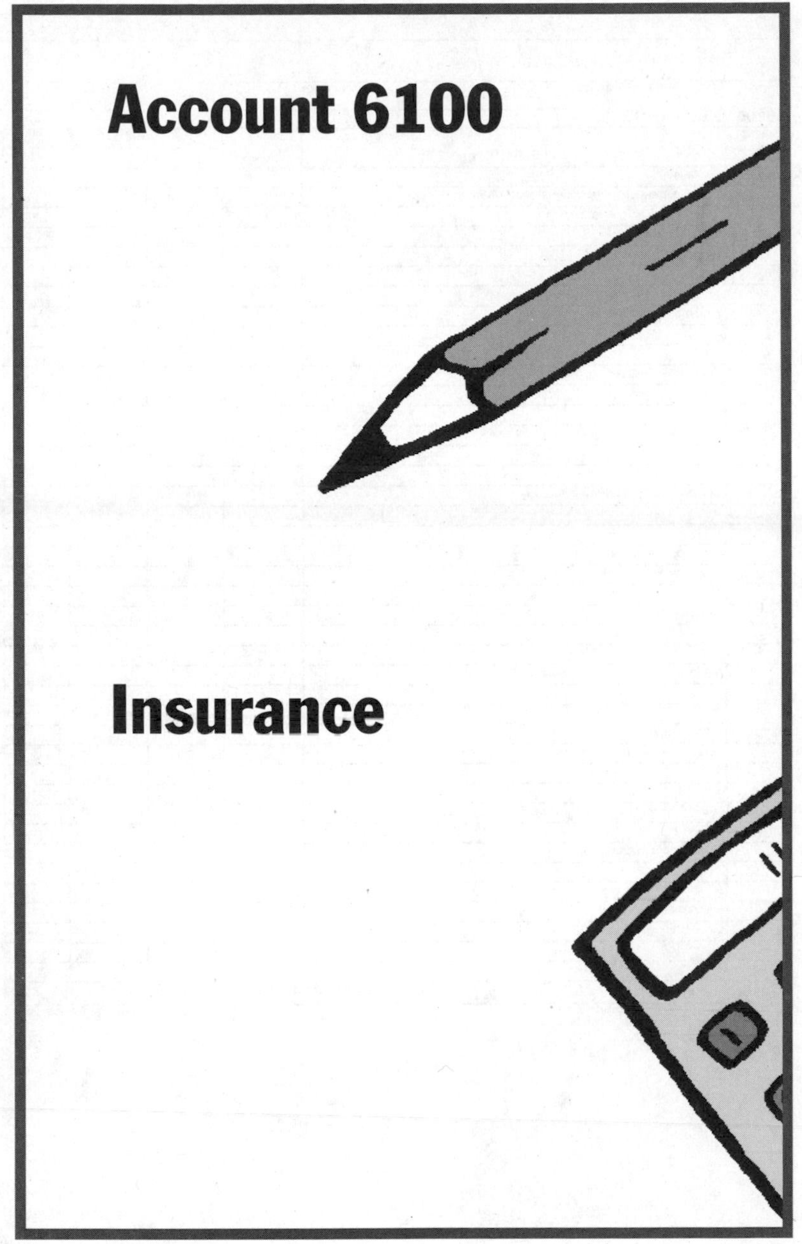

Insurance

PAGE NO. 49

PRODUCTION NUMBER	PRODUCTION TITLE	DATE

6100 INSURANCE

ACCT NO.	DESCRIPTION	AMOUNT	SUBTOTALS A	B	C
01	Package –				
	Total Budget Less - Producer(s) fee(s); Writer(s) fee(s);				
	Director/CAST (over 5 mil.) 13,584,149 x 1.7%				
	General Expenses				230,929
02	Negative Film Insurance				
03	Workman's Compensation Insurance				
04	Errors and Omission Insurance - Estimate				
05	Faulty Raw Stock, Camera and Processing				
06	Comprehensive Liability Insurance				
07	Set, Props, and Wardrobe Insurance				
08	Extra Expense Insurance				
09	Miscellaneous Equipment Insurance				
10	Other Insurance				
	Local Insurance Requirement				
11	Medical Exams - usually Director, D.P., Lead cast	1,000			1,000
25	Extra Riders/Additional Insurance				
85	Additional Expenses				
95	Miscellaneous				
99	Loss, Damage, Repair				
		SUBTOTALS			
		TOTAL ACCT 6100	231,929		

A - Fringeable/Taxes
B - Non-Fringeable/Taxable
C - Non-Taxable

6100—INSURANCE

ALL FILMS MUST BE INSURED. IT IS NORMAL TO estimate your insurance costs based on an overall percentage of the direct costs of the picture with certain exclusions, such as writers' fees, producers' fees, or other fixed above-the-line costs. All contractual surcharges such as the *completion bond* and *contingency allowance* are also excluded when calculating the cost of insurance.

The percentage used today is between one and one-half percent (1.5%) and one and seven-tenths percent (1.7%). For *The Conversation,* we are using 1.7%. The exclusions amount to: $620,129. We arrived at that figure as follows:

Producers fees	$	550,000
Writers fees	$	62,337
Writer's fringe	$	7,792
Subtotal A	**$**	**620,129**
Total Direct Costs	$	14,204,180*
Less Subtotal A	$	620,129
Total for Insurance Calculation	**$**	**13,584,051**

*(This figure includes totals for *above-the-line, below-the-line, post production*, and the following from the *other costs* area: *publicity, general expense*, and *fringe benefits/payroll.*)

Multiply the *Total for Insurance Calculation* above by the *insurance cost factor* (1.7%) and you will get:

Total Insurance Cost $ 230,929

If you have *essential elements* in the film, your premium will increase. Essential elements are major cast members and a major director. If anything should happen to one of your essential elements (illness, accident, death) your project will suffer financially. This is an area of your insurance which, if it applies to your film, you will have to negotiate a fee. (*See Cast Insurance, Account 6101.*)

If your project has any unusual areas of exposure such as: heavy duty car chases, stunts, special effects, location shooting on a Himalayan mountain you will be charged an additional percentage to cover the occurrence.

In 1995-96, deductibles and minimum premiums for production insurance rose markedly. Many productions, particularly those with heavy action sequences that pose risks of injury, will be facing premium totals closer to two and one-half percent (2.5%) or three percent (3%) of direct costs.

All your premiums are based on the value covered. Insurance carriers have the right to audit your production. If you go over budget then the declared value of your picture, which is based on cost, will increased and so may your premiums.

01: Cast Insurance

Normal *cast insurance* covers the director and up to five actors whom you designate. You can always cover additional cast members or other key persons, such as the DP, for an additional premium. Your cast and director are required to have physical exams before being covered. You will get a report if any preexisting conditions are excluded from coverage. If anyone becomes ill, have the person examined by a physician and notify your insurance agent immediately. If a covered actor dies, as was the case with Brandon Lee during *The Crow*, the insurance carrier can be liable for the total cost of the picture or the amount spent to that point, less a deductible of at least $10,000.

02: Negative Film Insurance

In the unlikely event that something disastrous happens to ruin your negative (e.g., the lab where your negative is stored burns down) the carrier is again liable for the total cost of the picture minus the deductible.

03: Workers Compensation

Workers compensation is a part of the budgeted amount in each of the fringe benefits sections.

04: Errors and Omissions

Errors and Omission coverage (E&O) is essential. Banks will not lend nor will bond companies assume liability until this coverage is in place. As with any preexisting medical conditions, carriers may find problems in your script. You should try to get full coverage by taking higher deductibles rather than accept exclusions.

05: Faulty Raw Stock, Camera, and Processing

Damage to your negative whether inherent or caused by camera or processing is covered here. Certain other problems, such as flicker because of faulty HMI lights, are also covered.

07: Sets, Props, and Wardrobe Insurance

Deductibles range from $1,000 to $5,000 per incident. Premiums adjust accordingly.

08: Extra Expense

This covers other unforeseen problems which can affect your production. Weather problems and *force majeure* events (aka **ACTS OF GOD**) such as earthquakes or wars are usually not covered. You may want to secure an *umbrella policy* or additional rider to cover catastrophic problems in any category that exceeds policy limits.

09: Miscellaneous Equipment

Covers cameras, lights, etc. Most vendors now require binders which names them as additional insured on your policy before they will release equipment to you.

10: Other Insurance—Local Insurance Requirement

Certain municipalities may require higher liability limits than the normal $1 million when you shoot within their jurisdictions. This is also true of any special locations where damage would be quite expensive.

10: Other Insurance—Guild Accident and Travel
This is a union requirement.

Account 6200

General Expense

PAGE NO. 50

PRODUCTION NUMBER	PRODUCTION TITLE	DATE

6200 GENERAL EXPENSE

ACCT NO.	DESCRIPTION		AMOUNT	SUBTOTALS A	B	C
01	Secretary					
02	Messenger Service					
03	Janitor/Cleaning Service					
04	Courtesy Payments (Also See Accts 4029 & 3717)					
05	Shipping (Also See Acct 3010)					
06	Accounting Service					
07	Production Services					
08	Entertainment					
	Meals (Also See Acct 4009)					
	Wrap Party					
09	Bank and Foreign Currency Exchange Cost					
10	Facility Sales Tax					
30	Rentals					
	Telephone & Telegraph (Also See Acct 4016)		ALLOW			55,000
	Installation Charges (Also See Acct 4016)					
	Office (Also See Acct 4013)	8 mos.	8,000			64,000
	Office Equipment (Also See Acct 4014)					
	Office Furniture (Also See Acct. 4014)	8 mos.	ALLOW			12,000
	Duplicating Machine (Also See Acct 4014)		ALLOW			10,000
	Parking (Also See Acct 4095)		ALLOW			4,000
	Data Processing		ALLOW			12,500
	Storage					
40	Purchases					
	Office Supplies (Also See Acct 4012)					
	Stationery		ALLOW			12,500
	Postage (Also See Acct 4011)					
	City License					
	MPAA Code Seal Fee		ALLOW			8,000
85	Additional Expenses					
	Legal Fees		ALLOW			125,000
	Legal Research					
	Accounting Fees					
	Preview Expenses		ALLOW			25,000
90	Sales Tax					
95	Miscellaneous		ALLOW			5,000
	Wrap Party/Wrap Gift		ALLOW			15,000
99	Loss, Damage, Repair					
			SUBTOTALS			348,000
	TOTAL ACCT 6200			348,000		

A - Fringeable/Taxes
B - Non-Fringeable/Taxable
C - Non-Taxable

6200—GENERAL EXPENSE

06: Accounting Service

INSURANCE AUDITS OR TAX REPORTING ARE ITEMS which occur after your production accountant is no longer needed full time and has gone on to another show. Later there may be residuals or royalties to pay. On a studio picture, its *Accounting Department* will take on these tasks. Independent producers may arrange with an accounting firm to handle such requirements.

09: Bank and Foreign Currency Exchange Costs

These range from checking account fees to wire transfers to interest on your production loan.

40: Purchases—MPAA Code Seal Fee

This certificate is usually a delivery requirement. This fee works on a sliding scale. Higher budgeted pictures will pay higher MPAA fees.

85: Additional Expense—Legal Fees

As with insurance you may estimate the cost of production legal as a percentage. One percent (1%) is the rule of thumb, and many production attorneys and/or firms will contract for the legal work for a total fee in this range.

These fees may vary depending on how complicated the deals for your show are. If you are obtaining production financing based on a number of distribution deals for different markets or have many profit participant deals, expect to pay more. The production attorney will be responsible for reviewing all contracts for the show including your actors' run-of-show deal, foreign sales, music clearance, etc. Also you as a producer will want to have your own attorney in addition to the production attorney. On an hourly basis, rates can vary from $125 to over $450 per hour depending on the lawyer's experience.

Preview Expenses

This covers research previews with recruited audiences, as well as press screenings.

Account 6900

Fringe Benefits and Payroll Taxes

PAGE NO. 51

PRODUCTION NUMBER | PRODUCTION TITLE | DATE

6900 FRINGE BENEFITS AND PAYROLL TAXES—OTHER COSTS					
ACCT NO.	DESCRIPTION	PAYROLL	& PENSION	HEALTH & WELFARE	TOTALS
01	DGA $	%	%	%	
05	IATSE $ 32,425	% 16	% 11.72	% 4	10,285
03	NABET $	%	%	%	
	OTHER $	%	%	%	
	or Allow				

SUBTOTALS				

TOTAL ACCT 6900	10,285
TOTAL ABOVE THE LINE	6,279,160
TOTAL BELOW THE LINE	5,723,706
TOTAL POST PRODUCTION	1,804,004
TOTAL OTHER COSTS	629,239
TOTAL DIRECT COST	14,436,109

A - Fringeable/Taxes
B - Non-Fringeable/Taxable
C - Non-Taxable

6900–FRINGE BENEFITS AND PAYROLL TAXES

ANY PUBLICITY PEOPLE OR OTHERS FROM this subsection should have fringes on their salaries entered here. There may not be any.

Also use this page to recap all the subtotals thus far. The total of all those amounts will be the *direct cost*. This figure will be the base amount upon which the *contractual costs* in the next section are derived.

—— *Notes* ——

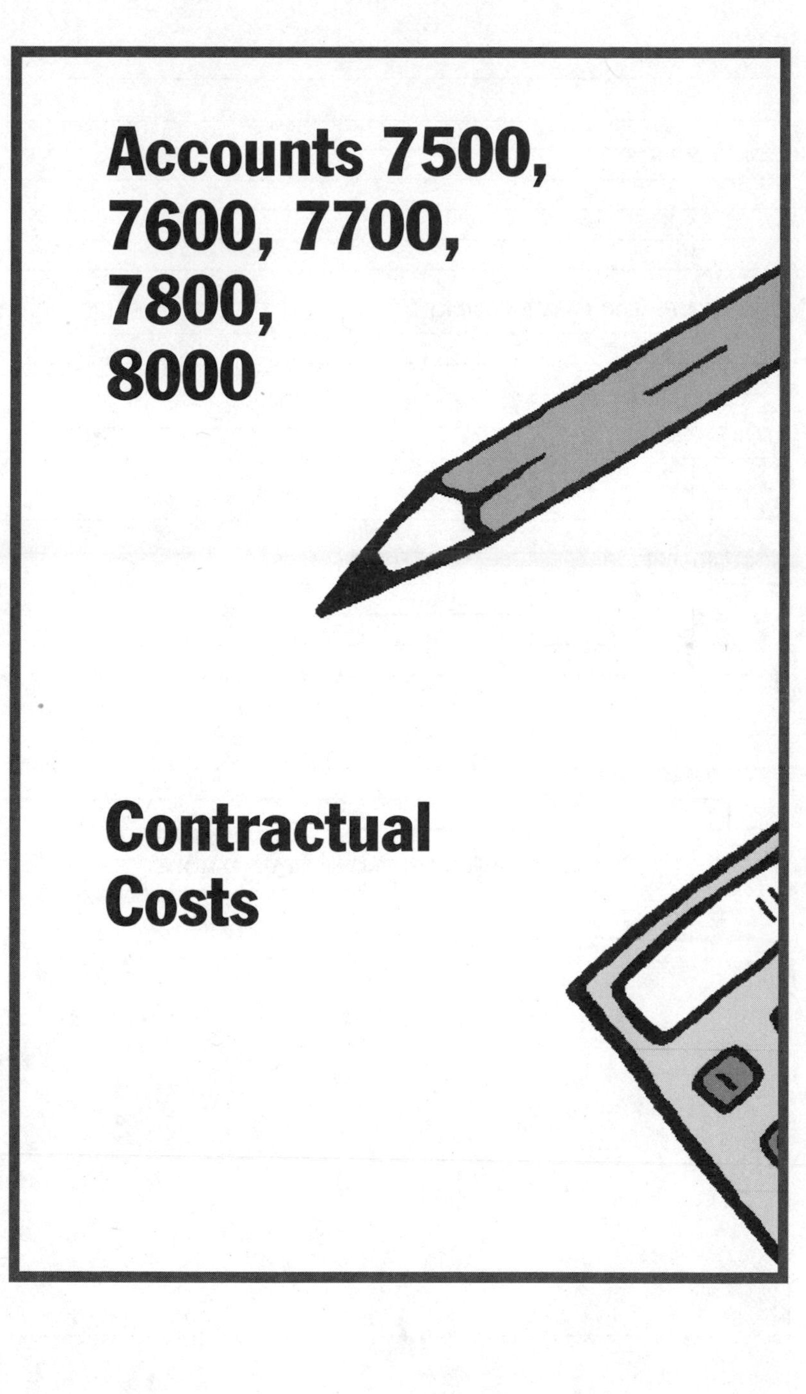

Accounts 7500, 7600, 7700, 7800, 8000

Contractual Costs

PAGE NO. 52

PRODUCTION NUMBER	PRODUCTION TITLE	DATE

7500 CONTINGENCY		
ACCT NO.	DESCRIPTION	TOTALS
01	* 10% x $ 14,436,109 (Total Direct Cost)	1,443,621
	TOTAL ACCT 7500	1,443,621

7600 COMPLETION BOND (OPTIONAL)		
01	* 6% x $ 14,366,082 (Total Direct Cost)	
	TOTAL ACCT 7600	430,982

7700 OVERHEAD		
01	____% x $____	
	TOTAL ACCT 7700	

7800 INTEREST, FINANCING CHARGES, FINDERS' FEES		
01	Interest	
02	Financing Charges	
03	Finders' Fees	
	TOTAL ACCT 7800	
	TOTAL NEGATIVE COST	

8000 DEFERMENTS				
01	DATE PAYABLE	TO WHOM	AMOUNT	
			TOTAL ACCT 8000	
			TOTAL NEGATIVE COST (INCLUDING DEFERMENTS)	13,996,545

A - Fringeable/Taxes
B - Non-Fringeable/Taxable
C - Non-Taxable * – Estimates – % could be lower.

CONTRACTUAL COSTS

7500: Contingency

ON INDEPENDENT PRODUCTIONS, YOU WILL NEED TO ADD a contingency figure of approximately ten percent (10%). The percentage is based on *below-the-line* costs only. On lower budget shows, a bond company may require a higher overall contingency and/or specific contingencies for areas of the budget which are deemed too tight. Even if a contingency is not required by a third party, having a higher contingency on low-budget productions is smart.

On higher-budgeted films, the bond company may ask for a much higher percentage than the standard ten percent (10%.) *[Note: On a recent film, the bonding company asked for a 20 percent (20%) contingency since the film was a period action, film which had many scenes in the water (ocean and tank). The production company agreed to the higher percentage in order to be bonded.]*

On studio films, there is no contingency required, as the studio is self-insured (meaning it will provide the money to cover any cost overruns.)

To arrive at our contingency figure here, we took ten percent (10%) of the *below-the-line costs* ($5,723,706) and arrived at $572,371.

7600: Completion Bond

If you are working on an independent film, you will need a *completion bond* —a guarantee to the financing entity that the film will be completed—no matter what. The bonding company guarantees to pay for any cost overruns on your show, in return for the right to approve many production decisions. These decisions include your choice of certain production personnel such as director, production manager, assistant director, production designer, director of photography and so forth.

With first-time directors, bond companies may require additional evidence of proficiency from shot lists to storyboarded sequences. As inducements, they may require letters from the director and others warranting that they have reviewed the script, schedule, and budget and can work within these parameters.

Director, producer, and others will have to sign and initial every page of these and other documents. The bond company will have certain takeover rights if your show falls significantly behind schedule and/or over budget. They may even send a set representative out to help you with these or other problems as they arise. Currently, there are three companies in the United States which provide completion bonds: Cinema Completion International (CCI); International Film Guarantors (IFG); and Film Finances. all located in Los Angeles. CCI and IFG deal with most of the larger budgeted pictures.

The average cost for a bond is two to three percent (2%–3%) of your budget minus the following items: Writers' fees and their fringe benefits; fees for cast members who are paid in excess of $5 million; fees for the any director who is paid in excess of $5 million.

If either the cast member or director is paid exactly $5 million or less, then their fee is kept in and calculated as part of the total cost. This $5 million number is the present benchmark in the industry.

Since *The Conversation* only qualified in one of these areas (Writer plus fringe benefits), we compute the following:

Direct Costs (including Insurance)	$14,435,109
Less Writers' Fee (includes Fringes)	$ 70,129
Subtotal	$14,366,082
Completion Bond Fee (3%) =	$ 430,982

I would recommend using three percent (3%) as the average fee charged for bonding a film. Your fee may be slightly higher or lower depending on the individual difficulties of your project. Also, depending on the arrangement with the bonding company, you may be entitled to a rebate of a portion of your fee if you meet certain requirements. Conversely, your fee may be higher if you don't meet certain requirements and/or have invaded your contingency amount. These are all negotiable points to discuss when meeting with prospective bonding companies.

7700: Overhead

When you work on a major studio lot, the production company will charge you an amount for overhead. Someone has to pay for the salaries of the studio executives, the cost of sweeping the sound stages, the food in the commissary, and so forth. Thirty-five percent is about average for this figure.

7800: Interest

If you have borrowed money from a bank or other money-lending institution you will have to pay interest on the loan, and that money must be accounted for.

8000: Deferments

If your budget is extremely tight you may wish to defer some payments. It is possible to ask your crew and/or cast to accept a percentage of their normal salary and to defer the rest until after the film is released, or makes a profit. It is not usual for an employee to defer the entire salary figure, but this is rare.

More often the employee will defer part of the salary, along with a little incentive or over-scale, until after the picture is released. The deferments are then paid out of the first moneys received from any source (box office, foreign sales rights, etc.) The DGA has a low-budget side letter which specifies conditions that permit partial deferments of salaries if agreed to by all parties.

[Note: As we were going to press, the DGA released a letter announcing an availability list for low-budget projects. This list will be given only to those production companies who are signature to the DGA's low-budget side letter. The Low-Budget Agreement provides for reductions in initial fees and deferments for films bud-

geted in the $2 million to $5 million range. Fees are set at 60% of scale for films in the $2–$3 million range, and 70% of scale for films in the $3–$5 million range.]

Computer Budgeting

COMPUTER BUDGETING

BUDGETING IS SOMETHING WHICH WORKS VERY well on computers. Unlike scheduing which is still a difficult fit as so much of it depends upon subjective judgment calls, budgeting is a more exact science. Spreadsheet programs such as Excel, can speed up your process remarkably by linking certain categories together. Therefore, a change in one category is reflected in many other categories, without having to make those changes individually by hand (and then, wondering late at night when you are working on yet another budget revision, if you have made all the necessary changes.)

If you are not an expert at spreadsheet programming, then buying one of off-the-shelf budgeting programs is a good good idea. The following is a brief rundown of the programs available, and stores which carry them, at presstime.

Each program has its benefits and limitations. The best way to find out about a program is to get the demonstration disk, if available, or arrange for a personal, or group, demonstration. Read the different companies' pamphlets, see several demonstrations and then take a second, private, demonstration of at least two programs where you can spend some time at the computer.

Our thanks to Walt Gilmore, former Chair of the Computer Committee of the Directors Guild of America, for his input and advice which follows.

> "The following is a list of available production programs. These programs cover a wide range of variable features and hardware requirements. Some of the programs work in a text mode, reducing the RAM and drive (or disk storage) capacity. Other programs operate in a graphics mode, requiring a graphics board and allowing more sophisticated displays (i.e., the Macintosh mouse-icon display) on the monitor. There are many other

variables between the programs which, on the surface, may be of less concern to the user (size of files, speed of printing, etc.) but may affect the user when working on very large, complicated projects. The *user-interface* (how the user operates the program) is probably of more concern to most people. If you are uncomfortable with the changes that you must make in your working environment to use the program, it will not satisfy you. That is why the buyer must be familiar with what is available and try at least two before purchasing.

"The descriptions below are by no means complete—merely attempts to reflect the major features and differences of each program. I have attempted to standardize the terminology used in the individual companies' brochures and reduce the information to the essentials. In this editing, my personal preferences are naturally included. Therefore, when shopping, please use this list as a guide to your own investigation. A checklist to use as a guide to shopping follows.

"Except as noted, all programs have some sort of security system on the master disk to stop usable copies from being made. A limited number of usable copies can be installed on hard disks."

—*Walt Gilmore*

PRODUCTION SOFTWARE SUMMARY

Compiled by Walt Gilmore
Directors Guild of America

DOTZERO, INC.

702 Third Street
Hermosa Beach, California 90254
Tel. 310/376-7732
FAX 310/379-5103
e-mail: dotzero@aol.com

Minimum system requirements

Macintosh: Not Available
MS-DOS: 550K available RAM, 2MB disk space.
Mouse and graphics adaptor not required.

Program Description

A very simple system which permits easy calculation of global and fringe benefits. It is the only system which has as an optional attachment a complete cost accounting system, capable of handling an entire production, including cost-to-complete, check writing, automatic daily balances, etc. The system was devised by Jack Smith, a well-known production auditor. His expertise is evident in its design.

Academy Award recipient for Technical Achievement.

Price: $49.95

A demo disk which allows you to try a limited version of the program for ten days is available for $8. Available as shareware on CompuServe and America Online.

FILM WORKS

Carlan, Graham & Associates, Inc.
1200 Riviera Street
Venice, CA 90291
Tel. 310/581-2311
FAX 310/581-2314

Minimum System Requirements

Macintosh: Not Available
MS-DOS: 400K RAM, 10MB Hard Drive

Program Description

This program has a very user-friendly interface without a mouse. Four function keys provide instant topical help screens, access to pop-up lists, list modification, copying repeated data and a pop-up calculator, which places results in numeric fields. Program prints strips on plain paper or can use Movie Magic strip holders. The budget program will also read Movie Magic and Toolkit files. The company provides 24 hour, seven days a week telephone support (via pager) and a user bulletin board system.

Price: Budgeting $199.

Ten percent discount to DGA members. (Scheduling program also available for $199.)

B.C. SOFTWARE, INC.

(Formerly MacToolkit)
11965 Venice Blvd., #405
Los Angeles, CA 90066
Tel. 800/231-4055, 310/636-4711
FAX 310/636-4688

Minimum System Requirements

Macintosh: Mac Plus
MS-DOS: Not available

Program Description

Originally a Macintosh version of FILM PRODUCTION TOOLKIT, the program is now independent with many original features. The program uses the Macintosh user-friendly interface. The companion budget program includes enhanced globals; a detail maker which allows designing of sheets for sets, effects, etc; and cost tracking. A new Rate Book on disk utility, published in association with *The Hollywood Production Manual* is available.

Price

Budgeting $279; Scheduling $299; or $499 for both.

MOVIE MAGIC

Screenplay Systems, Inc.
150 East Olive Avenue—Suite 305
Burbank, CA 91502
Tel. 818/843-6557
FAX 818/843-8364

Minimum System Requirements

Macintosh: MacPlus or better, System 6.0.5 or better, 1 MB of RAM, 2-3 MB hard drive and a floppy drive.

MS-DOS:

Movie Magic Budgeting: DOS 3.3 or better, 640K RAM, hard drive and floppy drive.

Movie Magic Scheduling: DOS 3.3 or better, 384K extended memory, Graphics card – EGA, VGA or Hercules, Microsoft compatible mouse, 3-4 MB of hard drive and a floppy drive.

Program Description

Movie Magic Budgeting is unequivocally the industry's number one budgeting program. It has a three-dimensional setup that makes accessing all parts of your budgeting significantly faster than the one-dimensional spreadsheet programs. Some key features include: automatic fringes; over 25 pre-made studio and production company budget forms; sub-groups which allow for multiple budgets within one file; hundreds of lines or detail; all files can be converted from DOS to Mac and back; and much more.

Price: Budgeting $595; Scheduling $695

ADDITIONAL RETAIL SOURCES

Some of the programs have representatives outside Los Angeles. When contacting the program manufacturers, ask if they have representation near you, or an 800 number for support. The following list is not all-inclusive, but are stores which cater to the motion picture industry.

THE WRITERS COMPUTER STORE
11317 Santa Monica Blvd.
Los Angeles, California 90025
Tel. 310/479-7774 • FAX 310/477-5314

CREATIVE COMPUTERS
1505 Wilshire Blvd.
Santa Monica, CA 90402
Tel. 310/394-7779 • FAX 310/394-5988

COMPUTRS
7 Great Jones Street
New York, NY 10012
Tel. 212/254-9191 • FAX 212/254-9664

THE WHOLE SHEBANG
205 7th Street
Hoboken, NJ 07030
Tel. 800/974-3226 • FAX 201/963-8563

BULLOCK ENTERTAINMENT

12000 Bay Street, Suite 703
Toronto, ONT M5R 2A5, Canada
Tel. 416/923-9255 • FAX 416/920-9134

SARGENT DISC LTD.

Pinewood Studios,
Pinewood Road
Iver Heath, Bucks
SLO ONH, England
Tel. 011 44 1 75-365-6631 • FAX 44 1 75-365-5881

LIKE MAGIC!

29 Beach Road
Callaroy NSW 2097, Australia
Tel. 011 61 2-9 971-1783 • FAX 011 61 2-9 971-2261

NEW MEDIA

1433 North Cole Place
Los Angeles, CA 90028
213/957-5000 • FAX 310/957-8500

STARCOMP

Tel. 818/609-0330
E-mail. rkoster@leonardo.net
http://www.leonardo.net/starcomp/
Contact: Robert Koster

[Download demos straight from Robert Koster's web page. A member of the DGA and a professional production person, you will always find good information and friendly responses from Bob.]

BUDGETING SOFTWARE CHECKLIST

The following list was prepared as an aide for comparison shopping.

CATEGORY	PROGRAMS 1	2	3
Hardware Requirements			
IBM or compatible, Macintosh	_____	_____	_____
RAM memory (256K, 1 MB, etc.)	_____	_____	_____
Hard Drive? Minimum Size	_____	_____	_____
Run on floppy? (Size)	_____	_____	_____
Mouse (Required or Optional)	_____	_____	_____
Wide and/or narrow carriage printer required?	_____	_____	_____
Printers supported:			
Laser	_____	_____	_____
Inkjet	_____	_____	_____
Other	_____	_____	_____
Program Features			
When was the program first introduced?	_____	_____	_____
What is the current version number?	_____	_____	_____
What is its release date?	_____	_____	_____
Is this a beta test version?			
What Is the customer base? (number in use)	_____	_____	_____
Menu type (Pull-down, Highlighted, Select Code)	_____	_____	_____
File Capacity	_____	_____	_____
Accounts (Budgets)	_____	_____	_____
Automatic backups?	_____	_____	_____
Entering			
Are there quick keys?	_____	_____	_____
Are lists available for repeated entries?	_____	_____	_____
Auto-entry features?	_____	_____	_____
Transfer of information between programs	_____	_____	_____
Is entry of information natural and/or sequence variable?	_____	_____	_____

CATEGORY	PROGRAMS 1	2	3
How are different versions of schedules maintained?	____	____	____
How are different versions of schedules compared?	____	____	____
Reports			
Overall look of form printouts?	____	____	____
Speed of printout	____	____	____
Are report forms adjustable?	____	____	____
Are there limits to reports?	____	____	____
Does program transfer information to a Production Report?	____	____	____
Does program transfer information to a Call Sheet	____	____	____
Does program print Day-Out-of-Days	____	____	____
Are Drop and Pickups shown?	____	____	____
Are Start, Work, Hold and Finish indicated?	____	____	____
Retail features			
Cost of program	____	____	____
Are additional programs required?	____	____	____
What optional programs are available?	____	____	____
Package deals?	____	____	____
Return policy?	____	____	____
Lease program?	____	____	____
Security	____	____	____
Copy protection system (key, limited installs, security module)	____	____	____
Number of installs allowed	____	____	____
Are installs limited (cost of new installs)	____	____	____
Can disk optimizers be used once the program is installed?	____	____	____
What are the phone support hours?	____	____	____
Does the company maintain an online help system or Web page?	____	____	____

CATEGORY	PROGRAMS 1	2	3
Are classes available?	_____	_____	_____
Is there on screen help?	_____	_____	_____
Upgrade policy (Free for ____ months, or cost per upgrade _____)	_____	_____	_____

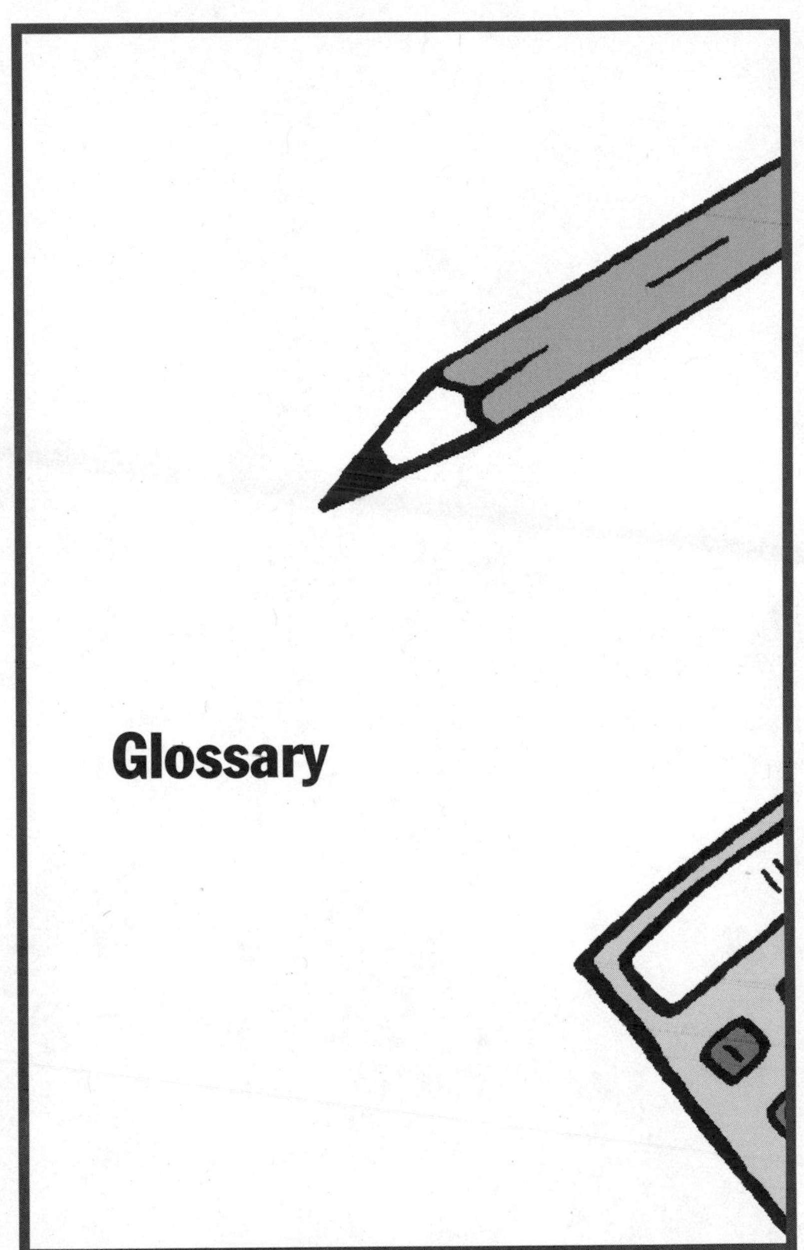

Glossary

GLOSSARY

A

ABOVE-THE-LINE

A film's budget is divided into two main sections: *above-the-line* and *below-the-line*. Above-the line expenditures are usually negotiated on a run of show basis and, generally, are the most expensive individual items on the budget. They include costs for story and screenplay, producer, director, and cast. Below-the-line costs include technicians, materials and labor. Labor costs are usually calculated on a daily basis. Also included in below-the-line costs are: raw stock, processing, equipment, stage space and all other production and post production costs.

ACTION TRACK

The film (picture) before any music, dialogue or effects tracks are added.

ACTS OF GOD

This phrase is usually inserted into contracts as a way of nullifying a contract, or certain portions of it, due to unplanned and uncontrollable events of nature such as hurricanes, earthquakes, tornadoes, fire, etc.

ADR

Abbreviation for *additional dialogue replacement.*

AMERICAN CINEMA EDITORS *(ACE)*

An honorary professional society of film editors. Membership is by invitation only.

AMERICAN FEDERATION OF TELEVISION AND RADIO ARTISTS *(AFTRA)*

This is the television, radio and videotape counterpart of the *Screen Actors Guild.*

AMERICAN SOCIETY OF CINEMATOGRAPHERS *(ASC)*

An honorary group whose members are some of the best cinematographers in America. The British counterpart is the British Society of Cinematographers (BSC), and the Canadian counterpart is the Canadian Society of Cinematographers (CSC).

ANSWER PRINT
The first composite (sound and picture) print that the lab sends for approval. Often it is necessary to strike several answer prints before all the required color corrections are made. Sometimes answer prints are silent (e.g., if the mix has not been completed.)

ARRANGER
The person who prepares and adapts previously written music for presentation in some form other than its original form. Often an arranger will work from a composer's sketch and create parts which then will be assigned to various voices and/or instruments by the orchestrator. Sometimes the composer does his own arranging and orchestrating. In the pop music idiom, the arranger and orchestrator are the same person. Often, in more legitimate music (film, symphony, etc.) the term *orchestrator* is used.

ART DEPARTMENT
The crew members who, under the direction of the production designer, are responsible for creating the *look* of a film as far as sets and locations are concerned. The cinematographer and costume designer also contribute to the overall *look* of a film. The art department staff usually includes the art director, an assistant art director, set designer, draftsman and apprentice.

ART DIRECTOR
The person who supervises and is responsible for every aspect of the film's decor and set construction. She must be knowledgeable in architecture as well as design.

ASSEMBLY
The first step of editing in which the editor has put together roughly cut scenes in script sequence in order to give the director a first look at the film.

ASSISTANT EDITOR
The member of the editing staff who works with the editor to synch dailies. The assistant editor also catalogues and keep the dailies organized and accessible, splices film, and keeps the editing room in working order. Having a good filing and coding system aids in keeping track of the thousands of feet of film. The assistant editor talks with the labs and effects companies and, in general, relieves the editor of having to do jobs other than editing.

ASSOCIATE PRODUCER
A title that varies from production to production. It can be the title given to the producer's second-in-command who shares business and creative responsibilities. It can designate an additional credit given to the production manager (the actual line producer when the producer is not always directly involved with the production on a daily basis.) Often it is an honorary title given to one of the financiers, or the person responsible for bringing the property to the producer.

ATMOSPHERE
1) The main emotional theme or mood of a film or scene or, 2) extras in a scene who lend a sense of realism to the action.

ATMOSPHERE VEHICLE

Any car, truck, motorcycle used in a scene by cast members other than principal players and/or actors with speaking parts. In other words, the human counterpart to atmosphere vehicles would be extras.

B

BACKGROUND *(BG)*

1) The part of the scene that is farthest away from the camera and still in view. 2) The real or artificial setting in front of which the action in a scene takes place. 3) Extras used for background action or ambience *(AKA atmosphere)*.

BACKGROUND NOISE

Sounds that provide general ambience or give the illusion of action off camera. Many of these sounds are added to the sound track in post-production.

BACK-UP SCHEDULE *(AKA COVER SET)*

An alternative film location and timetable which can be used in the event that shooting cannot proceed as planned. Often, exterior shooting is thwarted by weather. It is imperative to have a backup schedule of interior shooting which can be easily substituted.

BATCH NUMBER

The film manufacturer's code which designates the time of preparation of that emulsion. It was usually advisable to use stock from the same batch when shooting a particular sequence, so as to ensure consistent color and emulsion speed. Film processing has become so sophisticated that differences in emulsion can be corrected in the lab. Stock from different batches, therefore, can be used together.

BEST BOY

Two unions have jurisdiction over these positions—the electrician's local for the *best boy electrician*, and the grip local for the *best boy grip*. Officially, the term *best boy* has been replaced with ones that are less gender-specific, but the term still is commonly used. The best boy grip is in charge of the rest of the grips and grip equipment; the best boy electric is in charge of the rest of the electricians and the electrical equipment.

BG

Abbreviation for background.

BIBLE RUN

The complete, updated weekly computer run of all accounting activity on a motion picture production.

BILLING
The placement of names, titles and other contractual information in the credits. In addition to salary and points in a film, billing is a major issue when negotiating a deal. There are very definite rules and contractual terms which must be met in terms credit. Where the credit is placed, how it is placed on the screen, how many other names are on the card, as well as the size and kind of typography, are all taken into consideration. If any of these items is not deemed to be satisfactory, then you might be faced with a deal-breaker. Most guild and union contracts explain billing clauses in specific detail.

BIT OR BIT PLAYER
A small speaking part—usually two or three lines. Not to be confused with *silent bits.*

BLACKS
Cloths or drapes used to block daylight from windows or doorways when shooting night interiors, or to create the illusion of night when shooting a small, night exterior. An interesting exception: large portions of Universal Studios' back lot were blacked out when shooting *Streets Of Fire* as it was less expensive than shooting night for night.

BLACK TRACK PRINT
A silent (no sound, just picture) *answer print.*

BLANK
Ammunition that contains paper or plastic in place of the bullet.

BLUE PAGES
When a script has been fully prepared for production and distributed to all necessary people, it is necessary to distinguish added or changed pages from the original pages. The standard method is to issue script changes on different colored paper, beginning with blue, and then moving on to pink, yellow, green, etc. The date of the correction is marked on the top of the pages. Changes are usually noted with an asterisk in the margin by the change. They are printed on colored paper, first blue, then pink, etc.

BLUE-SCREEN SHOT *(PROCESS)*
A delicate and elaborate special effects process whereby the subject is filmed in front of a special, monochromatic blue background with normal film. Blue-sensitive mattes are made to replace the blue background with other footage. When combined, the subject and background look as if they were shot simultaneously. A very well known example is the flying bicycle scene in *ET: The Extra-Terrestrial. Jurassic Park, Independence Day*, and almost every film containing some visual effects employs this technique.

BODY MAKEUP ARTIST
According to union rules, a *makeup artist* may only apply makeup from the top of an actor's head to the breastbone, and from the tips of the fingers to the elbow. Everything else falls under the jurisdiction of the *body makeup* artist.

BOX RENTAL *(AKA KIT RENTAL)*

A daily or weekly sum paid to a crew member for the use of personal property *(e.g., makeup or hair dressing supplies, special tools)* during production.

BREAKDOWN *(AKA SCRIPT BREAKDOWN)*

1) (n.) An extremely detailed system of separating each and every element in the script. The UPM and First AD then rearrange the resulting breakdown into the most efficient and least expensive schedule for filming. 2) (n.) A detailed analysis prepared by the *script supervisor* for timing the script. 3) (v.) To separate individual shots from the dailies in the early stages of editing.

BUDGET

An attempt to estimate and list every possible expense necessary to make a film before the film is made. Accurate budgets can only be created after completely breaking down a script and preparing a production strip board. It is usually prepared by the production manager and also, for studio pictures, by the studio estimating department. It is not unusual to have many budgets prepared during the course of production as more information is supplied, or as extenuating circumstances occur.

BUS TO

As opposed to report to, this signifies a location day for the crew. Crew members' work day, and corresponding pay time, begins with the bus ride to the location and ends when they are dropped off after the completion of the day's work. *Golden time* does not begin until after 14 hours. When working at the studio, it begins after 12 hours.

C

CALL OR CALLTIME

The time and location for the next day's (or night's) shooting.

CALLBACK

1) An invitation for an actor to audition again, once the field of competition has been narrowed, having successfully completed a prior audition. For *SAG* members there is a limit to the number of callbacks an actor may have before being paid for his/her time. 2) An automatic invitation to continue working as a *day player* unless specifically notified by the end of the day that he is laid off.

CALL SHEET

A list traditionally posted or handed out at the close of each shooting day which was prepared by the *second assistant director* under the supervision of the *first assistant director* and approved by the *production manager*. The call sheet displays each cast and crew member's call times (report to the set or to the spot for prearranged transportation to location), which scenes to be shot, their order and which sets or locations will be utilized, cover sets, and any unusual equipment needed (crane, Steadicam, etc.)

CAMEO
A small part played by a well-known performer, usually to enhance the box office draw of a film.

CARRY DAY ***(AKA HOLD)***
A day for which the cast and/or crew are paid, but not required to work.

CARTAGE
The term for reimbursement to a musician for the cost of transporting certain musical instruments to the studio for music track recording. If they are brought by public carrier, the producer pays the courier company directly.

CAST
(N.) Generally, the performers appearing in a film. Specifically, on budget and breakdown forms, cast refers only to speaking parts, and not *extras*. *(V.) To* choose the actors for a production. In a large budget feature film, there is usually a *casting director* and an *extra casting director*. Very often, the casting of a film is done with box office considerations in mind.

CAST LIST
A compilation of actors' names (and the name of the character they play), their addresses, telephone numbers and agent contacts. This list is published either in alphabetical order or according to how the actors are on the production board. Usually, two separate lists are kept: one with confidential salary information for limited distribution among cast and crew (which must be submitted to *SAG* on all union pictures) and one without confidential information for general distribution.

CASTING DIRECTOR
The person (or company) responsible for interviewing, negotiating contracts with, and hiring most actors on a motion picture (television) project. She works under the supervision of the director and the producer.

CHARACTER
The person an actor is portraying in a production.

CHARACTER NUMBER
The number assigned to the character on the production board. Usually, the more scenes an actor has, the lower the number. For example, the stars in a production usually have numbers one through five.

CHILD ACTOR
Any actor under the age of 18. There are strict rules governing the working hours and conditions for child actors. In most cases, there must be a teacher or welfare worker on the set everyday when a child is working. It is best to check with the *Screen Actors Guild* for the most current rules.

CLEARANCE
Permission, paid for or not, to use someone else's copyrighted material (a book, song, poem, etc.) or a location in a film, video or television show.

CLOSED SET
A set in a studio or on location that is not open to any visitors or persons not immediately connected with the production. Sometimes when intimate scenes are to be shot, only a limited number of crew members will be allowed on the set.

CODE AND RATING ADMINISTRATION OF THE MOTION PICTURE ASSOCIATION OF AMERICA
The organization that classifies films' suitability for different audiences. They also rate trailers.

CODE NUMBERS
Small numbers put on the edge of picture and sound tracks with an encoding machine. Code numbers facilitate keeping picture and sound in sync while cutting.

COLOR CODING
1) A system used when breaking down a screenplay in order to create a production board. Individual items in the screenplay (cast, props, locations, etc.) are marked with different colors and then transferred onto breakdown sheets. A second color-coding system is used on the *production board* to differentiate interiors from exteriors, day from night, etc. 2) A system standard in the industry for designating later versions (revisions) of a script or script pages. The color sequence is as follows: white, blue, pink, yellow, green, and goldenrod.

COMPLETION GUARANTEE
A contractual understanding that a motion picture will be completed and delivered in accordance with certain specifications, usually time, cost and conformity to screenplay, and sometimes in accordance with specifications of creative elements. It usually provides that the guarantor will furnish moneys to pay costs over budget and contingency and, in many instances, gives the guarantor power to take over control of the production if it appears to be out of control *(i.e., over budget and over schedule).*

COMPLETION OF ASSIGNMENT FEE
A fee paid to certain members of the Directors Guild of America (production managers, assistant directors, etc.) which is usually one week's pay at scale to allow them to complete their paperwork at the end of a show before going off payroll.

COMPOSITE DUPE NEGATIVE
A duplicate negative that has both picture and sound in sync on the same piece of film.

CONDUCTOR
The person who interprets the score and directs the orchestra. Often the composer conducts his own music.

CONSTRUCTION CREW

Personnel who, under the supervision of the *construction supervisor*, perform the tasks necessary to complete the sets in and out of the studio. The crew is made up of *prop makers* and *laborers*.

CONTACT LIST

A compilation of the names, addresses and telephone numbers of all the vendors, supply houses, services, etc. That will be used by a motion picture company during production. This list is constantly updated with new information.

CONTINGENCY

A certain amount of money, usually ten percent (10%) of the total negative cost, that is included in the budget to cover unexpected expenditures. Usually a completion guarantee will not be approved by the completion guarantor unless a contingency is included in the final budget.

CONTINUITY

The orderly progression on action from shot to shot for proper development of the story in a film. During shooting, the script supervisor keeps track of scene details so there are no lapses in the continuity of dialogue, action, set dressing, props or wardrobe.

COST TO COMPLETE

The amount of money required, according to the budget, to finish a picture. The financial status of the production is reported weekly on cost reports.

COST REPORT

A detailed weekly analysis that identifies costs to date, costs this week, and estimates the cost to complete the film.

COSTS TO DATE

The amount of money per budget category that has been spent on a production to date.

COSTUME DESIGNER

The person who conceives and draws designs for the costumes (clothes) worn by the cast on a production. She contributes to the overall *look* of the film as well as the interpretation of the character portrayed in the film.

COSTUMER

The person responsible for taking care of the costumes on the set or on location during production. On television shows that do not have costume designers, the *wardrobe supervisor* is responsible for acquiring the clothes worn by the cast. This is a union category separate from costumer. The old-fashioned term for costumer was *wardrobe mistress*.

COVERAGE

1) Shooting a scene from different camera angles so that the same action is seen from different points of view. These shots are carefully edited to accomplish the dramatic objectives of the director–to create a scene that has movement, rhythm and drama. Coverage is made to accomplish the director's vision of a scene (how the scene will be seen). It accents performances, physical movement, rhythmic considerations of the scene, dramatic action, ambience (environment), etc. 2) The brief synopsis of story line and content of a project submitted for consideration, prepared by a story analyst. Usually the coverage includes a recommendation for any further action on the project.

COVER SET

An alternate set that can be used quickly when circumstances (weather, illness, etc.) Prevent shooting what was originally scheduled for that day.

COVER SHOT *(AKA INSURANCE TAKE)*

An additional printed take which can be used in the event the preferred take is unusable *(e.g., damaged film).*

CRAFT SERVICE

The member of a film crew that is responsible for the coffee, beverages and snacks on a set. The *craft service person* also sweeps up and does small chores. This is a union position on the West Coast.

D

DAILIES *(AKA RUSHES)*

Usually, scenes shot one day are rush processed and delivered by the lab for viewing the next day by the director, producer, cinematographer, editor, etc., Hence the name *dailies* or *rushes*. It should be noted that a set should not be struck until the dailies have been approved.

DAY OUT OF DAYS

A schedule showing the dates and times an actor will work.

DAY PLAYER

An actor hired by the day who has only a few lines or scenes. According to SAG rules, *day players* must be personally notified before the end of the day's work that they are laid off, otherwise they will automatically be *called back*..

DEAL MEMO

A short written statement outlining the terms of an agreement in plain English. Until formal contracts are drawn and signed, deal memos are fully binding to all parties.

DEVELOP/DEVELOPMENT
1) To submit film to a chemical process (done in a lab) that turns the latent image on the exposed film into a visible image. 2) The preliminary stage in the process of making a motion picture that includes acquiring the literary rights, writing the screenplay, scheduling, budgeting, scouting the locations, negotiating commitments of the director and principal cast and, in independent productions, raising money for production.

DEVELOPMENT DEAL
An agreement between a studio or production company and a producer, director or writer, to generate one or more film projects for eventual production.

DGA
Abbreviation *for Directors Guild of America.*

DIALOGUE TRACK
The portion of the sound track that carries the dialogue, as opposed to the music track, the effects track, etc.

DIRECTOR'S CUT *(AKA FIRST CUT)*
The director's version of the completed picture containing his audio and visual selections integrated into the completed picture. Under the *DGA Basic Agreement*, a film's director is entitled to the first cut of the film.

DIRTY DUPE *(AKA ONE LIGHT PRINT)*
A black and white, untimed reproduction of a workprint.

DISBURSING AGENT
The person in the accounting department who is in charge of paying out funds in a film, with the authorization of the financing entity or studio.

DOLBY®
A trade name for a noise-reducing system in sound recording and reproduction. Many theaters are now equipped with Dolby systems for better film sound reproduction, and the costs of *Dolby* should be included in the budget under post-production and distribution expenses. There have to be non-Dolby prints struck for theaters not equipped with Dolby systems. A competitive system known as ultra-stereo was recently developed and requires less expensive conversion for theater owners.

DOLLY
A movable, wheeled platform that holds the camera and its operator, for traveling (or dolly) shots. The dolly is operated by a *dolly grip*, a member of the grip department.

DOLLY TRACKS
Rails or planks upon which the dolly, carrying the camera and operator, moves smoothly toward, along side of, or away from the subject.

DOMESTIC VERSION
The cut of a film that is released theatrically in the United States, as opposed to the version (possibly altered) released overseas, or an edited version prepared for television.

DOUBLE TIME
Payment at twice the basic hourly rate for work performed on Saturdays, Sundays or union recognized holidays.

DRIVE ON *(AKA GATE PASS)*
Permission left by someone who works at a studio with the guard at the gate for an outsider to enter a studio lot for the purpose of visiting someone who works there or has an office there.

DROP AND PICK UP
A specific union rule applying to actors that states there must be at least ten free days between the last day that an actor works and the time he next works on a production, otherwise he must be paid for all intervening nonworking days. This can be done once per actor per production.

DUB *(A.K.A. MIX, LOOP)*
1) To combine the different sound tracks by mixing to produce a master recording from which the final sound track is then made. 2) To replace the dialogue with another voice or into another language. 3) Video term meaning to copy or to make a copy.

E

EDITING
The process of selecting, arranging and assembling a film and its sound track into a logical, rhythmical story progression. The stages of editing are: *rough cut*–the first logical assembly of the chosen footage, fine cut–a more finely hewn, worked over version, *final cut*–the version to which the negative will be conformed, from which release prints will be struck. The editing process is more one of evolution than one of finite stages, however.

EDITOR
The person responsible for editing the film. Many times, this job can entail as much creative input as the job of the director. A good editor can take banal footage and, by artful cutting, intercutting and Addition of a moving soundtrack, turn it into an exciting piece of film. It is not uncommon these days for an editor and assistant editor to start working on a picture during pre-production, begin assembling dailies during production, and if the picture is not too complicated, present a rough cut within four-to-six weeks after completion of *principal photography*.

EFFECTS TRACK *(ABBR. FX TRACK)*
The separate channel onto which *sound effects* are recorded.

ESTABLISHING SHOT
Usually a long or full shot at the beginning of a sequence to specify (establish) the location, mood setting, etc.

EXECUTIVE PRODUCER
The title usually given to the person responsible for either financing the film or securing the financing for the film. In some cases, the executive producer credit can be given to the UPM or some other person associated with the production. It can even be the star's agent.

EXPENDABLES
Those items that are purchased for use on a film that will probably be used up *(e.g., light bulbs, tape, gels.)*

EXPLOITATION
Advertising, publicity, merchandising, licensing and promotion of a film.

EXTRA
An actor who speaks no lines—except as part of a group—and who makes no gesture to set himself apart from the other extras.

F

FAVORED NATIONS
A shorthand phrase used in negotiations and in informal contracts to denote that a party will be afforded treatment equal to the best given by the producer. Often used in defining the profits for the participants (actors, director, etc.) The size and placement of billing or the calibre of dressing rooms, motor homes on the set, etc.

FINAL CUT
1) The finished version of the work print to which the negative is conformed in order to strike the release prints that will be shown in theaters. 2) An important point when negotiating a director's or producer's contract to determine who has the last word on the form and content of the version that will be released.

FIRST ASSISTANT CAMERA OPERATOR
A member of the camera crew who changes lenses, keeps the camera in proper working condition and maintains focus while the camera is in motion. If there is no second assistant camera operator, the first assistant also loads and unloads the magazines and fills out camera reports, marks the spots where the actors will stand, and takes the measurement between the object being photographed and the lens. On most productions, there usually is a second assistant camera operator.

FIRST ASSISTANT DIRECTOR

The main assistant to the director. The First Assistant Director (First AD) is a member of the Directors Guild of America *(DGA)* or another guild or union outside the United States which covers production people. The First AD is the liaison between the director and production manager, and can sometimes double as the production manager on smaller productions. During production, the First AD is responsible for the directing and placing extras, keeping the production moving, for the call (making sure that everyone and everything is in the right place at the right times.) It is the First AD's job to maintain order and discipline on the set. The First AD orders *"Quiet on the set!"* before a take and tells the camera operator to roll. Before production begins, the AD breaks down the script, determines the number of extras and silent bits needed for each scene, and, with the director's and production manager's approval, hires them. The First AD usually has an assistant called a *Second AD*.

FLATBED

A motorized editing device, where reels of film (sound and picture) run side to side during viewing (instead of upright, as on a *Moviola*). This makes it possible to easily run several different tracks simultaneously with the picture. Two name-brands are *Steenbeck* and *KEM*.

FOLEY

Any body movement sound or sound effect that is recorded in a studio as the picture for a scene is run, and is then cut into the film. For example, in a chase scene on foot, a *foley artist* would watch the scene to be foleyed and recreate the actions of the actor while creating believable sounds *(footsteps, panting, etc.)* . A punch might be created by slugging a piece of meat. In a musical, the sound of tap dancing would be recreated by the dancers on a *foley stage* while watching the dance footage.

FOLEY ARTIST

A specialist who is called upon to recreate certain body movements and other sounds. In television, the foley artist is sometimes a member of the editing staff.

FOLEY STAGE

One of several in a *foley studio*, these large rooms have various types of floor surfaces and other objects to create most of the sound effects needed for a picture.

FOLEY STUDIO

A specially designed recording studio that has facilities to project picture and sound simultaneously while recording new sounds which are being created by the foley artist(s). The sound effects are recorded on full track, usually three–or four-stripe, so as to give the editor three attempts at getting the right sound. The sounds are then cut into the film in sync.

FOLEY TRACKS

A 35mm copy of recorded *foley sounds* to be cut and synched into the film by the editor. The original foley master is stored for safekeeping until the completion of the film, when it will be mixed into the final *soundtrack*.

FORCED CALL

Violation of a union or guild contract by bringing a crew or cast member back to work before he or she has had the minimum amount of time off.

FRINGE BENFITS
1) Additional compensation (usually not in cash) over and above salary. If the individual is a member of a guild or union, vacation pay, as well as health, welfare and pension benefits are paid to the organization of which that person is a member. 2) Free screenings for studio employees, or a Christmas bonus from the boss, are some examples of fringe benefits a job might offer.

FRINGE RATES
Those wages in Addition to direct wage compensation that are paid on behalf of an employee *(e.g., Health and welfare, pension, taxes.)*

G

GAFFER
The chief electrician on the set who is responsible for the lighting of the set according to the instructions of the *director of photography*. The gaffer supervises his electrical crew's placement of lights before and during shooting.

GENERATION
Each step involved in going from original negative or tape, to final viewing (or listening) product. For example, to get from original 35mm negative to a release print, you can (though not Advisable) strike a print from the negative. That print would be second generation. More common is to go from a negative to a *CRI* to release print (third generation) or from negative to interpositive (IP) to dupe negative (*dupe neg.*)–also considered three generations, as IP/dupe neg is considered to be one generation. The quality is as good as, if not better, than a print from a CRI. Generally the more generations away from the original, the poorer the quality of the final product. A 1/2 inch video cassette made from a 3/4 inch cassette will have poorer quality than a 1/2 inch cassette made from a print.

GENERATOR
A movable power source used on location (or as backup power in a studio) that runs on gasoline or diesel fuel.

GENERATOR OPERATOR
The person who turns on the generator at the beginning of the day and turns it off in the evening, and makes sure it stays in good running condition throughout production.

GOFER *(AKA RUNNER)*
A person who "goes for" this and that. Another term for *production assistant.*

GOLDEN TIME *(AKA GOLDEN HOURS)*

A form of overtime payment. If an employee works in a studio, or reports to a location within the studio zone on a straight time day, any time worked beyond 12 consecutive hours is calculated at *double* the hourly rate. If the employee, who does not fall under the on call classification, works on a double time day (Saturday, Sunday, holidays) in a studio or on a location within the studio zone, any time beyond 12 consecutive hours is calculated at *four* times the basic hourly rate.

If the employee is working on a *bus to* location (where transportation is provided from the studio to the location) or distant location on a straight time day, the hours are calculated at *two and one-half* times the basic hourly rate after fourteen consecutive hours have elapsed. On a double time day, the rate is *five* times the basic hourly rate after fourteen consecutive hours.

GREENS PEOPLE

The crew members responsible for dressing the set with plants and trees, and maintaining them. Often, if a cut tree in a forest set (for example) has been on the set many days and has started to turn brown, the greens crew paints the leaves or needles green to make it look fresh and alive.

GRIP

A general term for a crew member who provides the labor on the set in various departments–in the theatre they would be called stagehands. There are various grips for various departments: lighting grips, who trim, diffuse and mold lights; construction grips, who build sets, backdrops, etc.; dolly grips, who lay and move dolly tracks, and push and pull the dolly, etc.

GRIP PACKAGE

A typical grip package contains all the equipment required to adjust or manipulate lights and camera. It usually consists of: apple boxes, packing quilts, sand bags, gloves, scrims, flags, various light stands, mechanic and carpenter tools, a 12' by 12' frame (with the same size silk and black cloth), a pole cat, box of wedges, high rollers and various reflectors.

H

HEADER

Cardboard strip about 4" wide and either 15" or 18 1/4" long on which are listed all the key elements that make up a script breakdown. This strip is the guide for all the smaller production strips comprised in a production strip board.

HIATUS

A planned interruption in the production schedule. This almost always applies to episodic television when, after shooting all the shows for a season, the company shuts down for two or three months before resuming production.

I

IATSE

Abbreviation for *International Alliance of Theatrical And Stage Employees.* The parent organization of some 1,000 local unions in North America representing every branch of production as well as employees in film distribution and exhibition.

INDEPENDENT CONTRACTOR

A person rendering services, but not as an employee on payroll.

INDEPENDENT PRODUCER

Formerly, the term meant a producer of low budget and/or nonunion films whose distribution would be limited–sometimes four-walled. Now, the term can refer to any producer not under contract to a major studio.

INDEPENDENT PRODUCTION

A production not financed by a major studio. Nevertheless, a film produced independently may be distributed by a major.

INSURANCE COVERAGE

As it is virtually impossible to predict accurately the cost of insurance on a feature film due to so many variables, an average percentage figure of between two and four percent of the total negative cost will be entered for insurance in the budget. This estimate will depend on the shooting schedule, locations, cast members, types of coverage needed *(e.g., negative, director, errors and omissions, workers compensation, etc.)*

INTERNEGATIVE/INTERNEG
(AKA CRI–COLOR REVERSAL INTERNEGATIVE)

A negative made from the original negative, using reversal film stock. This should not be confused with a dupe negative, which is a negative made from an interpositive.

INTERNS

Unpaid assistants usually used in the production office who work for experience or course credit. These jobs usually are short term. Productions need to be careful not to assign duties to interns that by DGA charter are actually duties of the DGA Trainee.

INTERPOSITIVE *(IP)*

A positive print made from the original negative, used to make dupe negatives, not used for projection. It can be recognized by its orange base. It is usually denser than positive release prints.

K

KEY NUMBER *(AKA EDGE NUMBER)*

The manufacturer's serial numbers printed on the edge of the film, used by the negative cutter when conforming negative to cut work print. They are also used by the editor when ordering effects–to tell the optical house where to begin and end the fades and dissolves. Edge numbers should not be confused with code numbers.

KEY SECOND AD

On a production having more than one second assistant director, the *Key Second* is in charge of the other seconds, coordinating their tasks and reporting to the first AD and to the production manager.

L

LINE PRODUCER

The supervisor of both above-the-line and below-the-line elements during production. The production manager reports to the line producer on below-the-line matters.

LIVE ACTION

Real actors filmed on sets or at real locations as opposed to animation or special effects made to look like real action.

LOAN OUT CORPORATIONS

A corporation specifically designed to allow a higher paid individual (director, actor, writer, etc.) to receive income as a corporation and not as an individual.

LOCAL LOCATION

Any spot within a 30 mile radius of the union agreed-upon center—*the studio zone*—to be used for shooting a film or television show. Any shooting location where cast and crew do not have to spend the night. In Los Angeles, it is usually 30 miles from the intersection of La Cienega and Beverly Boulevard. In Manhattan, it is defined as any place between 125th Street and the Battery (the southern tip of Manhattan.)

LOCATION

Any locale used for shooting away from the studio. Location shooting provides special problems for production managers who must arrange for food, shelter, toilet facilities, transportation to and from for cast and crew plus generators and other special equipment. Local locations are near a studio. Cast and crew will usually have a report to location call for a certain time, then return home that night. Distant, or overnight locations are any locations farther than local locations where cast and crew are obliged to stay overnight, and usually work six days a week.

LOCATION ACCOUNTANT *(AKA PRODUCTION ACCOUNTANT, LOCATION AUDITOR)*

The person assigned to account for all the money spent while shooting a picture on location.

LOCATION FEE

The compensation paid for the use of a site and facilities when shooting a motion picture or television show.

LOCATION MANAGER

The person who reads the script to find out what locations are needed, scouts for locations, evaluates their suitability then takes photographs which are shown to the director and production designer. After a location has been approved, the location manager arranges for permission and negotiates the terms for using the location for shooting. He is then responsible for organizing all the details that relate to that location–permits, parking, catering, police, firemen, etc. The *location manager* is responsible for drawing up a budget for all locations.

LOCKED

Unchangeable. Finished. Not to be changed.

LOOP

(N.) 1) The length of film in the camera or projector not engaged in the sprockets, that absorbs the vibrations of the projector or camera motor as the film passes through (momentarily stops at) the gate. 2) A length of magnetic sound film or tape joined head to tail, that forms a circle, or loop, so that the recording is repeated again and again as it goes over the player head. *(V.)* The act of dubbing in (looping), or replacing, newly recorded sounds or speech with previously recorded sounds or speech. Usually the principal actors will be called back during post production to rerecord lines that were not recorded properly, or need to be changed or added.

LOT

The real estate on which a studio is located (office buildings, sound stages, dressing rooms, etc.) with guards at the front gate to regulate entry of non-employees.

M

MAGNETIC FILM *(MAG FILM)*

A perforated film base the same size as motion picture film, coated with iron oxide instead of light-sensitive emulsion, for recording sound. This is used for editing, not production sound. The perforations allow synchronization with the picture track.

MAGNETIC RECORDING
Sound recorded in sync with motion picture film on magnetic tape that will be transferred later to MAG film for editing, then, after the final mix is completed, transferred back to film on an optical track.

MAGNETIC STRIPE
A coating of ferromagnetic iron oxide that runs along the edge of perforated 70mm Dolby film onto which sound is recorded.

MAGNETIC TAPE
A high quality polyester or mylar based tape coated with a substance containing iron oxide, for recording sound, or for recording sound and picture on videotape. Professional size is 1/4 inch and generally runs between 7-1/2 and 15 ips for high quality recording. This is five times faster than home recording.

MAG/OPTICAL PRINT
A release print containing both magnetic and optical sound tracks for use in theaters that have either system.

MAIN TITLE (S)
Although specifically referring to the title card containing the name of the film, it more generally refers to all credits appearing at the beginning of the film. Under the terms of the DGA contract, the director's credit is the last to appear before the beginning of the film.

MASTER *(AKA MASTER POSITIVE)*
Film or tape from which dupe negatives are made for striking release prints–or, in the case of sound or video tape, the material from which subsequent listening or viewing copies are made.

MATTE
A specially designed mask with one or more specified areas cut out so that when placed on a camera or printer lens, the areas not masked are exposed. Mattes are used in special effects for combining separate images onto one piece of film, changing backgrounds or the tone of an image.

MATTE ARTIST
A member of the special effects department who designs and helps construct backgrounds or mattes for matte shots. One of the legendary matte artists is Albert Whitlock, whose work appears in such films as *The Birds, Marnie, The Sting, Earthquake, Ship Of Fools.* He won an Academy Award for his work on *The Hindenburg.*

MATTE BOX *(AKA SPECIAL EFFECTS BOX)*
An adjustable filter holder attached to the front of the lens. It shields the lens from unwanted light, and holds mattes and filters in place when shooting.

MATTE SCREEN
A specially treated projection screen, in which the brightness of the images appears the same from all viewing angles.

MATTE SHOT
A shot combining many layers of moving elements in a live action scene with a pro-photographed background.

MEAL PENALTY
A fine paid to a crew or cast member who has not been given enough time off for a meal, or the beginning of whose meal break has been delayed longer than permitted by union regulations

M&E TRACK
Abbreviation for music and effects track. The sound track containing everything but the dialogue. It is particularly useful when doing foreign language versions, as new dialogue can be recorded without interfering with the music or effects.

MOVEMENT LIST
An information sheet listing the means by which everyone connected with the production is getting to and from a location.

MOVIOLA
The trademark of a device used for viewing interlocked picture and sound tracks. It is used extensively in editing for building sound tracks. It has variable speeds and can be stopped at a single frame so that the editor can mark the cuts, optical effects, etc. The film runs up and down through the viewer instead of side to side like a flatbed.

MPAA
Abbreviation for *Motion Picture Association of America*, the organization that gives films and their advertising (trailers, etc.) Their ratings. All major distributors are members. The *MPAA* also employs ex-FBI agents to track down film pirates both in the united states and abroad. They are also the chief lobbying arm of the film industry. They represent the interests of major distributors of the motion picture industry in financial, legal, ethical, trade and foreign trade matters. *The Motion Picture Export Association (MPEA)* is the foreign office of the *MPAA*, and acts as a trade organization for the American motion picture industry abroad.

MPAA CODE SEAL
A certification that a film, its trailers and advertising have been made and rated in conformity with the regulations and standards of the MPAA.

MUSIC CONTRACTOR
The person responsible for hiring musicians and coordinating all business and financial activities for music (recording) sessions. He/she must be present at all recording sessions.

MUSIC TRACK
That channel of the soundtrack onto which the music is recorded, separate and distinct from the dialogue and the effects tracks.

N

NABET
Abbreviation for *National Alliance of Broadcast Engineers and Technicians.*

ND
1) Abbreviation for nondescript *(e.g., This scene will require 25 ND office worker extras.)* 2) Abbreviation for neutral density *(i.e., A neutral density filter or gel that evenly reduces the amount of light on the film or on the scene being lit on the set.)*

NEGATIVE
Exposed and processed film whose image is the opposite of the original subject *(i.e., The reverse of a positive.)* The term sometimes refers to unexposed film stock *(AKA raw stock),* or stock in the camera before processing.

NEGATIVE COST
All expenses required to achieve the final negative, from which release prints are made. The term, or an equivalent term, is usually defined in financing and participation agreements. These special definitions vary from contract to contract, especially with respect to indirect costs *(e.g., overhead)* and contingency costs, and will govern the interpretation of each respective contract.

NG
Abbreviation for *no good*, usually referring to a bad take.

NIGHT-FOR-NIGHT
Night sequences that are actually shot at night. For the most part, night exteriors, or night interiors where night exteriors need to be seen *(i.e., through windows)*, are shot night-for-night.

NIGHT PREMIUM
An adjustment made to the basic rate of pay per various unions and guilds, for work conducted after a certain hour, usually 8:00 PM.

O

ON A BELL

When a film company is actually shooting, a bell is rung by the sound mixer and a red light goes on outside the door of the sound stage as a signal that all activity around the set is to stop and no one is to come on or off the stage. This happens every time the camera rolls. When shooting on location there is no red light, but the bell is still sounded to warn everyone that a shot is about to begin. When the take is finished, the bell sounds twice for *all clear.*

ON CALL SALARY

A fee (usually one day's regular wages) paid to an actor or crew member, who may or may not be used the following work day, but must remain available and cannot accept other employment.

ON-CALL

An actor, or crew member, who may or may not be used the next day, but must remain available.

OPTICAL SOUND TRACK

Sound track reproduced on photographic film by optical means that creates sound when read by an optical sound reader, as opposed to magnetic sound track which is recorded on magnetic tape or film. The sound is reproduced by light waves, electronically converted to sound impulses during projection.

OPTION

An agreement in which a prospective buyer, for a fee, has exclusive rights to represent (develop, sell, etc.) a property or one's services for a specific period of time. Technically, an option is merely an offer to enter into a contract, but the potential seller cannot revoke the offer during the option term, because the potential buyer (option holder) has paid for it.

ORIGINAL

Usually refers to original negative.

ORIGINAL SCREENPLAY

A screenplay written especially as a movie, and not adapted from another medium *(e.g., novel, short story, play).*

ORCHESTRATOR

The person who takes the composer's or arranger's sketch and assigns parts to the various voices and/or instruments. Sometimes the composer does his/her own orchestrations.

OS

Abbreviation for *off screen*, that is, not seen by the camera.

OVERAGES *(AKA COST OVERRUNS)*

Production costs that exceed the amount in the prepared budget.

OVERHEAD

The fixed costs of maintaining offices, facilities and personnel for a studio or individual production/ production company. In the case of a studio, these costs are passed on the production companies or producers renting facilities as a percentage of their budgets.

P

PA

Abbreviation for *production assistant (AKA gofer, runner).* This is now a *union (DGA)* position.

PANAGLIDE

Trade name for a body frame for a motion picture camera developed by Panavision. It allows smooth, steady movement of a hand-held camera.

PAN AND TILT

A special fitting on the tripod that allows the camera to pan (move horizontally) or tilt (move vertically).

PANAVISION

1) Trademark of a motion picture camera system often used in shooting feature films. It is a wide screen process using 35mm film and an anamorphic lens. Panavision 70 (super Panavision) uses 65mm film and an anamorphic lens. The 65mm film is used in the camera for shooting, while 70mm film is used for release prints. The extra 5mm are for the magnetic sound stripe on the edge. 2) International company which manufactures motion picture equipment which can be purchased or rented.

PANAVISION 70 WITH TODD A-O SOUND

A 65mm unsqueezed negative printed on 70mm film stock. The extra 5mm is for additional stereophonic magnetic sound tracks (that is, in addition to the normal optical sound track) on either side of the perforations. There are five sprocket holes per frame in this film as opposed to the four in 35mm film.

PAY OR PLAY

A contractual obligation which guarantees the employer will pay the employee whether or not the services are performed or required. This kind of guarantee is usually given only to high-level people in the industry (stars, directors, writers, etc.) It is usually considered a deal breaker if not contractually agreed to.

PER DIEM
A specific amount of money calculated on a daily basis to cover costs incurred by the member of the company while shooting on location. Such costs can include meals, lodging, laundry, etc. Travel costs are usually additional.

PERFORMER
Any actor in a production who has a speaking, dancing or singing part. Extras or walk-ons are not considered performers..

PERK
Short for perquisite. A fringe benefit, privilege or profit over and above a salary. There are many perks in the film business used as incentives for people to take a job, or to keep them in a job *(i.e., cars, expense accounts, wardrobe from films, etc.)* Often perks are not left to fate, but are written into contracts.

PICTURE CAR
Any vehicle which is going to be shown on-camera in a film or television project, as opposed to those vehicles used behind-the-scenes for the production of the project.

PRACTICAL
Refers to a prop or piece of set dressing that actually works, *(e.g., shower, door lock, lamp, sink.)* Also a light on a set that works.

PRE-PRODUCTION
The period of preparation before principal photography begins. Most of the work of preparing the script, script breakdown, budget, location scouting, costume design, set construction, is done during pre-production. In other words, everything you need to do in order to shoot a film.

PRINCIPAL PHOTOGRAPHY
That segment of time during which all scripted material covering all the speaking parts is filmed. Second unit material may be shot at approximately the same time. Second unit can be shot, however, either before or after principal photography.

PRINCIPAL PLAYERS
Those members of the cast who are the main featured actors in the film or television show.

PROCESS SHOT
Used primarily for moving automobile or train shots, the previously filmed background of the shot is projected through a transparent screen, while the actors sit in the process body and perform.

PROD
Slang for independent production or independent producer.

PRODUCER

Ideally, the first person on a project and the last person off. The producer's role is to find and develop a project, hire the writer/s and develop the script, hire the director, actors, and others. It is also the producer's responsibility to arrange for financing, oversee the production, on this and any other projects he or she may be producing concurrently. (In episodic television, this person is called the *Executive Producer.*) Also, the producer may be involved in the release and exploitation of the film. Some directors and actors who initiate their own projects act as their own producer.

PRODUCTION ASSISTANT *(ABBR. PA, AKA GOFER, RUNNER)*

An entry-level member of the production crew whose job it is to do menial, but necessary, jobs for the producer, director, production manager, production office coordinator, etc.

PRODUCTION AUDITOR *(AKA LOCATION AUDITOR, LOCATION ACCOUNTANT)*

That member of the production staff whose primary responsibility is to maintain up-to-date, accurate financial records of the costs entailed in the production of the film or television show. This position may be covered by a union. The production auditor works directly with the production manager and the financing entity.

PRODUCTION DESIGNER

An honorary title awarded to art directors by the producer or producers of a film project. It is not uncommon for big-budget productions to have a production designer supervising one or more art directors.

PRODUCTION OFfiCE COORDINATOR *(POC)*

A clerical member of the production staff who works directly for the production manager and acts as a liaison between the production office and all other groups during the production. In some parts of the united states, this is a union position.

PRODUCTION REPORT

A daily report itemizing all elements used for that particular day's (or night's) shooting. The *key second assistant director prepares the production report* and submits it to the *production manager* for approval. It is then sent to the *producer, director, production auditor*, the studio (if any), and any other party concerned with the daily costs of the production. The report includes such items as: the scenes shot, the number of pages completed, amount of footage exposed, any abnormalities that would explain any overage or underage of material covered, any penalties incurred and their reasons, which crew members and actors were used, etc.

PRODUCTION STRIP BOARD

A scheduling tool used by production managers and first assistant directors to determine exactly how much time it will take to shoot the film, and who is needed for each scene. Each scene in the script is marked on a separate strip according to whether it is an interior or exterior, day or night. These strips are then laid out on the board, which consists of many panels, arranged to show the most efficient and least expensive order in which to shoot the project.

R

RATING, MPAA

The *Motion Picture Association of America's* established system of categorizing feature films according to viewer audience suitability. The categories are as follows: *G–General Audiences, PG–Parental Guidance Suggested, PG 13–Children Under The Age Of 13 Are Not Admitted Without A Parent Or Guardian, R–Restricted,* and *NC-17—No One Under 17 Allowed With A Parent Or Guardian.* The MPAA also rates trailers. There are two ratings: *all Audience* and *Restricted.* A restricted trailer may only play with an *R-* or *NC-17* rated film.

REAR SCREEN PROJECTION

A system of projecting film onto the back of a translucent screen–as opposed to the front of the screen as in standard projection. Although it is sometimes (though rarely) used in theaters, its main use is in production, as an exterior background more easily shot in a studio. For example, a shot in which two characters are driving in a car. From the car's window we see scenery (streets, buildings, trees, mountains, etc.) passing by. The live action is shot in the studio against the projected background (stock footage, or footage shot by a second unit), making sure that the camera and projector are carefully synched to prevent flickering. This is referred to as a process shot. For extremely large scenes, the more complex matte shot (or traveling matte) is used.

RELEASE PRINT

A final composite print ready for distribution to theatres.

REPORT SHEETS

Logs or data sheets filled out daily by the camera and sound departments listing each take and noting which ones are to be printed and which ones are NG (no good).

REPORT TO

An instruction written on the call sheet to indicate that crew members are working at a studio or at a local location, and their workday begins upon their arrival at the set.

RESIDUALS

Additional compensation similar to a royalty paid to an author of a book that is paid to actors, writers, directors, et al, according to each union's contract. Not all union members receive residuals.

ROOM TONE

The existing presence or ambience in a quiet room. It is recorded onto a buzz track and later mixed in with the dialogue track. This room tone makes a scene sound more realistic and hides cuts in the dialogue track.

ROUGH CUT

The first stage of editing, in which all scenes in the film are placed in their approximate order to tell the story.

ROYALTY
A negotiated percentage of income based on sales.

RUNNERS
1) Scaffolding on which lights, backdrops and other equipment can be hung. 2) The production assistants *(AKA gofer)* who run errands for the producer, director, production manager and others.

RUN-OF-SHOW
A contractual term usually used when negotiating an actor's salary and work days. With a *run-of-show* deal, the production company agrees to pay that actor a negotiated salary figure in exchange for the actor's promise not to accept any other employment during that time.

S

SCALE
The minimum wage established by each union or each individual job category. Usually, an experienced crew member (or well-known actor) will receive more than scale.

SCALE PLUS TEN
A common practice in which the production company agrees to pay employee union scale rate plus an extra ten percent to cover the employee's agent's fee.

SCREEN TEST
An audition recorded on film or tape to see if an actor is right for a part, or to see how someone looks on film.

SCRIPT SUPERVISOR *(AKA CONTINUITY CLERK)*
A member of the crew who records detailed notes on every take, including dialogue, gestures, action, lens used, costumes, makeup, etc. These notes help ensure continuity from shot to shot and scene to scene. Films are usually shot out of sequence, so these notes are vastly important to the continuity of the finished product. The script supervisor submits her notes at the end of each shooting day. They are an essential tool for the editor and director when putting the film together. Some feel that the script supervisor's job is the second most important one on the set after the director. Without the help of the script supervisor, the director's job would be infinitely more difficult as there are so many details to keep track of while shooting a film.

SECONDARY LOCATIONS
As with principal players and supporting players, there are locations that are deemed more important (primary locations) and those that are less important (secondary locations). When scouting locations, it is advisable to find the primary locations, then find secondary locations nearby.

SECOND ASSISTANT CAMERA OPERATOR

A member of the camera department who reports to the first assistant camera operator and prepares the camera equipment for the first assistant camera operator. He loads and unloads magazines from the camera, fills out the camera reports, slaps the clapsticks at the beginning or end of each take.

SECOND ASSISTANT DIRECTOR

A production position who reports to the first assistant director and the production manager, and is generally responsible for all cast and crew. Duties include: preparation and distribution of daily paperwork (call sheets, production reports, actor's time sheets, extra's vouchers, etc.) The Second AD also maintains a liaison between the production manager and/or the production office and the first assistant director. The Second AD assists the First AD in the placement of extras and in the maintenance of crowd control. She also helps supervise and direct the work of any *DGA trainee* assigned to the project. On union productions, the Second is a member of the *DGA* or some equivalent union covering production personnel *(e.g., Directors Guild of Canada, Directors Guild of Great Britain).* Can be upgraded on second unit to *First AD*.

SECOND SECOND ASSISTANT DIRECTOR

On a production requiring more than one second assistant director, additional second assistant directors—*Second Second AD's*— are hired. They report to the *key second assistant director*. They are usually hired on a day-to-day basis and are called upon to help with a large cast or extra call, or to manage large crowd scenes.

SECOND UNIT

An additional production crew used for shooting sequences that do not involve principal players, such as background shots at remote locations, backgrounds for process shots, large-scale sequences shot with multiple cameras, and inserts. This crew is handled by the second unit director. Often the second AD becomes the first AD of the second unit. On nonunion productions, the camera operator may become the second unit director of photography.

SET

The exterior or interior location where a film or television show is shot. The person responsible for the look of a set is the production designer or art director.

SET DECORATOR

The person responsible for dressing the set with furnishings relevant to the various scenes.

SET DESIGNER

The person responsible for planning the construction of the sets, from the description and drawings of the art director/ production designer.

SIGNATORY

A company that has signed an agreement with a union or guild obligating them to comply with the rules and regulations of that union or guild.

SOUND TRACK

1) The audio portion of a film that is divided into three or four separate tracks or channels: dialogue, music, effects and a spillover track for additional effects. An optical sound track is made from the mixed tracks, then is printed onto the side of the film in the lab. It is not uncommon for many separate units (there can be hundreds) to be individually edited and then be mixed to produce the final sound track. 2) another term for the recorded version of a film's musical score, available on albums, tapes and compact discs.

SPOT

To go through a film and choose where certain elements need to be added, such as sound effects, live replacement, music, etc.

SPOTTING SESSION

A time during post production when the director, composer, editor and music editor determine where the music (score) for a film should fall.

STANDARD SCRIPT FORMAT

The preferred form in which screenplays are typed or written. If other formats are used, it can affect a production manager's calculations in judging how long it will take to shoot the piece.

STATION 12

A department of the Screen Actors Guild which confirms that an actor is an active member in good standing of SAG and that all dues have been paid in full.

STEP DEAL

A development arrangement whereby the decision to proceed is made after approval or completion of certain steps *(e.g., synopsis, treatment, first draft, final screenplay.)*

STILL PHOTOGRAPHER

The person responsible for taking stills on a movie set, to be used for matching/continuity in later shots *(e.g. hair, costumes, makeup, set decoration)*, or later on, for publicity purposes.

STORY ANALYST

A member of the story department who reads and analyzes literary material (screenplays, treatments, magazine articles, books, etc.) That is submitted each week to the story department. The resulting synopses prepared by the story analyst are called coverage, and are submitted to the story editor for review.

STORYBOARD

A series of drawings or photographs that show the progression of shots in a film sequence (generally an action sequence that is expensive to shoot) or for an entire film. Alfred Hitchcock was famous for never beginning to shoot his films without having complete storyboards showing each shot in detail. 2) Storyboards are used extensively in the production of commercials. They are created by the advertising agency for sponsor approval, then are distributed to production companies for bids.

STORY EDITOR

A member of a studio's story department and supervisor of several story analysts. The job entails reviewing the coverages submitted by the analysts, then passing them on to the production VP's with recommendations as to whether or not the property should be acquired and/or developed.

STRIKE

1) To tear down a set when shooting has been completed. It is advisable not to strike any set until the dailies have been approved. 2) To refuse to work due to a labor grievance. 3) To create a print from a negative *(i.e., to strike a print).*

STUDIO *(LOT)*

1) *(lot)* physical location and facilities (offices, sound stages, etc.) Existing for use by either in-house or independent production companies for development, production and post production of motion pictures and television shows. 2) A film shot *in a studio* means shot in specially built sets on sound stages or studio back lots (e.g., *New York, New York,* which was shot primarily on sound stages and back lots in *Los Angeles),* as opposed to being shot on location (e.g., *Mean Streets*, shot on locations in *New York*.)

STUDIO *(MAJOR)*

An organization that develops, produces and distributes motion pictures and television shows. In the old days of Hollywood, the studios were much more powerful and self sufficient than their modern day counterparts. They kept their own stable of producers, directors, actors and writers under contract, as well as having ongoing art, costume, makeup, publicity, etc. Departments. They had everything necessary for every phase of making movies, from concept to completion, to distribution and exploitation and even exhibition. These days, studios hire as needed for the most part, instead of keeping large numbers of people on staff full time. There are some departments, however, *(e.g., legal, story, advertising, distribution, etc.)* which are maintained on an ongoing basis.

STUDIO TEACHER

See Welfare Worker/Teacher.

STUDIO ZONE

Many major cities have specified areas, of a certain radius from a central point. In *Los Angeles*, it is a radius of 30 miles from the old *AMPTP* headquarters at *La Cienega* and *Fairfax*. Anything outside that area is considered to be a distant location. More precisely, any location where the cast and crew are required to spend the night is considered a distant location. Anything else is considered to be within the studio zone. If the location is a long drive, but not far enough away to necessitate spending the night (local location), then employees are compensated for mileage.

STUNT ADJUSTMENT

The premium paid in Addition to the Guild (*SAG or AFTRA*) day rate to the stunt person by the production company. The amount is commensurate to the complexity, relative danger or level of expertise required.

STUNT COORDINATOR
A member of the crew responsible for the organization and coordination of all stunts on a production.

T

TAFT-HARTLEY
A labor law that permits anyone to accept a job and continue working for 30 days before being required to join any union or guild that might be affected.

TECHNICAL ADVISOR
An expert consultant on a motion picture or television show who ensures that details in his/her specialized area are authentic. For example, a retired airline pilot may be asked to offer advice on the workings of a 747, or a native of Bali to verify details in the script *(e.g., costumes, dialogue, makeup).*

TECHNICAL COORDINATOR
The person responsible for assisting the director on a multi-camera project (scene, episode, feature film, etc.) photographed continuously either before a live audience or as if there were one present. The coordinator's chief responsibility is to supervise the movement of each camera throughout the show.

TIMING
1) An actor's ability to create the proper tempo in a scene through the rhythm and flow of his or her performance. 2) A lab technician's evaluation of the density and color balance of each shot of the film, so as to achieve the desired contrast and color balance. 3) Referring to the actual running time of a proposed motion picture, the script timing is usually performed by the script supervisor. It is a detailed analysis of exactly how long (to the second) each scene will run. Having a script timed early on in the preparation of a project can save the producer a great deal of money. Scenes that appear to be too long can be cut down in the writing instead of waiting until the editing room.

TRACKING SHOT *(AKA DOLLY SHOT, TRAVELING SHOT, TRUCKING SHOT)*
A moving shot where the camera follows the action in a scene. The camera is placed on a dolly that moves on tracks, or on a camera car or other vehicle.

TRAILER

Usually a visual synopsis of a motion picture that has its own structure–not necessarily corresponding to that of the film. It is used to create an audience awareness of and interest in an upcoming release. Teaser trailers run less than ninety seconds and may be attached to the beginning of another feature film released by the same studio. Regular trailers may be of any length, but are usually less than two minutes. They are rated by the Motion Picture Association of America. Today, trailers are considered to be an art form in their own right, and reflect highly sophisticated aesthetic techniques combined with carefully determined marketing strategy.

TRAINEE, DGA

A person learning to become a *Second Assistant Director* in the *Directors Guild of America.* Very few applicants are accepted each year in the *DGA Training Program.* The trainee must pass a rigorous written and oral examination. Usually, there are more than 1,500 candidates who apply each year for not more than two dozen places.

TREATMENT

A very detailed story outline or synopsis that usually includes sample dialogue as well as narrative.

TURN-AROUND TIME

The minimum and specific number of free time that must be given according to union contract before that person may return to work without incurring a penalty. For example, an actor must be given 58 hours between completion of work Friday before beginning again on Monday.

U

UNION *(AKA GUILD)*

A labor organization that determines work standards, wages, hours credits, etc., on behalf of its members. Depending on how strong and well-organized the union/guild is, it may also offer legal advice, health and pension benefits, dental plan, have an internship program, a film society, etc.

UNION CARD

The identification slip issued to each dues paying member in good standing. The member should be able to produce his card when working on a production.

UNIT MANAGER

A production department member assigned to act as local business and production head of a particular film unit *(e.g., second unit while shooting on location).* Also another term used for UPM.

UNIT PRODUCTION MANAGER *(UPM, AKA PRODUCTION MANAGER)*
The producer's executive assigned to the production, responsible for coordinating and supervising all administrative, financial and technical details of the production, and overseeing the activities of the entire crew.

VEHICLE
Any car, truck, motorcycle, etc., used on the production.

VIDEO ASSIST
A system often used these days where vieo tape is shot simultaneously with film through the lens of the principal camera. This allows the director and others to view the shot immediately after the end of the take.

VOICE OVER *(VO)*
Dialogue or narration which comes from off screen. The source of the voice is not seen.

WALLA
Background-people noise, indistinguishable voices.

WAIVER
To give up something that is called for, or required, by contract.

WELFARE WORKER/TEACHER
A person who is in charge of following and maintaining the strict rules governing the working conditions of minors.

WARDROBE TESTS
Similar to a *screen test*, although what is being tested this time is the wardrobe and how it looks on screen.

WORK PRINT
An untimed print assembled from dailies with tape splices. When the work print reaches the final cut stage, the negative is conformed to it.

WRAP
Generally, it refers to the end of a day's shooting, but can also specifically refer to the completion of a particular assignment or location, and to the end of principal photography.

WRANGLER
A member of the film's crew whose job it is to deal with the care, feeding training, and performance of the animals working o the production. Another term for *animal handler* or *animal trainer*.

WRITERS GUILD OF AMERICA *(WGA)*
The official collective bargaining union for screenwriters in the motion picture and television industry.

WRITTEN BY
A *Writers Guild of America* designation meaning that the original story and screenplay were by the same writer.

Index

INDEX

Note: Numbers in *italics* are Glossary entries.

SYMBOLS

A

D

J

K

L

M

Q

R

S

Z

OTHER BOOKS BY THE AUTHOR

Books by Ralph S. Singleton

Film Scheduling:
Or, How Long Will It Take To Shoot Your Movie?
Film Scheduling/Film Budgeting Workbook
Movie Production & Budget Forms. . .Instantly!
Filmmaker's Dictionary

These and other fine books and directories on the entertainment industry are available directly from Lone Eagle Publishing. For a free catalog, please *call* 1.800.FILMBKS (1.800.345.6257); *fax* your request to 310.471.4969 or *email* us at info@loneeagle.com. Or, you can always *mail* your request together with a self-addressed, stamped envelope to:

Lone Eagle Publishing Company
1024 N. Orange Drive
Hollywood, CA 90038